JOURNAL FOR THE STUDY OF THE OLD TESTAMENT SUPPLEMENT SERIES
339

Sheffield Academic Press
*A Continuum imprin*t

Three Faces of Saul

An Intertextual Approach to Biblical Tragedy

Sarah Nicholson

Journal for the Study of the Old Testament
Supplement Series 339

Copyright © 2002 Sheffield Academic Press
A Continuum imprint

Published by Sheffield Academic Press Ltd
The Tower Building, 11 York Road, London SE1 7NX
370 Lexington Avenue, New York NY 10017-6550

www.SheffieldAcademicPress.com
www.continuumbooks.com

British Library Cataloguing-in-Publication Data

A catalogue record for this book is available from the British Library

Typeset by Sheffield Academic Press
Printed on acid-free paper in Great Britain by MPG Books Ltd, Bodmin, Cornwall

ISBN 1-84127-248-5

CONTENTS

Face I
SAUL IN 1 SAMUEL

Face II
SAUL IN LAMARTINE'S *SAÜL*

Face III
HENCHARD IN HARDY'S *THE MAYOR OF CASTERBRIDGE*

ACKNOWLEDGMENTS

I wish to thank the staff of St Mary's College at the University of St Andrews, who were invariably supportive during the writing of the thesis that became this book. I am greatly indebted in particular to Peter Coxon, in whose classes I began to appreciate the literary genius of biblical narrative, for all his efforts as my supervisor and for his continuing concern. I also wish to thank Robin Salters, who advised me during the final stages and offered me assistance and support afterwards with a view to getting the thesis published. I am also grateful to the St Mary's College office staff, particularly Vera Prunty and Susan Millar, for support beyond the call of duty.

I would like to express my gratitude to friends who in various ways were highly supportive in connection with this book, especially Eilidh Whiteford for her patience as I regularly bent her ear about literary theory, and Sonia MacDonald for many insightful and challenging questions. I also owe special thanks to my brother Alec Nicholson for chauffeuring me to libraries, for the gift of a printer, and for research assistance. I wish to thank Luciano Kovacs for help with Italian texts and translation, and Duncan Robertson for initial help with funding and for the computer on which this book was written.

My personal debts are no less compelling. My parents, Marilyn and David Nicholson, provided immense support in ways which are too numerous to mention, but their financial and emotional support and the unexpected piano were greatly appreciated. I am also indebted to Donnie and Mina Smith, and Christina and Iain for welcoming me so warmly into their family and for much-needed encouragement. I wish to express my thanks to my husband, Calum Smith, for supporting me materially and emotionally and for his professional proofreading skills which have eliminated many embarrassing errors. Any which remain are my own responsibility.

Finally, I would like to thank my baby daughter Anna for allowing me to get enough sleep to finish this on schedule.

ABBREVIATIONS

ANET	James B. Pritchard (ed.), *Ancient Near Eastern Texts Relating to the Old Testament* (Princeton: Princeton University Press, 1950)
BibInt	*Biblical Interpretation: A Journal of Contemporary Approaches*
BibRes	*Biblical Research*
BZ	*Biblische Zeitschrift*
CBQ	*Catholic Biblical Quarterly*
JBL	*Journal of Biblical Literature*
JSOT	*Journal for the Study of the Old Testament*
JSOTSup	*Journal for the Study of the Old Testament*, Supplement Series
JTS	*Journal of Theological Studies*
MLN	*Modern Language Notes*
PMLA	*Publications of the Modern Language Association of America*
RivB	*Rivista biblica*
RSV	Revised Standard Version
SBLDS	SBL Dissertation Series
SJOT	*Scandinavian Journal of the Old Testament*
VT	*Vetus Testamentum*
ZAW	*Zeitschrift für die alttestamentliche Wissenschaft*

INTRODUCTION

Show them the ways of the king who shall reign over them.
1 Sam. 8.9b

For several centuries many people, in different ways, have attempted to demonstrate the ways of the first king who reigned over the people of Israel. Scholarship has focused on aspects of Saul's reign by means of approaches from the historical and archaeological to the source-critical and discourse-critical. Poets and novelists, painters and composers have interpreted elements of the story of Saul and remodelled these elements in their own creative work. There are so many means of approaching the account of Saul's life and death in 1 Samuel, and so much work already done, that yet another investigation into the story of the first king of Israel might be regarded by some as superfluous. However, it is perhaps witness to the creative genius in the story itself that it prompts and allows for such a plethora of investigation, interpretation, inspiration and speculation. This study will involve a substantial investigation into the story as viewed by the poetic eye rather than simply the critical, namely in the work of Alphonse de Lamartine and Thomas Hardy, who have offered very different accounts of their engagement with the biblical narrative.

The Story of Saul as History and as Literature

Much of what has been written about Saul by critics is work that has been done from a historical perspective, and thus raises questions about the dating of Saul's kingship, the authorship of the books of Samuel or its literary units, the manner in which the cult of Yhwh functioned, and the geographical features of the land in which Saul lived.[1] Although historical criticism has often been concerned (particularly in the last two centuries) with the concept of scientific and critical objectivity, it nonetheless recog-

1.   See, for example, Bernhard W. Anderson, *The Living World of the Old Testament* (London: Longman, 3rd edn, 1978), pp. 161-64.

nizes its limitations, not least that the primary sources for investigating this history are the texts of the Hebrew Bible which are neither numerous nor (as most Old Testament historians would acknowledge[2]) intentionally objective. Since it is the case that as other sciences have developed they have informed this historical approach, it is evident that any approach to the Hebrew Bible that takes account of the historical may draw on a huge base of erudition. Archaeology is an important example of just such a development.[3] This historical work has been crucial to the evolution of literary approaches to the Hebrew Bible and provides much of the background on which exponents of literary criticism draw. However, historical criticism sometimes tends to treat the Hebrew Bible as if it had been written with modern historical criteria to fulfil, and it often displays tensions between a modern conception of history and the function of the text in its original context, which may be addressed by means of the investigation of ancient historiography.

Therefore, divergent from the study of the Hebrew Bible as 'a history' is the concern with this function in context: the Hebrew Bible as 'history'. Saul has also been the object of much work from this perspective. Source criticism's attempt to trace texts anterior to the texts that form the Hebrew Bible as it has been received by the source critics has led to a wide range of opinion on the aims and intentions of Saul's near-contemporaries. This has involved discerning discrete authors in the texts and assuming a process of frequent redaction, either oral or in written form. The task is aided by textual criticism and the availability of versions in Greek, Syriac and Aramaic, together with discoveries such as the Qumran texts. Curiously, although scholars with historical perspectives on the Hebrew Bible have made efforts to observe methodological considerations, it appears that proponents of source criticism, or diachronic criticism, have been less inclined to examine their methodological presuppositions, but simply choose a model and work within it. Moshe Garsiel, writing about 1 Samuel, makes the point that

> Most studies denominated 'literary' in fact offered a literary, historical-diachronic analysis—that is, a hypothetical reconstruction of the book's

---

2.   Iain Provan, making a similar point, cites Lemche and Ahlström. Provan argues against the separation of story and history. See Iain W. Provan, 'Ideologies, Literary and Critical Reflections on Recent Writing on the History of Israel', *JBL* 114 (1995).

3.   See, for example, Martin Noth, *The Old Testament World* (trans. from the 4th German edn by V.I. Gruhn; London: Adam & Charles Black, 1966), pp. 107-109.

developmental processes—and displayed no interest in the literary-synchronic question of the text as it now stands.[4]

However, despite a degree of lack of methodological rigour in some
quarters, this diachronic approach has been valuable in raising questions
concerning the attitudes of the writers and redactors of 1 Samuel to the
issue of kingship and the cult of Yhwh which must inevitably inform the
synchronic perspective.

Most critics who use vocabulary such as 'biblical narrative', and the
'art' or 'poetics' thereof, are associated with this synchronic approach:
Shimon Bar-Efrat, Robert Alter, Adele Berlin and Meir Sternberg are
among the most prominent critics who advance this perspective. The
principal departure of this method from those which preceded it is the
insistence on the presence of meaning in the received text with no appeal
to sources in interpretation. Perhaps one of the reasons (though by no
means the only one) for discussing the text as it stands rather than as
reconstructed by source critics is that there are simply so many conflicting
theories concerning any single received text as to how it came to be that
way, particularly in the case of that source criticism and textual criticism
that recommends a redistribution of the content of the text. This is not to
say that source-critical work should be abandoned or ignored by those who
favour a synchronic approach, since source criticism's aims to discern the
political and theological presuppositions and intentions of the narratives'
authors must inevitably colour any search for meaning in art. Dale Patrick
and Allen Scult trace the principle of the extant text to the followers of
James Muilenburg's rhetorical criticism, but express concern that many
proponents of this principle have 'lost touch with the insights into the pre-
canonical exchanges with audiences that had been identified and studied
by source, form and traditio-historical critics'.[5] Nevertheless, many critics
who concern themselves with this type of literary approach do not intend
to preclude discussion of textual rhetoric. They may, however, be concerned with rhetorical exchanges with other audiences, such as their own
cultural contemporaries.

The influence of postmodernism and poststructuralism has become
strong in the field of literary-synchronic approaches, and inherent in many
postmodern and poststructuralist theories is a concern with political sub-

---

4. Moshe Garsiel, *I Samuel: A Literary Study of Comparative Structures,
Analogies and Parallels* (Ramat Gan, Israel: Revivim Publishing House, 1983), p. 16.

5. Dale Patrick and Allen Scult, *Rhetoric and Biblical Interpretation* (JSOTSup,
82; Sheffield: The Almond Press, 1990), p. 17.

version and denaturalization of the material of rhetorical exchanges. Bar-Efrat comments on the tendency of the 'avowedly historical approach' to 'regard the narratives as a means of uncovering the historico-cultural reality, such as the "setting/function in life" (*Sitz im Leben*) or the changing views, institutions and religious customs'.[6] Since Bar-Efrat identifies with structuralist perspectives, he is not particularly concerned with a contemporary political viewpoint, and he emphasizes the texts' 'being' rather than their 'becoming'. The rhetorical challenge to the historical approach comes with techniques such as, for example, deconstructions of patriarchal motivations in texts. Examples of this line of approach are to be found in the work of Ellen van Wolde, for example. Thus the cultural agenda that historical-critical work embraces, and which structuralist literary approaches neglect, may be reappropriated by postmodern or poststructuralist methods, yet usually with the difference that it is twentieth-century western culture that is in focus rather than attempts to determine a text's *Sitz im Leben*.

The literary-synchronic approach is, however, about much more than simply interpreting the extant text as opposed to discerning its sources. The four critics mentioned above (Bar-Efrat, Alter, Berlin and Sternberg) are interested in an understanding of narrative technique which is outside the scope of historical-critical and literary-diachronic approaches. Discussion focuses on matters such as characterization, perspective and viewpoint, stylistic devices and narratorial ideology. This focus draws the centre of interpretation away from the author and towards the reader, which causes discomfort among critics of the literary-synchronic approach. Consequently Sternberg, for example, devotes plenty of space to the matter of 'Getting the Questions Straight', and tackles the question of the propriety of a discourse-oriented approach to the Bible. He concludes,

> It is on the pervasiveness rather than in the occurrence of the [strong aesthetic] principle that my claim of the Bible's literariness rests, and with it my case for poetics.[7]

There is, nevertheless, evidence of a pervasive rift in biblical scholarship between those who consider that reader-oriented criticism is trendy and arbitrary and those who argue that author-oriented criticism is outmoded and autocratic.

---

6.   Shimon Bar-Efrat, *Narrative Art in the Bible* (JSOTSup, 70; Sheffield: The Almond Press, 1989), p. 10.

7.   Meir Sternberg, *The Poetics of Biblical Narrative: Ideological Literature and the Drama of Reading* (Bloomington: Indiana University Press, 1985), p. 43.

The position of the literary-synchronic approach to the Hebrew Bible in relation to its predecessors and contemporaries has, it seems, been fraught with difficulty. While Sternberg voices concerns about taking a literary (interpretive) approach in isolation, V. Philips Long outlines three possible relationships: 'mutual condemnation', 'division of labour' and 'dialogue'.[8] Most critics who consider these possible relationships prefer to take the latter approach in their own work as this represents an inclusiveness towards perspectives that define the ontological character of the Hebrew Bible as religious or theological. In practice, however, there may be methodological tensions with this line of approach, since these different perspectives tend to embrace different philosophical movements in criticism. For example, the emphasis in much historical work on scientific objectivity is often underlined by the techniques of what in literary theory is represented by the New Criticism, while the models involved in literary-diachronic criticism are often formalist or structuralist, and the literary-synchronic approach frequently employs the deconstruction techniques of poststructuralism, though there is also a strong tradition of structuralism. Nevertheless, even the apparent opposition in literary theory of poststructuralism to structuralist methods, or of structuralism to formalist, may give way in practice to a method in which the two are held in a balance. Furthermore, some scholars declare an adopted method but operate by means of rules or categories that are in conflict with this method. David Jobling, for example, has embraced structuralism and specifies the theoretical system of A.J. Greimas, among others. He adopts Greimas's actantial schema as a means by which 'narrative can be analyzed according to its participants, or 'actants' ...*who need not be people*, and their relationship to the movement of the narrative'.[9] His diagram, however, is almost entirely made up of characters. Terry Eagleton has this to say about Greimas:

> A.J. Greimas's *Sémantique structurale* (1966), finding Propp's scheme still too empirical, is able to abstract his account even further by the concept of an *actant*, which is neither a specific narrative even nor a character but a structural unit.[10]

---

8. V. Philips Long, *The Reign and Rejection of King Saul: A Case for Literary and Theological Coherence* (SBLDS, 118; Atlanta: Scholars Press, 1989), pp. 10-11.

9. David Jobling, *The Sense of Biblical Narrative: Structural Analyses in the Hebrew Bible (1 Samuel 13–31, Numbers 11–12, 1 Kings 17–18)* (JSOTSup, 7; Sheffield: JSOT Press, 1978), p. 15, my emphasis.

10. Terry Eagleton, *Literary Theory: An Introduction* (Oxford: Basil Blackwell, 1983), pp. 104-105.

Jobling does not explain how a character is or is not a structural unit; nor does he discuss the possibility that this reversion to character might perhaps be considered, by Greimas at least, just the sort of empiricism that the actantial schema was designed to discard. This example is not intended as censure of Jobling but rather as an example of the discrepancy between a literary theory that resists the pursuit of meaning and a literary critical practice that (almost inevitably) aspires to it.

The story of Saul has been found by literary-synchronic critics to be eminently suitable for their purposes. First, it is written as narrative, rather than as a legal text or a chronicle or other genre which would be less conducive to the literary-synchronic approach. Second, it is a lengthy narrative, and thus provides sustained examples of the features central to such an approach: for example characterization, multiple viewpoints and stylistic devices. Bar-Efrat has discussed the characterization of Saul and David, the repetitions in the plot as a means of stressing matters of importance and differing viewpoints, the role of conversation in the narrative, and the function of stylistic features such as rhythm and metaphor. Alter has discussed the story of Saul as 'historicized prose fiction', the technique of rendering an event as dialogue as a means of 'obtruding the substratum', the characterization of Michal, and composite artistry in some of the supposedly contradictory pericopes. Berlin has also discussed the characterization of Michal, and she has discussed point of view in differing accounts (such as the two accounts of Saul's death). Sternberg has focused on thematic concerns, such as the motif of good looks in Samuel, and omniscience in the account of David's anointing. However, very little has been written about the characterization of the deity in 1 Samuel,[11] and this is one of the gaps that this thesis will address. I will also go more closely into the question of repeated material in 1 Samuel than has been possible in the work of the critics discussed above, since their focus has been wide enough to cover narratives throughout the Hebrew Bible and my focus shall be purely on 1 Samuel.

I have thrown into the preceding paragraphs some terms that I have not defined and which are associated with movements in literary theory and criticism. Within this field the definitions of such terms are varied and

11. Although Sternberg, for example, has discussed God's nature, Burke O. Long's criticism is persuasive. For Sternberg, God's character never changes. Long attributes this to the invocation of 'an ahistorical principle: God is exempt from the confusions and limitations that define other participants in biblical narratives' (Burke O. Long, 'The 'New' Biblical Poetics of Alter and Sternberg', *JSOT* 51 [1991], pp. 71-84 [82]).

sometimes even conflicting. I will now, therefore, turn to literary theory and give a brief but necessary overview of some of the movements involved and their consequences for biblical scholarship.

Literary Theory and Methodology

A literary approach to biblical narrative, particularly a literary-synchronic approach such as this thesis proposes, should engage with movements in literary theory that exist in literary fields, and not only with those developments that have occurred in the field of literary approaches to biblical narrative. This brief overview of literary theory can hardly do justice to the massive amount of work that has been done in recent years any more than my brief overview of the historical approach to biblical scholarship could do justice to that field. My chief purpose here is to outline the main areas of literary criticism and to determine which is the most suitable for the present study of the story of Saul.

Literary criticism has been practised since antiquity. Jane Tompkins comments on the equation of language with power which was 'characteristic of Greek thought at least from the time of Gorgias the rhetorician',[12] and she goes on to describe the effect of this on the status of the literary text. Literature in Greek thought is not considered an end in itself, but rather a means of producing behavioural results. Consequently, in antiquity the chief preoccupations of literary criticism were rhetorical and moral. Control over literary techniques and production were vital since it was believed that poetry or literature could have potentially harmful results, hence Plato's exclusion of poetry from the ideal state. Those who did not go as far as Plato's stand for exclusion contended that control should be exercised by the state.

This stance towards the written word changed at the time of the Renaissance. Although literature continued to be defined in respect of its value in shaping public morality, the audience had changed since classical times. Tompkins argues that

> while poetry is believed to have a social function, as it did in antiquity, the content of that function does not remain the same because the social, economic, and political structures that define it have changed.[13]

12. Jane Tompkins (ed.), *Reader-Response Criticism: From Formalism to Post-Structuralism* (Baltimore: The Johns Hopkins University Press, 1980), pp. 203-204.
13. Tompkins, *Reader-Response*, p. 208.

Literature, and other forms of art, were dependent on patronage and, in addition to the wider civic role, literature became a primary source of economic support to its producers.

Gradually, from the mid-eighteenth century, literature came to be written in order to evoke an emotional response rather than a purely behavioural one, and criticism's goals changed with the same movement. By the nineteenth century, the appropriate function of poetry was regarded as providing a model of perfection or a goal for aspirations. The critical response was formalism. Since, according to this theory, poetry is regarded as higher than life, formalism is not concerned with the content of a story but with its nature. In formalism the response of the reader is meaningless because poetry is an end rather than a means. It involves an opposition of the concrete to the abstract. Form alone is of consequence and content is merely a surplus having no significant value.

The appearance of New Criticism, which retained a formalist bent, came in response to attacks on the integrity of poetry. In New Criticism language is nothing, but context is everything. This perspective is grounded in the kind of positivist epistemology which was until recently (and is still in some quarters) the underlying presupposition of scientific endeavour. It is perhaps the advent of quantum mechanics, in which the result of an experiment may be determined by its very observation, which has led to a change in this positivism in science. New Criticism is associated with the technique of 'close reading', which some critics claim renders it unsuitable for longer narratives, although it might be argued that J.P. Fokkelman, for example, employs the technique, despite his structuralist methodology. The result runs to thousands of pages[14] and it is perhaps for this reason that the technique is considered unsuitable for longer narratives.

A change of tactics in literary theory led to structuralism and reader-oriented criticism. Structuralism is concerned by and large with examining the structures of a text. There is an imputed analogy between the 'grammar' of a sentence and the 'grammar' of literature. Structuralism has a tendency to 'de-emphasize individual consciousness in favour of systems of intelligibility that operate through individuals'[15] and in its social-scientific context examines 'the tendency to construct the world in terms

---

14. See J.P. Fokkelman's four-volume commentary on Samuel: J.P. Fokkelman, *Narrative Art and Poetry in the Books of Samuel: A Full Interpretation Based on Stylistic and Structural Analyses*. II. *The Crossing Fates (I Sam. 13–31 & II Sam. 1)* (Assen: Van Gorcum, 1986).

15. Tompkins, *Reader-Response*, p. xix.

of binary oppositions',[16] which tendency forms models for social behaviour. Within these systems, the structural units have meaning only in relation to one another and not to anything outside the frame of reference. Structuralism provides a set of laws by which signs are organized into meanings.

The science of semiotics emerged out of structuralism, particularly with respect to poetry and poetic devices. A sign, or signifier, relates to a signified arbitrarily, and meaning is produced on the basis of difference; thus 'cat' signifies a furry house pet only because it differs from 'bat', 'rat' and every other signifier. Discerning meaning is not one of structuralism's aims; rather it aims to reconstitute the rules that govern the production of meaning. Along similar lines, narratology also grew out of structuralism and is concerned with models by which narration relates to narrative. Beginning with unwritten texts, such as myths, it has been argued (in the work of Claude Lévi-Strauss)[17] that the structures are produced not by individual minds but by the myths themselves through social codes, as a way of organizing reality. This then led to a focus on other kinds of narrative and its analysis by categories (in the work of Gerard Genette)[18] such as 'distance' and 'perspective'.

The questions most often raised in response to structuralist theory are set out in Eagleton's work:

> Was language really all there was? What about labour, sexuality, political power? These realities might themselves be inextricably caught up in discourse, but they were certainly not reducible to it. What political conditions themselves determined this extreme 'foregrounding' of language itself?... What had happened to the concept of literature as a social *practice*, a form of *production* which was not necessarily exhausted by the product itself?[19]

It was these kinds of questions which, combined with the political failure of the student movement in France in 1968, led French theorists away from the systematization of the whole that was structuralism.

---

16. J. Cheryl Exum and David J.A. Clines (eds.), *The New Literary Criticism and the Hebrew Bible* (JSOTSup, 143; Sheffield: JSOT Press, 1993), p. 16.

17. See e.g. Claude Lévi-Strauss, *The Raw and the Cooked: Introduction to a Science of Mythology* (trans. John and Doreen Weightman; London: Jonathan Cape, 1970).

18. See e.g. Gerard Genette, *Narrative Discourse: An Essay in Method* (trans. Jane E. Lewin; Oxford: Basil Blackwell, 1980).

19. Eagleton, *Literary Theory*, pp. 111-12.

Eagleton writes, 'Unable to break the structures of state power, post-structuralism found in possible [*sic*] instead to subvert the structures of language. Nobody, at least, was likely to beat you over the head for doing so'.[20] Within post-structuralism there is a prevailing claim that reality is based in language. Therefore a study of language may take on a political character, which was lacking in structuralism. However, this is not an inevitable consequence of poststructuralism: involvement in political concerns is generally associated with the French theorists, and generally avoided by Anglo-American theorists. This distinction implies two 'schools' of poststructuralist theory. Eagleton points to Michel Foucault's early interest in language, which gave way to a concern with political and historical aspects of poststructuralist theory.

Deconstruction is one of the central tools of poststructuralism. It intends to undermine structuralism's binary opposites, or to show that they undermine each other. Deconstruction of a text is concerned with the text's fragilities which undermine it, exposing its inadequacies. Thus the technique 'implies an operation involving the dismantling of something into discrete component parts and suggests the ever-present possibility of putting the object back together in its original form'.[21] This latter, however, is rarely a consequence of its operation. For followers of the French school, the motive for deconstruction is political, and therefore deconstruction of texts 'relativizes the authority attributed to them, and makes it evident that much of the power that is felt to lie in texts is really the power of their sanctioning community'.[22] For Derrida[23] deconstruction is a technique of 'desedimenting' the text, the purpose of which is to allow the already-inscribed to float to the surface.

The Anglo-American school, on the other hand, sees in deconstruction a freedom from political posturing, since it emphasizes the limitations of discourse which continually undermines itself. However, in adopting this perspective, the Anglo-American critics peddle meaninglessness rather than ambiguity. Eagleton notes that

> Meaning may well be ultimately undecidable if we view language contemplatively, as a chain of signifiers on a page; it becomes 'decidable', and

---

20. Eagleton, *Literary Theory*, p. 142.

21. Josué V. Harari (ed.), *Textual Strategies: Perspectives in Post-Structuralist Criticism* (London: Methuen, 1980), pp. 36-37.

22. Exum and Clines (eds.), *Literary Criticism*, p. 20.

23. See e.g. Jacques Derrida, *Of Grammatology* (trans. Gayatri Chakravorti Spivak; Baltimore: The Johns Hopkins University Press, 1976).

> words like 'truth', 'reality', 'knowledge' and 'certainty' have something of
> their force restored to them, when we think of language rather as something
> we *do*, as indissociably interwoven with our practical forms of life.[24]

Furthermore, seeking to avoid a political stance is as much a political
decision as declaring a political stance, and may itself be deconstructed. It
seems more honest to expound the limitations of one's discourse, despite
the inevitability of undermining oneself.

A poststructuralist perspective on the Hebrew Bible remains a comparatively new endeavour. Its advantages are precisely the eclecticism and
'methodological adventurousness' to which Cheryl Exum and David
Clines drew attention in 1993.[25] However, the decision of the contributors
to that volume 'not to linger over the theoretical niceties' may invite the
sort of criticism that Burke Long makes of Alter and Sternberg (that they
'largely dismiss, and hence refuse to engage with, a considerable body of
philosophical thought that questions the very traditionalism they represent'[26]). Long criticizes Alter and Sternberg for their neglect of poststructural theory; those who advance poststructural perspectives without
discussion of methodological niceties may face criticism of their neglect
of other philosophical movements. Such criticism, however, is unlikely to
come from Long, since he hopes that critics will avoid any temptation to
normativity but rather that they will engage in 'a resistive criticism that
assumes the necessity of de-mystifying continually all acts of criticism'.[27]
In other words, it is the attempt to limit criticism to which Long, together
with other proponents of poststructural criticism of the Hebrew Bible,
objects. It seems to me that this refusal to be bound by limitations is the
most compelling reason to adopt a poststructuralist methodology, or even
a plurality of methodologies. If we accept the proposition that our environment, at this moment in time, is postmodern[28] then our methodological
concerns need not make the claim to 'have any truly satisfactory answer
that serve[s] for now as well as for then',[29] or for now as well as for a time

---

24. Eagleton, *Literary Theory*, p. 147.

25. Exum and Clines (eds.), *Literary Criticism*, pp. 12-15.

26. Long, 'Biblical Poetics', pp. 73-74.

27. Long, 'Biblical Poetics', p. 84

28. Cf. Exum and Clines (eds.), *Literary Criticism*, p. 15.

29. David M. Gunn, *The Fate of King Saul: An Interpretation of a Biblical Story*
(JSOTSup, 14; Sheffield: JSOT Press, 1980), p. 17. Gunn is discussing the insights of
Aristotle, Longinus, Sidney and Johnson, which, he feels, do not provide such an
answer.

to come. The only limitation we will accept, then, is that which we impose on ourselves: that of our political milieu. Furthermore, the methodological pluralism of which Harari writes may be a fitting response to the concern that close methodological identification becomes 'the result of a disciple mentality' and that 'methodology can kill research instead of stimulating it and can close critical horizons instead of opening them'.[30]

The Intertextual Perspective

The concept of intertextuality derives from the notion that all texts are constructed out of other texts, not merely by a process of source or influence but in the sense that each component part of the text has been reworked out of other texts that surround it. There is no original text and there is no ultimate meaning, since the codes and signifiers upon which a text depends point inexhaustibly to further codes and signifiers. Thus intertextuality is not about discerning sources or influences, as has been traditional in critical practice, but rather it studies a text's participation in discursive space and discursive practices. Since many of the texts that surround the text under examination are anonymous or unidentifiable, intertextual studies are usually carried out among texts whose boundaries are more easily fixed, even if theoretically the boundaries are arbitrary. This practical narrowing of the field entails the consequence that

> one either falls into source study of a traditional and positivistic kind (which is what the concept was designed to transcend) or else ends by naming particular texts as the pre-texts on grounds of interpretive convenience.[31]

However, this only becomes a problem if the critic wishes to argue for the universal legitimacy of her or his criticism. In applying practical, if arbitrary, boundaries to a theory resistant to the drawing of lines of delimitation, the critic must recognize the limitations of the critical product. Nevertheless, to establish some degree of closure is not the same as to insist on a totality of interpretation.

The term 'intertextuality' is most often used in practice as an umbrella term for approaches that investigate the relationships between (usually written) texts. A frequent assessment of these relationships is that they are troubled; that the anterior text is displaced by the posterior text and also

---

30. Harari (ed.), *Strategies*, pp. 10-11.
31. Jonathan Culler, 'Presupposition and Intertextuality', *MLN* 91 (1976), pp. 1380-96 (1388).

undermined by it. This displacement is often termed 'decentring' since the anterior text's authority is stirred but not shaken. The centre has been moved but not destroyed. Peter Miscall writes,

> Textual authority and status are in question because the original text no longer has the necessary site and center to exercise its previous authority. But the authority and status are 'in question' and are not totally removed or denied.[32]

Thus there is a confrontation between intertexts in which they vie for power. This is the case even if we are not able to speak of one text as anterior and another as posterior. Such a view is based on the poststructuralist identification of language with power and the location of reality within language. The confrontation may become especially apparent if the intertexts in question are not written texts but social texts: an example might be the intentional use of intertextual methods to displace claims of interpretive totality on the part of Higher Criticism.

However, this confrontation may be tempered by reading intertextually forwards as well as backwards. Such reading may be accidental: if one happens to read Muriel Spark's *The Only Problem* before one has read Job, subsequent reading of the biblical material will result in reading forwards. Reading backwards has often been accompanied by the concept of the 'death of the author'; intertextual readings are often thoroughly unconcerned with what an author meant to say, with the circumstances of the author's life, or with the author's imagined audience. In short, the author loses his or her privilege. Since these homicidal tendencies are in practice politically motivated, the assassination of the author with the intention of gaining privilege for the reader may be seen as revolutionary or alternatively as gratuitous violence. To insist on the death of the author may be to go beyond decentring and cause the hermeneutic to lose its centre altogether. Accordingly, it appears that the best solution is to exercise caution; to allow the author some degree of significance but to assert the reader's power at least equally.

Intertextual approaches to the Hebrew Bible have tended to remain intra-canonical; that is, texts within one book have been compared and contrasted with texts from another. Some scholars have worked on the relationships between verses in the Prophets and the quotations of these verses in the

---

32. Peter D. Miscall, 'Isaiah: New Heavens, New Earth, New Book', in Danna N. Fewell (ed.), *Reading Between Texts: Intertextuality and the Hebrew Bible* (Literary Currents in Biblical Interpretation; Louisville, KY: Westminster/John Knox Press, 1992), pp. 41-56 (45).

New Testament. These are clearly in some kind of source relationship, but the fact has not been a deterrent. An exception to this intra-canonical approach is Hugh Pyper's article on the book of Job as a pre-text for Muriel Spark's *The Only Problem*, which is a highly cogent analysis.

The concept of source need not be considered alien to intertextuality, yet neither need it be privileged. Principles of intertextuality may be used to discuss material that is clearly related by source in order to obviate privileging either anterior or posterior texts. The question of source becomes relevant to such discussion but is no longer the prevailing question; more important to this type of discussion are questions about the nature of other textual relationships, comparisons and contrasts, and the success (or lack thereof) of a text within its own framework.

For the most part this thesis presents a diachronic (or text–text) view of intertextuality despite the synchronic approach to the biblical material in the first two chapters. This alternation between a synchronic and a diachronic perspective provides a wider scope for interpretation. Nevertheless, the synchronic approach to intertextuality is not to be disregarded, since its operation is inevitable even to a diachronic view, and furthermore, since the purpose of this thesis depends on it! The primacy of the synchronic view entails other problems: if applied to a common notion in this field, that 'the genotext only becomes a text or only achieves significance through what the phenotext makes of it',[33] then a logical extension could be that the Bible only achieves significance through a woman in Scotland reading a nineteenth-century French play (or through others reading her thesis). This is clearly missing the point of the theory, since 'no reader is an island', but it highlights a tension whereby the synchronic view can become an endless loop. Nevertheless, the two views work best if they function in symbiosis and contribute to the concept of a plurality of methodologies for which I have already argued. It may be claimed on the basis of the work of David Gunn, Lee Humphreys and Cheryl Exum that a synchronic approach to 1 Samuel is the most successful for treating the concept of the tragic vision, since Humphreys's diachronic approach is ultimately less convincing. However, a purely synchronic intertextual approach to the work Lamartine and Hardy would fail to take account of the most fascinating aspect of their perspectives, viz. the relationships with the text of 1 Samuel.

---

33. Ellen van Wolde, 'Trendy Intertextuality?', in S. Draisma (ed.), *Intertextuality in Biblical Writings: Essays in Honour of Bas van Iersel* (Kampen: Kok, 1989), pp. 43-50 (45).

The Story of Saul as Tragedy

If there is one arena where intertextuality can be most widely appreciated it might be the arena of tragic drama, which has been a pervading influence in western culture. Poets and dramatists throughout several centuries have tendered their own versions of myths that date back to Homer and beyond. Furthermore, the philosophical positions of Plato and Aristotle were informed by the progress of tragedy[34] and understandings of tragedy since Plato and Aristotle have depended on their assessments. The views expressed in Aristotle's *Poetics* in particular have been extraordinarily tenacious in critical approaches to tragedy. Walter Kaufmann remarks, 'For more than twenty-one centuries, no other theory of tragedy attracted anywhere near so much attention'.[35] Yet Aristotle's definition in the *Poetics* has elicited much debate, not least over the meanings of words such as '*mimesis*', '*eleos*', '*phobos*' and '*catharsis*'. Kaufmann is very persuasive in his discussion of the meaning of such words.[36] he objects to 'imitation' for '*mimesis*' and instead suggests 'pretend' (in the sense of 'make-believe'), though he cautions that Aristotle's use of the term is not univocal. He also suggests 'ruth' for '*eleos*' (cf. Milton[37]) and 'terror' for '*phobos*'. Armed with these definitions he examines the ideas of catharsis and of hamartia and the six elements that Aristotle claims are necessary for tragedy (plot, character, diction, thought, spectacle and music). Plot is of supreme importance to Aristotle, and in particular two themes—reversal (peripeteia) and recognition (anagnorsis)—are essential in stirring emotions. Kaufmann draws attention to facets of tragedy with which Aristotle does not engage; for instance, where Aristotle speaks of 'thought' he is referring to the thoughts expressed by the characters rather than the tragic poet's thought. Terms that many scholars use without discussion are challenged by Kaufmann: hubris, he argues, is often assumed to refer to pride or arrogance, yet the term is used only once in the *Poetics* and elsewhere *hybrizein*, *hybris* and *hybrisma* have a range of meanings: 'to

34. Walter Kaufmann, *Tragedy and Philosophy* (Princeton, NJ: Princeton University Press, 1968), p. 1: 'the two greatest Greek philosophers [did not] merely come *after* the greatest tragedians; their kind of philosophy was shaped in part by the development of tragedy'.

35. Kaufmann, *Tragedy*, p. 228.

36. See Kaufmann, *Tragedy*, pp. 34-59.

37. 'Look homeward Angel now and melt with ruth' (*Lycidas* 163), quoted in Kaufmann, *Tragedy*, p. 52.

wax wanton or run riot…wanton violence and insolence…lust and lewd-
ness…outrage, violation, rape'.[38] Thus it appears that Aristotle's terms,
which many scholars take for granted, do not have straightforward
translations or meanings and merit closer attention. Larry Bouchard, for
example, writes quite unselfconsciously of the 'elicited response' in
tragedy, 'the arousal of pity and fear'; and is unconcerned in rendering
'*mimesis*' 'imitation' in his discussion of tragic method.[39] His insistence
that '*hamartia*' in Greek tragedy is not to be identified with a Christian
conception of sin might follow a different path if his definition of hubris
were closer to Kaufmann's rather than the recurrent 'overweening self-
projection' which 'remains a challenge to the divine order'.[40]

Questions of Aristotle's meaning, of definitions and translations, become
important in view of the fact that Aristotle's *Poetics* is still considered by
many to be the definitive pronouncement on tragedy. Many scholars who
wish to avoid strict Aristotelian categories in their interpretations of tragedy
feel obliged to make apology for their positions yet feel no corresponding
obligation to the work of Hegel and Nietzsche. However, the work of these
two philosophers has been highly influential.

Hegel has contributed several insights to the discussion of tragedy. He
has been widely criticized, on the grounds that his ideas are based solely
on *Antigone* and on the grounds that he found no flaw in Antigone's
character. Nevertheless, Hegel's discussion of tragedy has contributed
some ideas to the field which have become common parlance in interpretations of tragic drama. Most striking is his concept of tragic collision.
Hegel holds that fundamental to many (but not all) tragedies is a collision
between moral powers that oppose each other. Louis Ruprecht states that

> Nowhere does Hegel insist upon a collision between '*equal* and opposite'
> moral powers (whatever that would mean)—a theory that is more physics
> than poetics, more Newton than Hegel.[41]

Kaufmann, however, quotes from the *Werke*:

---

38. Kaufmann, *Tragedy*, p. 74.
39. Larry D. Bouchard, *Tragic Method and Tragic Theology: Evil in Contemporary
Drama and Religious Thought* (University Park: Pennsylvania State University Press,
1989), pp. 20-21.
40. Bouchard, *Tragic Method*, pp. 25, 31.
41. Louis A. Ruprecht Jr, *Tragic Posture and Tragic Vision: Against the Modern
Failure of Nerve* (New York: Continuum, 1994), p. 74.

> The heroes of ancient classical tragedy encounter situations in which...they
> must necessarily come into conflict with the equally justified ethical power
> that confronts them.[42]

The word here translated 'equally justified' is *gleichberechtigt*, and
Kaufmann argues that Hegel is wrong to insist on this equality. Furthermore, the implication is not that each side of the collision is morally
flawed but that each side of the collision has a claim to moral right.

Not only is moral conflict a necessity, but also, as Ruprecht contends,
'For Hegel, just as tragedy is in its essence an affirmative genre, so too is
the dialectical collision of extremes actually *constitutive* of the moral
life'.[43] Another of Hegel's chief tenets of tragedy follows from this conclusion: tragic heroes play a part in their own ruin. For Hegel this entails a
notion of 'truly tragic suffering', which is only possible if it comes in
consequence of some action of the hero's. Hegel thereby makes a distinction between Fate and Destiny: Fate is blind and unprejudiced, whereas
Destiny is a personal matter. Kaufmann comments that this notion of
'truly tragic suffering' is problematic since it only applies to tragedies that
depend on a tragic collision; he finds it narrow since it applies to suffering
in which the hero is morally innocent. For Aristotle, this scenario would
be shocking rather than tragic. However, Kaufmann concedes that the
concept of 'truly tragic suffering' refines Aristotle's idea of hamartia,
resulting in 'a subtler insight into innocence and guilt'.[44]

Nietzsche has frequently been considered to hold views thoroughly in
opposition to those of Hegel. Perhaps his scathing criticisms of Hegel are
part of the foundation of this opposition; and certainly his Dionysian
position points to a ravine between his views and those of Hegel. However, there are points at which their understandings of tragedy converge.
An example is the notion that tragedy is not interested in the end, that it is
beyond optimism and pessimism. In fact, for Nietzsche, optimism was the
cause of the death of tragedy. Ruprecht identifies several recurring themes
in Nietzsche's work on tragedy: the necessity of redemptive suffering,
which is a matter of deriving pleasure from overcoming resistance in life;
the conception of heroic stature, which is not universal but rather limited
to those who can learn the lessons of tragedy; and the existence of a
peculiarly Hellenistic pessimism that is authentically tragic and differs

42. Kaufmann, *Tragedy*, p. 327.
43. Ruprecht, *Posture*, p. 118.
44. Kaufman, *Tragedy*, p. 243.

from any other kind of pessimism and involves a rejection of the modern world.[45]

Ruprecht's emphasis is on Nietzsche's Dionysian stance 'against the Crucified', with its imagery of two gods in a battle only one can win; Kaufmann deals more with Nietzsche's ideas about the death of tragedy. Nietzsche wrote that the birth of Attic tragedy came about as the result of a marriage of the 'Apolline art of the sculptor and the non-visual [to the] Dionysiac art of music'.[46] The earliest tragedy always presented Dionysus as the hero, and later tragic heroes are merely masks of Dionysus. Tragedy's death, according to Nietzsche, was a tragic one, a suicide. Euripides was responsible: his style involves dialectic which is rational, and through the hero's pleading his case he risks losing tragic pity and inspires optimism. Thus rationalism and optimism are the causes of the death of tragedy. Nietzsche admires Aeschylus as the tragic poet who unites the Dionysiac and the Apolline in the character of Prometheus. He claims that Euripides intended to excise the Dionysiac elements from tragedy, but that he failed in his attempt to base tragedy purely on the Apolline. Sophocles' rendering of the Oedipus myth is ineffective because 'such is the truly Hellenic delight in this dialectical unravelment that it casts a sense of triumphant cheerfulness over the whole work, and takes the sting from all the terrible promises of the plot'.[47] Kaufmann takes issue with a number of these conclusions: he argues that Aeschylus has the most optimistic world view of the 'Big Three', that tragedy's cause of death is not optimism but despair, and that Nietzsche was 'wrong in supposing that a superabundance of dialectics was necessarily a sign of optimism'.[48] It is worth mentioning that *The Birth of Tragedy* was Nietzsche's first book, eagerly anticipated by his academic contemporaries but denounced immediately it appeared, causing a certain amount of harm to his career. He later condemned much of it himself, though he argued that parts of it contained new insights.

Unfortunately there is not enough space here to consider others, such as Paul Ricoeur and René Girard, who have been influential in more recent times. Neither has it been possible to discuss the peculiarities of Shakespearian tragedy. However, this brief overview of the theory and philosophy

45. See Ruprecht, *Posture*, pp. 150-68.
46. Friedrich Nietzsche, *The Birth of Tragedy out of the Spirit of Music* (trans. Shaun Whiteside; ed. Michael Tanner; London: Penguin Books, 1993), pp. 14, 27.
47. Nietzsche, *Tragedy*, pp. 46-47.
48. Kaufman, *Tragedy*, p. 315.

of tragedy, while by no means exhaustive, sets out some of the central presuppositions and tools with which poets and critics work when they explore the tragic vision. The transition from discussing Attic tragedy to the concept of a tragic vision in the Hebrew Bible has not been an easy one, fraught as it is with methodological and philosophical difficulties such as authorial intention and the idea of a monotheistic Weltanschauung, yet the transition is facilitated by employing literary theories that emphasize the role of the reader, and in some ways this postmodern stance is closer to the world of ancient Greece than to the pre-modern world.

Is there evidence of tragedy in the Hebrew Bible? Not according to George Steiner, who argues in *The Death of Tragedy* that

> Tragedy is alien to the Judaic sense of the world. The book of Job is always cited as an instance of tragic vision. But that black fable stands on the outer edge of Judaism, and even here an orthodox hand has asserted the claims of justice against those of tragedy... God has made good the havoc wrought upon his servant; he has compensated Job for his agonies.[49]

Later, in the *Antigones*, he qualifies this view. Writing of Kierkegaard and Abraham, he opines that

> Abraham's concept of destiny is antithetical to that of the ancient Greeks... It is a destiny which comports the pathos of sterile alienation, not the essential fruitfulness of tragedy. Hence the arresting fact that Judaic sensibility, with its immersion in suffering, does not produce tragic drama.[50]

While this may be true of Abraham, it is certainly not true of Saul. Furthermore, even if Job could be dismissed as being on the outer edge of Judaism, surely Saul and David are at its very centre. Steiner does not discuss Saul either in *The Death of Tragedy* or in *Antigones*, and Exum criticizes his position in the former, in which he 'perceives the Bible as speaking univocally'.[51] He also perceives several centuries of ancient Hebrew thought and culture as speaking univocally. The Judaic sense of the world expressed in Genesis differs vastly from the Judaic sense of the world expressed in Daniel. Perhaps one obstacle for Steiner is that, like Kaufmann, he belongs to the school that insists on dramatic form in authentic tragedy, and this is absent in the Hebrew Bible. However, if one

---

49. George Steiner, *The Death of Tragedy* (London: Faber & Faber, 1961), p. 4.
50. Steiner, *Tragedy*, p. 25.
51. J. Cheryl Exum, *Tragedy and Biblical Narrative: Arrows of the Almighty* (Cambridge: Cambridge University Press, 1992), p. 7.

allows for the expression of a 'tragic vision'[52] in literature, the necessity of a particular genre is obviated. Exum argues for using the term 'tragic' for texts that share the tragic vision,[53] and this pushes back traditional boundaries and extends the scope of interpretation.

Northrop Frye has several things to say about tragedy and biblical literature. Contrasting tragedy and comedy, he argues that the perception of misery as tragic is a Greek conception; 'The Bible's vision of misery is ironic rather than tragic, but the same dialectical separation of the two worlds [happy and wretched] is quite strongly marked'.[54] His aim is a complete reading of both the Hebrew Bible and the New Testament in terms of their central *mythos* and he suggests that the Christian myth is a comic version of the Oedipal myth, whereas the account of Reuben's approach to one of his father's women in Genesis 35 has an outcome more in line with that of the Greek myth: he loses his inheritance. A contribution that has had some influence is Frye's idea of plot shape—in comedy a U shape; in tragedy an inverted U shape. This theory has been taken up by Exum and William Whedbee but criticized by Gunn.[55] Its chief problem is, as Gunn remarks with reference to *Macbeth*, *Hamlet* and *Lear*, that restorative and ambiguous endings do not fit the model. Kaufmann has made a similar point with respect to Greek tragedy. He argues, against Steiner's statement 'Tragedies end badly', that Aristotle does not say this,[56] and moreover that many Greek tragedies do not end badly (for example *Oedipus at Colonus* and all but one of Aeschylus's tragedies).

Frye argues that Saul is 'the one great tragic hero of the Bible'; a position with which many later scholars, such as Exum, generally concur. According to Frye, Saul achieves his tragic stature by a kind of 'inspired blundering' on the part of the narrator who 'has not simply made the elementary though very common error of identifying God with the devil' but who has 'managed to add the one element that makes the story of Saul genuinely tragic',

---

52. Exum and Humphreys use this approach, taking the term 'tragic vision' from Sewall. See Exum, *Arrows*, Humphreys, *Tragic Vision* and Sewall, *Vision*.

53. Exum, *Arrows*, pp. 4-5, 154.

54. Northrop Frye, *The Great Code: The Bible and Literature* (London: Routledge, 1982), p. 73.

55. See J.C. Exum and J.W. Whedbee, 'Isaac, Samson and Saul: Reflections on the Comic and Tragic Visions', in J.C. Exum (ed.), *Tragedy and Comedy in the Bible* (Semia 32; Decatur, GA: Scholars Press, 1985), pp. 5-40; David M. Gunn, 'The Anatomy of Divine Comedy: On Reading the Bible as Comedy and Tragedy', in Exum (ed.), *Tragedy and Comedy*, pp. 115-29.

56. Kaufmann, *Tragedy*, p. 50.

viz. 'the suggestion of malice within the divine nature'.[57] I cannot decide whether Frye's tongue is lodged firmly in his cheek or whether he means to state quite explicitly that (1) the narrator of 1 Samuel had a conception of 'the devil' and (2) this entity is enough like God that humans (or narrators?) constantly confuse them. Certainly Frye's volume abounds with remarks such as this, though we must note that he states quite emphatically that he is not a biblical scholar;[58] the purpose of his work is not biblical scholarship, and it would be pointless to expect it of him.

Gunn does not raise the question of a tragic vision in the Hebrew Bible in *The Fate of King Saul*; his is a straightforward interpretation of Saul's story as a tragedy of fate. Perhaps this is because at the time he was writing the debate had not yet begun to rage. A few years later, Lee Humphreys discusses the tragic vision in some detail, commenting that there is a consensus that denies the existence of formal tragedy in the Hebrew tradition, and argues for the existence of a tragic dimension in ancient Hebrew literature. He links the Hebrew tradition to the Greek by means of the Ancient Near Eastern *Gilgamesh Epic*. Humphreys contends that there is a common historical situation in societies' production of tragedy, that ages that have fostered tragedy 'stood between the more or less dramatic breakup of older and long-enduring patterns of thought and action and the emergence of new patterns to replace them'.[59] In ancient Israel there were two such situations: the formation of the Davidic empire and the death of the nation of Israel in 587 BCE. However,

> The Hebraic tradition did not produce tragedy in any sustained way or much material informed by the tragic vision. But at their best, expressions of that tradition had behind them intimations of the tragic.[60]

This historical and formal perspective is avoided by Exum in *Tragedy and Biblical Narrative*; she prefers to interpret inductively and heuristically. She does not attempt to account for the existence of a tragic vision in the Hebrew Bible, but begins her first chapter with juxtaposed quotes from Steiner and Sewall arguing respectively against and for the existence in its cultural milieu of a tragic sense of 'the world' or 'life'. By 1992 the precedent for tragic interpretations had been established, and Exum's contribution is highly significant by virtue of its fresh insights and approach,

57. Frye, *Code*, p. 181.
58. Frye, *Code*, p. xiv.
59. W. Lee Humphreys, *The Tragic Vision and the Hebrew Tradition* (Philadelphia: Fortress Press, 1985), p. 134.
60. Humphreys, *Tragic Vision*, p. 140.

which are less idiosyncratic than those of Gunn or Humphreys and employ the latest literary-critical techniques and methodology.

Yair Zakovitch, responding to Exum and Whedbee's article in *Semeia* 32, advances the common criticism that the terms 'comedy' and 'tragedy' are 'borrowed from the world of Greek drama [and] entirely alien to biblical literature'.[61] He is concerned that the questions to be addressed are those that arise from the biblical text, rather than 'imported' questions, that the 'story of Saul' is the work of many hands, and ultimately that the greatest contributions are to be made where authors 'let the texts speak for themselves—where interpretation is grounded in close and careful reading and not dependent on categories drawn from outside the Bible'.[62] This caution is important, but essentially stems from a different methodological perspective from that of Exum and Whedbee (and indeed from mine). Proponents of theories such as reader-response, poststructuralism and intertextuality might rejoin that reading is an interpretive activity, and that it is not politically appropriate to privilege the author's intentions. While authorial intention may remain an interesting question, it need no longer be the most important question.

Technical Matters

There remain a few procedural points to mention. The decision that 1 Samuel 8–31 be the interpretive unit is not necessarily the most obvious choice, since Saul does not appear until ch. 9 and his death is lamented in 2 Samuel 1. However, ch. 8 deals with Israel's desire for a king and the response of the deity is significant for Saul's progress. Saul's death in ch. 31 is the end of his participation in the narrative, and he can respond neither to David's lament nor to the alternative account of his death. The end of his life is the end of his story, and it is on Saul that this thesis focuses. The majority of scholars working on the Saul story have set the boundaries at either ch. 8 or 9 and at either ch. 31 or 2 Samuel 1. My preference is for the former in both cases.

There are many interpretations and renderings of the Saul narrative, but I have chosen to treat only two: Hardy's *The Mayor of Casterbridge* and Lamartine's *Saül: Tragédie*. Lamartine and Hardy are by no means the only examples of a creative (rather than a critical) approach to the legend

---

61. See Yair Zakovitch, '∪ and ∩ in the bible', in Exum (ed.), *Tragedy and Comedy in the Bible*, pp. 107-14 (109).
62. Zakovitch, '∪ and ∩, p. 114.

of Saul: elements of the story have been painted by Brueghel and Rembrandt, set to music by Handel and Israels, dramatized by Gide and Lawrence, and committed to verse by Browning and Byron, to name but a few. While Breughel's painting and Handel's oratorio are fascinating, the decision to limit myself to the literary field rather than to art in general was made on the basis that, although the theory of intertextuality may allow for a discussion of the relationships between written texts and brush strokes and crotchets, in practice intertextual experimentation tends to remain within the confines of written texts (and usually sources and their issues at that). 1 Samuel is in a source relationship to both Hardy's novel and Lamartine's drama, but each poetic eye has seen a different vision. Lamartine attempts the monumental task of dramatizing the story, though since the play is not performed it can only be regarded as a written text in these times. Hardy's trajectory is one of more extensive adaptation and remains within the narrative form. Arguably the best work of both Hardy and Lamartine is their verse, and their work in other media is characterized by their poetic vision. There are three reasons for the choice of these two rather than other texts, all of which are concerned with contrast: first, they are of different genres: one is a play and the other is a novel. Second, one is written in French, the other in English. Third, and perhaps most importantly, Lamartine's drama is barely known, even to Lamartine scholars, while Hardy's novel is very popular and widely available: it has been read by millions, televised by the BBC, and can be purchased for £1.00 in high street bookstores. All three of these reasons have political implications.

Translations from French and Italian are mine and, unfortunately, more literal than poetic. All quotations, whether prose or verse, and words that are not English are italicized except (1) those which have been appropriated into English usage, such as 'Weltanschauung', and (2) names of characters and places in the French and Italian dramas. This latter is to facilitate distinctions between references to Lamartine's drama *Saül* and the character 'Saül' within the drama. Translations from Hebrew are also my own, though sometimes based on RSV. In designating the deity I shall in general use the name Yhwh. Where I make reference to a specific verse I shall designate אלהים 'God' and יהוה 'Yhwh'. I do, however, consider God to be generally identifiable with Yhwh as a character within the narrative. Since the narrator refers to the deity as 'he' I shall retain this pronoun, since, as Exum comments, this 'helps underscore the status of the deity as a character in the biblical narrative'.[63] Similarly, with refer-

---

63. Exum, *Arrows*, p. xiv.

ence to Lamartine's drama, I shall refer to the deity as 'God' in order to reflect Lamartine's *Dieu* but as 'Yhwh' where I am making comparative remarks concerning the deity of 1 Samuel.

My chapter titles are fragments taken from the work of Thomas Hardy.

Face I
SAUL IN 1 SAMUEL

Chapter 1

TO EVERY BAD THERE IS A WORSE:
THE MECHANICS OF BIBLICAL TRAGEDY

Introduction

Several scholars have recently worked on the elements of tragic vision within 1 Samuel and on Saul as a tragic hero. Cheryl Exum and David Gunn in particular have contributed much insight to this field, though neither of them deal in great depth with the concept of a theory of biblical tragedy. Exum explains:

> My use of the term 'tragedy' is heuristic: it provides a way of looking at texts that brings to the foreground neglected and unsettling aspects, nagging questions that are threatening precisely because they have no answers. I offer neither a theory of tragedy nor an investigation of the genre as such.[1]

Exum thus speaks in terms of 'tragic dimension' and 'tragic vision', though she considers that the story of Saul is the only biblical narrative that fulfils its initial tragic potential. In this she aligns herself with Northrop Frye and Gerhard von Rad.[2] Her work on the narrative centres on the concept of 'the hostility of God', and she juxtaposes the Saul story and the Samson story in order to emphasize the contrast between the tragic dimension of Saul's relationship with Yhwh and the comic dimension of Samson's relationship with Yhwh. This raises some interesting points, such as the profusion of similar plot events which have quite contrasting consequences.[3] Another interesting comparison is the use of repetition in

---

1. Exum, *Arrows*, p. 2.
2. See Exum, *Arrows*, p. 17. She quotes Frye, *Code*, p. 181 and Gerhard von Rad, *Old Testament Theology* (trans. D. Stalker; New York: Harper & Row, 1962), p. 325.
3. For example, Exum notes that both Saul and Samson die fighting Yhwh's battles against the Philistines'. But although both men die by their own hand, Samson's death is not suicide. Samson dies through a divine act which vindicates him, while Saul dies in isolation from Yhwh and truly by his own hand.

the Samson story and in that of Saul. Exum cites Frye in her interpretation of the repetitions in the Samson narrative as a signal of the comic, yet she does not make the corresponding conclusion with respect to the Saul narrative. Samson repeatedly does the same things and encounters the same obstacles, and as Exum points out, 'we see over and over again that Samson bounces back, and we come to expect it'.[4] However, she mentions a 'cumulative effect' of repetition in the Saul story (such as 'hazy' details in the first account clarified in the second, cf. 1 Sam. 13 and 15), yet she does not make the connection that this is part of the mechanics of the tragic vision in the narrative. I would strongly assert that this is indeed the case.[5]

Gunn's interpretive locus is also in a sense heuristic, although he does not use the term. In his introduction he acknowledges his concern that an interpretation be 'workable', that it should 'stay with a reader on subsequent readings of the text', which concern is more congenial to him than providing 'evidence': 'To set out all such working can kill off the essay— to no advantage'.[6] Gunn's work is therefore inductive and has certainly acquired the tenacity he hoped for, as witnessed by the indebtedness of subsequent scholars to his interpretation.

In viewing the Saul story as tragedy Gunn focuses on the concept of a 'tragedy of Fate'. In so doing he does not deny Saul's flaws, but points to the tensions between fate and flaw, and asks which is ultimately the cause of Saul's fall. Thus in his examination of ch. 13, he acknowledges Saul's failure, but concludes that no account is taken of Saul's defence, that 'the question [of God's rejection of Saul in this chapter] resolves itself into one about the motives of Samuel and Yahweh',[7] Similarly, following his examination of ch. 15 Gunn concludes that 'the privilege of interpretation belongs…to God, and God, allowing no explanation on Saul's part, *chooses* to interpret as he does'.[8] Thus Yhwh's motives (and Samuel's) are at issue in Saul's rejection. This underlines Gunn's focus on fate, since Saul's disobedience 'is neither wilful nor flagrant'. Saul's flaw is not a moral one. The sense of fate that is involved in Saul's rejection becomes if anything more pronounced with the entrance of David. 'By the cruellest of fate's tricks' the newly anointed David is brought to Saul as a means of cure from

---

4.   Exum, *Arrows*, p. 26.
5.   See discussion below, pp. 53-55.
6.   Gunn, *Fate*, p. 17.
7.   Gunn, *Fate*, p. 40.
8.   Gunn, *Fate*, p. 56.

his torment, and after Saul's outburst of jealousy in 18.8 'he [Saul] becomes locked (unknowingly?) in a contest with the will of fate, represented by the 'man after Yahweh's own heart', David'.[9]

In his final chapter Gunn examines more closely the portrayal of Yhwh in the story, having concluded that Saul's is primarily a tragedy of fate, and that his fate is inextricably bound up in the person of Yhwh. Gunn links Yhwh's attitude towards Saul with Yhwh's attitude to kingship, leading to the eminently quotable conclusion that 'Saul...is kingship's scapegoat'.[10] Finally, Gunn raises the problem of evil and stresses the dark side of God. He remarks, 'For David, Yahweh is "Providence"; for Saul, Yahweh is "Fate" '.[11]

Lee Humphreys has also done some excellent work on Saul as a tragic hero. His series of three articles focuses on the structures of the Saul story and traces a pattern which he claims portrays Saul initially as a tragic hero and culminates in a portrayal of Saul as a villain. He begins by drawing attention to a destructive phase following a constructive phase in each of the units he identifies, and each constructive phase follows an encounter with Samuel (in the third occurrence with Samuel's ghost). By means of this examination of the structures he concludes that narrative contains 'complex characterization and development of human relationships... We plumb to the depths of the human psyche'.[12] This analysis leads him to the question of the vision of the deity. Humphreys addresses this question in his second article by recourse to narrative strata, arguing that there has been a recasting of Saul's character, shifting the emphasis from Saul's 'compelling grandeur' and 'heroic or even tragic stature' to the dominance of Samuel and David, and Saul's corresponding villainy. Humphreys' interest here is not in the historical origins of these different strata but rather in recognizing that there is a variety of viewpoints represented by different sources in the 'proposed unified accounts formed from them'.[13] He emphasizes Saul's failures and flaws rather than his fate, although he acknowledges that 'This tragic potential is most apparent in the development of the relationship between Saul and his god'.[14] Humphreys's

---

9. Gunn, *Fate*, pp. 78, 80.

10. Gunn, *Fate*, p. 125.

11. Gunn, *Fate*, p. 116.

12. W. Lee Humphreys, 'The Tragedy of King Saul: A Study of the Structure of 1 Samuel 9–31', *JSOT* 6 (1978), pp. 18-27 (25).

13. W. Lee Humphreys, 'The Rise and Fall of King Saul: A Study of an Ancient Narrative Stratum in 1 Samuel', *JSOT* 22 (1980), pp. 74-90 (77).

14. Humphreys, 'Rise and Fall', p. 79.

manner of expression places the emphasis on Saul's perception of 'his god', neglecting the issue of Yhwh's attitude to Saul.

In Humphreys' third article he contends that the early narrative stratum that he has isolated, telling of the rise and fall of Saul, 'contains motifs and characteristics that reflect a cultural sphere distinct from that of ancient Israel; in fact, clear links with the Aegean world of early Hittite and Greek culture are apparent'.[15] This is consonant with the view expressed in the previous article that by being informed by the tragic vision it 'stands apart from most Israelite literary tradition'.[16] However, this view is in direct conflict with Exum's later work on Jephthah and his daughter, and on the house of Saul (where she uses material from 2 Sam.).

It is at this juncture that Humphreys comes to discuss the nature of the deity portrayed in the Saul story. He argues that in this early stratum the deity is 'in many ways…a savage god', and he discerns a 'tension between human guilt and accountability on the one hand, and divine order and control on the other'.[17] There is an apparent anxiousness to avoid the conclusion that Gunn and Exum draw: the conclusion that evil originates in the divine and consequently afflicts Saul. Humphreys contends that there are no morals to be drawn and no lessons for life in this tragedy. Perhaps this is because if one were to draw morals one might implicate Yhwh. Yet to do Humphreys justice, he acknowledges that Saul's story 'must temper all assertions of beneficent divine order or of justice, or of divine beneficence toward humankind'.[18] This, however, does seem startlingly like a lesson in life.

Humphreys finally identifies other perspectives in the story of Saul in 1 Samuel: the portrayal of Saul as a villain comes from a northern prophetic circle, while the portrayal of Saul as rejected comes from a southern royalist circle. He claims that the redaction of 'the deuteronomistic historian' was a mere light brushing. In summary, Humphreys's diachronic approach

---

15. W. Lee Humphreys, 'From Tragic Hero to Villain: A Study of the Figure of Saul and the Development of 1 Samuel', *JSOT* 22 (1982), pp. 95-117 (95). Humphreys notes an incident parallel to the necromancy at Endor in the Gilgamesh epic (see *ANET*), and refers to other scholars' work on Hittite and Greek material making a similar comparison with 1 Sam. 28. However, this is Humphreys's sole example of a 'link', and the designation of the dead individual as a אלהים is not prescriptive in the tragic vision in the story of Saul. What is needed in support of Humphreys's argument here is a clear link with Hittite and Greek literature rather than with culture.

16. Humphreys, 'Rise and Fall', p. 80.

17. Humphreys, 'Hero to Villain', p. 100-101.

18. Humphreys, 'Hero to Villain', p. 102.

differs significantly from that of Exum and Gunn and most others who
have discussed the tragic dimension in the story of Saul, and his work is at
many points illuminating. However, his discussion of the nature and
activity of the deity is marred slightly by neglect of certain aspects of the
narrative, most crucially the activity of the evil divine spirit, which he
consistently evades, preferring to write instead of Saul's madness, on
which he is quite cogent.

Having outlined the work of three major scholars on tragedy in the Saul
narrative, I will continue in this chapter by outlining the tragic themes that
are in evidence in 1 Samuel, and then I will look more closely at an example of tragic collision in 1 Samuel: that between father and son. Having set
out the background to the tragic vision and focused on an example, I will
proceed by discussing the mechanics of the tragic vision, by investigating
the repetitions and type-scenes as the manner in which the tragic vision is
expressed. This discussion will therefore offer a theory of biblical tragedy
in the story of Saul.

Overview of the Tragic Vision

It will be useful to outline the events that occur in the narrative of 1
Samuel that have led to the claim that there is evidence of the tragic vision
in the story of Saul. I shall deal here largely with the events that lead to
Saul's rejection: 1 Samuel 13 and 15, and the background to those events.

The events that seal Saul's fate begin in 1 Samuel 8 when the people of
Israel come to Samuel and demand a king, 'like other nations', to govern
them and lead them in battle. Yhwh's reaction to this is one of jealousy;
the people have rejected him from being king over them, and he instructs
Samuel to reprove the people with a catalogue of the disasters a human
kingship would entail, including the withdrawal of divine sympathy: 'And
in that day you will cry out because of your king, whom you have chosen
for yourselves, but Yhwh will not answer you in that day' (8.18). Yet in
living memory, under Yhwh's kingship, the ark has been captured by the
Philistines and Eli's sons slain and Eli himself killed. The people wish to
be ruled by a just ruler, and their reason for wanting a king is given as the
fact that Samuel is old and his sons, whom Samuel has made judges over
Israel, are greedy and corrupt. However, Yhwh views their demand as a
sign of infidelity and complains bitterly of their rebuff. Despite his perception of this demand as a personal rejection, Yhwh agrees to let Samuel set
a king over them, yet in the event Yhwh supervises the choice. At this
point Yhwh appears to be more positive about the appointment of a ruler,

claiming that he has seen the suffering of his people and consequently intends the king to save them from the hand of the Philistines. So Saul is directed to Samuel to be anointed, and then to a band of prophets, whereupon the spirit of God possesses him and sends him into a prophetic frenzy. Samuel tells him that from that point he is to do what he sees fit to do because Yhwh is with him. For the time being, Yhwh seems to be well disposed towards Saul, and Saul's only opponents are some individuals whom the narrator terms 'worthless fellows' and who 'despised him and brought him no present' (10.27).

God's spirit comes on Saul again in 11.6, when Saul hears of the Ammonite threat to the inhabitants of Jabesh-gilead. His early military success brings him the admiration of the people, but Samuel is still determined to force the people to acknowledge their sin in asking for a king. At his instigation, Yhwh sends thunder and rain at the time of the wheat harvest, and Samuel warns them that if they do not obey God, they and their king shall be swept away.

Obedience appears to be the key to the success of the kingship, and Saul soon makes a mistake which is to cost him his sovereignty. In ch. 13, Saul brings his army to Gilgal. After Jonathan's defeat of their army at Geba, the Philistines are so provoked that they prepare for a serious attack. Saul's army is outnumbered and therefore rather apprehensive. Naturally the prudent military procedure would be to begin battle at once, but Samuel has commanded Saul to wait for seven days until Samuel comes to Gilgal to offer a sacrifice before the battle, and to show Saul what to do (10.8). When Samuel does not arrive, and in desperation at the sight of his army deserting him, Saul offers the sacrifice himself. At once Samuel appears and tells him he has done foolishly, that he has disobeyed God's commandment, that God has rejected him and his line, and in fact has chosen another man to be king.

The crucial question at this point is whether Saul's error is in offering of the sacrifice himself, rather than waiting for the 'man of God' to perform the offering, or whether he was prepared to go into battle without the further instruction of God through Samuel, thus rejecting the help of God and being content to fight on his own merits. One suggestion is that he has infringed a cultic rule in which only a priest may offer a sacrifice.[19] But Samuel is not a priest, and his words to Saul imply that Saul's mistake was in breaking a specific command, namely that he was to wait for Samuel.

19. For example, Harold Lindsell in the Eyre & Spottiswoode Study Bible [RSV] heads the section 13.8-15 with the note 'Saul intrudes into the priest's office.'

As Exum has noted, there is quite a disparity between his accusing 'What have you done?' (13.11) and his injunction to Saul at the anointing: 'do what your hand finds to do, for God is with you' (10.7).[20] In fact, Samuel's arrival just at the end of the sacrifice verges on suspicious. The original instruction was ambiguous, and Saul acted only when he had waited the seven days required of him, and even then only because of his desperation at seeing his army sneak away. The gravity of the military situation is strongly emphasized: the people hid in caves and holes and in rocks and tombs and cisterns, they followed Saul trembling, they began to slip away. Saul is facing a Philistine army of thirty thousand chariots, six thousand horsemen, and troops whose number was 'like sand on the seashore', and Saul must lead into battle an ever diminishing army of conscripts. He is desperate at Samuel's unexplained absence and apparently has no conception that in sacrificing he is risking his kingship. In his attempt to win Yhwh's favour before the battle, he loses God's favour for the remainder of his life, and not just for himself, but also for his descendants. Yhwh's attitude towards him allows no room for leniency or second chances; another king has already been chosen. Saul is guilty, but this is not the only issue here. The crucial factor is not only the fact of Saul's error, but also the attitude of Yhwh towards the king of Israel. Having chosen a king for the people, Yhwh now finds him unequal to the task for which he has been chosen and proscribes his leadership.

Although Yhwh has rejected Saul as king over Israel, he does not wrest the throne from him; Saul retains his position and status. In ch. 15 Samuel gives Saul Yhwh's command to annihilate the Amalekites, and all that belongs to them. So Saul takes his army, warning the Kenites, who live among the Amalekites, to disperse, and he exterminates the Amalekites. However, he brings back their king, Agag, and some livestock. Yhwh complains to Samuel that Saul has not obeyed the command, and Samuel is furious. Saul protests that he did in fact do what was commanded of him, in that he killed all the Amalekites, and that the people brought back the animals to sacrifice to Yhwh. Samuel argues that 'to obey is better than sacrifice' (15.22), and Saul soon concedes that he did it because he obeyed the voice of the people, whom he respected, and is repentant. But from Yhwh's perspective Saul has rejected his commandments, and now Yhwh is determined to relieve him of his throne.

Once again, Saul seems to have misinterpreted the instruction—why else would he be so forthright about the fact that they spared the king and

20. Exum, *Arrows*, p. 28.

brought back the sheep and cattle? One would presume that if he believed himself to be guilty he would be trying to conceal these things from Samuel. He defends himself by shifting all the blame onto the people. Nevertheless, for whatever reason, he has not followed the instruction he was given and his guilt remains. Yhwh regrets having made Saul king, and Samuel never sees Saul again, though he grieves over him. The interpretation of the command is evidently Yhwh's prerogative, and in choosing to find Saul's interpretation unacceptable, Yhwh condemns him.[21] Though Saul is portrayed as devoted to Yhwh, and as having good intentions, he fails repeatedly, and his intentions are irrelevant to Yhwh. There is irony in Samuel's assertion that Yhwh will not repent, since Yhwh has used exactly the same word to describe his attitude to Saul.[22]

Despite having rejected Saul's kingship, Yhwh does not actually remove him from the throne. Saul continues to govern the people and to lead them in battle, but in the meantime Yhwh has chosen another king, and sends Samuel to commit treason by anointing him. One may conclude that Yhwh had chosen David some time previously, for in ch. 13 Samuel tells Saul that Yhwh 'has sought out a man after his own heart, and Yhwh has appointed him to be ruler over his people', and again in ch. 15 'Yhwh has torn the kingdom of Israel from you this very day, and has given it to a neighbour of yours who is better than you'. The situation, then, is somewhat bizarre. Saul has the throne and the loyalty of the people, yet David has been anointed king and it is with him that Yhwh's favour rests. In effect, Yhwh is now tolerating two kings simultaneously—an unexpected development considering his initial antipathy towards the notion of any kingship. There is a collision here between two valid claims: between Saul's claim that his kingship has been established, and David's claim to be the ruler 'after [Yhwh's] own heart', and this collision must inevitably lead to catastrophe. The circumstances have as their substructure the struggle between the divine and the human, a struggle that is complicated not only by the fact that Yhwh has done what Samuel says Yhwh does not do—repented—but also by Yhwh's ambivalence in rejecting Saul's kingship while at the same time permitting him to continue to be king.

Exum notes that 'Yhwh has an ambivalent attitude towards kingship'.[23] It is evident that from ch. 8 Yhwh has been ambivalent about the whole issue of kingship, and this puts the perspective on his disposition towards

21. Gunn makes a similar point: *Fate*, p. 56.
22. On Yhwh's repentance, see below, pp. 58-59.
23. Exum, *Arrows*, p. 35.

Saul under suspicion. Does Saul deserve such harsh judgment? Peter Miscall sees Saul's errors as providing the motivation behind God's treatment of Saul: 'Saul rejects the Lord, and the Lord rejects Saul.'[24] Yet on the two occasions when Saul's actions are found wanting, his intention has been to gain God's favour by sacrifice. As Gunn remarks, 'Saul is not disloyal to Yahweh'.[25] Nevertheless, it may certainly be argued that Yhwh is disloyal to Saul. The ambivalence of the deity in the face of two valid claims on the throne entails other collisions which work themselves out on many different levels, and perhaps the most striking example is the father–son relationship. We shall therefore examine this in more detail.

The Father–Son Collision

One of the categories in George Steiner's five tragic conflicts is that between the young and the old.[26] Nowhere is the potential for tragic drama more effective than when this conflict arises between parent and offspring, and hence it is hardly surprising that a troubled paternal– (or maternal–) filial relationship has remained a central feature of the tragic vision; the majority of those works that are perceived as tragic deal with this issue to no small extent. Walter Kaufmann writes,

> The writer who deals with relationships in which his readers and his audi-
> ence are involved has an obvious advantage over writers who portray
> exceptional relationships of which most men lack first-hand experience. No
> wonder most of the greatest tragedies deal with the relation of lovers or that
> of parents to their children and children to their parents.[27]

And indeed throughout the ages writers of tragic drama and tragic fiction have been concerned with the range of possibilities for human suffering that can arise from such a relationship. Sophocles' *Oedipus Rex*, is perhaps the most prominent example: the hero is guilty not only of patricide but also of producing offspring by incest. The approaches of other writers are no less compelling; the destruction of Lear by two of his daughters, and

---

    24. Peter D. Miscall, *1 Samuel: A Literary Reading* (Bloomington: Indiana University Press, 1986), p. 117. Miscall points out that the people have rejected the Lord but that the Lord does not reject them, and that we do not know why the Lord rejects Eliab. This reading is consistent with the understanding of a tragic dimension in Yhwh's rejection of Saul.

    25. Gunn, *Fate*, p. 124.

    26. George Steiner, *Antigones* (Oxford: Clarendon Press, 1984), pp. 231-32.

    27. Kaufmann, *Tragedy*, p. 137.

the impossibility of reconciliation with the third, engages the darkest of human fears. Even the curse of childlessness on Macbeth's kingship[28] is a function of the working out of the tragic. Furthermore, the extreme horror of infanticide, such as that committed by the unwitting Heracles in subjection to divine manipulation, or, more chilling still, Medea's murder of her sons, is a recurrent theme in the tragic vision. Hence in the tragic vision worked out in 1 Samuel, Saul ultimately fails in his role as parent, and his offspring fail in their duties to their father: Saul treats Michal and Jonathan with contempt while they contest his authority. Exum's discussion of the fate of Saul's house is extremely valuable in drawing attention to the tragic dimension not only of Michal and Jonathan but also Abner, Ishbosheth and Rizpah (Saul's concubine according to 2 Sam. 21). None of Saul's children are given the opportunity to further Saul's line. Such a theme as the troubled parental–filial relationship is arguably an essential element in the tragic vision; Tolstoy's assessment of family life at the opening of *Anna Karenina* is one of literature's finest comments on this phenomenon: 'Happy families are all alike; every unhappy family is unhappy in its own way'.[29]

The collision between Saul's claim on the throne and David's equally valid claim is one that also involves Jonathan as Saul's potential successor. The sense of collision is heightened by the network of familial and pseudo-familial relationships between the three men. There is a strong undercurrent of a father–son type of relationship between Saul and David which threatens the relationship between Saul and Jonathan, while at the same time the relationship between David and Jonathan threatens that between Saul and David (20.30-34; 22.8). The absence of a threat to David's position in the tense relationship between Saul and Jonathan

28. *Macbeth*, Act III, i. Macbeth, speaking of Banquo:
> He chid the Sisters,
> When first they put the name of King upon me,
> And bad them speak to him. Then prophet-like,
> They hailed him father to a line of Kings.
> Upon my head they plac'd a fruitless crown,
> And put a barren sceptre in my gripe,
> Thence to be wrench'd with an unlineal hand,
> No son of mine succeeding: if't be so,
> For Banquo's issue have I fil'd my mind,
> For them, the gracious Duncan have I murther'd...

29. Leo Tolstoy, *Anna Karenina* (trans. Joel Carmichael with an introduction by Malcolm; New York: Bantam Books, 1960), p. 1.

prevents a triangle forming which might alleviate the sense of tragedy, since David's claim would in that case be weakened. The relationship between Saul and Jonathan does not threaten David because Jonathan's loyalty is to David and not to Saul.

Even before David is introduced in the narrative there is tension between Saul and Jonathan. In 14.1 Jonathan omits to tell Saul about his planned attack on the Philistine garrison, as possibly he omitted to do in 13.3. On both occasions the ensuing battle is outside Saul's strategic control. Saul has no knowledge of Jonathan's military manoeuvres and Jonathan has no knowledge of Saul's oaths. There is an implied disagreement between them over military strategy and procedure, and it results in Saul's sentencing Jonathan to death. This tension is characteristic of their relationship throughout 1 Samuel. Whenever Jonathan appears, even when his name is mentioned in his absence, his words or actions are incompatible with the concerns of his father. On the tension in 14.39, J.P. Fokkelman remarks,

> This tension arises from the impossibility of Saul's plan and shows the falseness of his language and intercourse with God. Another is that Saul always says 'Jonathan my son' when he speaks of the prince... This has a false ring in a father–son relationship which has been so totally disturbed; 14.1 prepared us for this by disclosing their lack of communication and at the same time using the (apparently redundant) opposition.[30]

David Jobling has drawn attention to the problem of succession in 1 Samuel and has worked on the portrayal of Jonathan as a possible successor to Saul. In his 1976 article he focuses on ch. 14 and its position between the two rejection episodes, and the statement in 13.14 that Yhwh has chosen Saul's (unnamed) successor.[31] In ch. 14 Jonathan is 'a charis-

---

30. Fokkelman, *Narrative Art*, pp.75-76.

31. Niels Peter Lemche ('David's Rise', *JSOT* 10 [1978]) and Walter Brueggeman ('Narrative Coherence and Theological Intentionality in 1 Samuel 18', *CBQ* 55 [1993], pp. 225-43) both point out that Saul is the first to discern that it is David who will succeed to his throne. Later Jonathan and Abigail express this knowledge. However, Good draws attention to the difference between Saul's 'knowledge' of the identity of his successor and the 'knowledge' of the reader, who has had the benefit of the account of David's anointing. Saul 'does not know it in the full sense. We do know it, however, and that knowledge renders deeply ironic Saul's efforts to overcome David, which cannot succeed' (Edwin M. Good, *Irony in the Old Testament* [Sheffield: Almond Press, 2nd edn, 1981], p. 76).

matic hero approved and empowered by Yhwh'.[32] Saul is unfavourably contrasted with Jonathan throughout the chapter: he attempts to take credit for Jonathan's successes and he misconceives his religious duty. Jobling's aim is to uncover the literary prehistory of the passage, but he nevertheless argues that the redaction of chs. 13–15 has produced a unified account. He concludes by raising the problem of the implied rejection of Saul's line in 13.14 and suggests that the answer may be found in Jonathan's mediatory role in the transition from Saul to David. In fact the inclusio to which Jobling points extends beyond the fact of rejection to Yhwh's choice of successor. Jobling does not mention the connection between 13.14 and 15.28 (where Samuel tells Saul of his successor), but this connection is vital in the context of the succession. Jobling develops this idea of a mediatory role in his 1978 structural analysis, arguing that

> In relation to Saul, [Jonathan] moves between close identification and an independence which frequently suggests his replacing Saul. In relation to David, he moves between close identification and a self-emptying into David, a readiness to *be replaced* by him.[33]

Thus Jonathan as a character is in the service of the plot. Jobling contends that his attitudes and actions lack any normal motivation. The problem with this is that it fails to take account of the narrative as art. Unexpected ('normal' is a culturally loaded term and hence questionable) motivations capture the attention of readers or audiences. Furthermore, what is 'normal' about David's motivation in proposing to fight with the Philistine armies against the Hebrews, or Abigail's motivation in defying her wealthy and powerful husband at the threat of a few bandits? It is precisely in this unexpected motivation, in Jonathan's abdication in favour of David, that the seeds of tragedy are sown. Likewise, Jobling's claim that Saul's attempt on Jonathan's life is 'without narrative logic'[34] fails to take account of themes that point to the tragic vision.[35]

Jobling returns once again to succession in his 1986 sequel, where he examines succession in the context of deuteronomic political theory. He compares and contrasts 1 Samuel 1–12 with Judges 6–9 and concludes that

32. David Jobling, 'Saul's Fall and Jonathan's Rise: Tradition and Redaction in 1 Sam 14.1-46', *JBL* 95 (1976), pp. 367-76 (369).

33. David Jobling, *Structural Analyses*, p. 11.

34. Jobling, *Structural Analyses*, p. 14.

35. The narrative logic is in the relationship between this incident and Saul's attempts on David's life and in characterizing Saul. See below, pp. 63-64.

heredity is assumed to be intrinsic to kingship, but that the concept of primogeniture is discredited. This throws up a problem which Jobling has not addressed in relation to Jonathan: that Saul has other sons who might expect to succeed despite Jonathan's abdication. However, Jobling still refrains from addressing this question in his conclusion, where he contends that

> In David, Israel received a royal system that was permanent, an everlasting dynasty; but, just before this was established, the impossible possibility of a royal dynasty's coming to an end was achieved by means of Jonathan's 'abdication'.[36]

In fact, in 2 Samuel, when David has claimed the throne, one of Saul's sons survives and retains some of the northern territory, and David's expansion begins only after that son's death. I would therefore assert with Jobling that Jonathan's 'abdication' is significant in 1 Samuel for David's succession, but against Jobling that this significance lies primarily within the narrative rather than in historical or theoretical reconstruction. In other words, while Jonathan's 'abdication' is significant as a figure of plot and characterization, any understanding of models of kingship based on this figure is fraught with problems.[37] The problem caused by the existence of other sons of Saul is precluded in the narrative framework by their nominal status, since the problem of succession is a feature of the tragic vision and the possibility of succession by other sons is not advanced within the story. This is not to say that Jobling's discussion of theological concerns is invalid, but that such concerns might benefit from a relation to literary concerns. For instance, Jobling's assessment, which Exum picks up—that Jonathan 'accomplishes little else of lasting significance'[38]—cannot go unchallenged. Jonathan's role in Saul's first victory over the Philistines informs the Saul–David sections of which Jobling comments, 'there seems to be nothing in them that would be different if Jonathan did not exist'.[39] The tension between Saul and his son, which is a crucial factor in the tension between Saul and David, is already present in the material prior to the Saul–David sections, which then develop this theme. This

---

36. David Jobling, *The Sense of Biblical Narrative*. II. *Structural Analyses in the Hebrew Bible II* (JSOTSup, 39; Sheffield: JSOT Press, 1986), p. 87.

37. It appears that Jobling is attempting here to use the methodology of literary theory in order to draw historical conclusions, and he is not entirely convincing.

38. Exum, Arrows, p. 75.

39. Jobling, *Structural Analyses*, p. 7.

is the plot, after all, which the character of Jonathan supposedly serves (so Jobling).

It is by means of literary techniques that Robert Lawton proceeds in analysing the relationship between Saul, Jonathan and David. Lawton points to the separation between Saul and Jonathan and to Saul's bitterness over the loss of David's allegiance, for which he holds Jonathan responsible (1 Sam. 22.8). In 1 Samuel 14, Saul expresses no regret that his son is to die. Lawton compares David's relationship with Jesse to Saul's relationship with Jonathan and concludes that there is a similar distance. Saul's repeated use of the relational designation 'son of Jesse' when referring to David is, Lawton argues, not a term of contempt, but a sign that Saul is jealous of Jesse and wishes David were his own son. In ch. 24, David's use of 'father' and Saul's use of 'son' with respect to each other points to an emotional relationship which goes beyond that of king and subject. Lawton concludes that

> The narrator's development of a deeper and more subtle relationship between Saul, Jonathan and David puts a profound psychological dimension at the service of this larger theme. In Saul's twisted heart, David is more his son than Jonathan is. He is the one who *should* succeed Saul.[40]

Lawton's insistence on following MT ואבי ראה גם ראה at 24.12 is crucial, since the only reasons given for rejecting this are based on its unusual repeated imperative. As Lawton points out, it is grammatically correct. Furthermore, the unusual quality, which Lawton describes in terms of David blurting it out, may be associated with a technique discussed by Patricia Willey with reference to the episode in 2 Samuel 14, where the woman of Tekoa in her confusion 'blurts out' garbled answers to David's questions.[41] When translators attempt to make sense of intentionally nonsensical text, or when scholars reject it in favour of other versions, they may be missing the point of the difficulty. The emotional bond between Saul and David is demonstrably in contrast to Saul's distant relationship with Jonathan, and this gives depth to the tragic vision. However, Lawton's conclusion that Saul imagines David should succeed him is not so plausible. Saul is portrayed as experiencing a constant struggle in his relationship with David, a struggle that is informed by the involvement

---

40. Robert B. Lawton, 'Saul, Jonathan and the Son of Jesse', *JSOT* 58 (1993), pp. 35-46 (46).

41. Patricia A. Willey, 'The Importunate Woman of Tekoa and How She Got her Way', in Fewell (ed.), *Reading*, pp. 115-32 (115-17). See also below, pp. 74-75.

of Yhwh's evil spirit. Although Saul eventually acknowledges that David will succeed him (24.20 [ET 24.19]), he does not accept it, and continues to pursue David (ch. 26). This conflict within Saul's emotions points once again to the tragic vision.

Nevertheless, Lawton's work points very strongly to father–son typology in the relationship between Saul and David, and on the basis of this, it will be useful to consider the work of David Pleins on 'Son-slayers and their Sons'. Pleins contrasts the Aqedah with Saul's attempt on Jonathan's life in 20.33, and concludes that Abraham acts in obedience to God while Saul does not. He also compares the broader rhetorical function in terms of the theme of securing an heir. He argues that in 1 Samuel 'Saul has failed the test of his worthiness to supply an heir to the throne',[42] which is curious in view of the fact that there is no suggestion anywhere in 1 Samuel that Saul is being tested in any such way. In fact, from 13.14 it is implied that Saul's line as well as Saul has been rejected, which seems to conflict with any reference to the Aqedah. However, the question of the identity of Yhwh's second chosen king, Saul's successor, has been raised in the same location. Pleins, like Lawton, argues for father–son typology between Saul and David and draws attention to Saul's many attempts on David's life. Pleins sees in the episodes in ch. 24 and ch. 26 a necessity of comparison with Genesis 22, in which

> David is brought into a conscious father–son relationship to demonstrate the basis of his worthiness to serve as Israel's legitimate heir to the throne.[43]

This notion of a father–son relationship as the basis for succession has been dismissed by Jobling, as discussed above. However, Pleins argues in contrast to Lawton that elsewhere this motif is downplayed, that Saul is termed Jonathan's 'father' and that the comparison with Genesis 22 compounds the 'sad irony of the father–son relationships in 1 Samuel'.[44] While this may be the case, the question of obedience is where Pleins's argument falls down. He maintains that Jonathan's disobedience disqualifies his succession,[45] and that conversely David 'obeys' by bending before the

---

42. J. David Pleins, 'Son-Slayers and their Sons', *CBQ* 54 (1992), pp. 29-38 (33).

43. Pleins, 'Son-Slayers', p. 35.

44. Pleins, 'Son-Slayers', p. 36.

45. It is interesting to note in this connection Exum's contention that Jonathan's eating the honey 'has a 'coincidental' quality about it reminiscent of the 'coincidental' appearance of Jephthah's daughter' (*Arrows*, p. 77). One might also draw a comparison with the sense of coincidence in the appearance of Samuel at the end of Saul's sacrifice in ch. 13.

father who would kill the son, thus displaying more active and demonstrative obedience than Isaac's. While the case for Isaac's obedience can be argued by comparison of Genesis 22 with the Targums, the notion of obedience is in fact largely absent from 1 Samuel 24 and 26. Although it is true that David does not kill Saul at either opportunity, the emphasis in the narrative is not on any sense of 'obedience' (obedience to what exactly, one might ask), but on the power differential between Saul and David and the force of the encounter between them. For while it is the case that Saul makes several direct attempts on David's life and pursues him with the intention of killing him, in neither ch. 24 nor ch. 26 does Saul directly threaten David's life, and both episodes conclude with a nominal reconciliation. This points once again to a complex network of relationships between Saul, Jonathan and David which resists straightforward explanation but which shapes the tragic vision in 1 Samuel.

Furthermore, Pleins does not deal with Saul's attempt to kill Jonathan in ch. 14, which occurs before David's entry in the narrative. It seems to me that this episode is crucial, since although the threat to Jonathan's life is not portrayed as a deliberate attempt on Saul's part to have his son put to death, the theme is certainly present in this episode. The threat to Jonathan's life comes about precisely because of Saul and the reprieve comes about only because the people will not permit the carrying out of Saul's death penalty. If we are to understand the function of Jonathan's role as being concerned with the problem of succession (cf. Jobling), then we must also take this episode into account. Crucial to the account is the issue of Jonathan's actual guilt. Saul enquires of Yhwh, Yhwh does not answer, Saul perceives that a sin stands in the way of the answer and draws lots to find the guilty party. The lot finds Jonathan guilty. This whole episode demonstrates that according to Yhwh Jonathan is deserving of death. Perhaps this goes some way towards providing an explanation to the problem of succession which is not fully addressed by Jobling's idea of a mediatory role, or Pleins's idea of disobedience.

It is curious that neither Pleins nor Lawton gives a detailed analysis of Jonathan's relationship with David. Jobling touches on this when he argues that Jonathan's character is without 'normal' motivations, but generally refrains from close analysis of the relationship. It is my contention that the relationship between Jonathan and David provides a key to understanding Saul's relationship with both these 'sons'. Neither the widespread assessment that Jonathan loves David and gives up his right to the throne to him for this reason, nor the symbolism of the gift of clothes, fully explains the network of relationships. Moreover, the question of why

David and not Jonathan succeeds Saul has been answered theologically
and psychologically and these answers go some way towards providing
explanations as to how the writer or redactor of 1 Samuel addressed the
question of succession, but it is the tragic vision which contextualizes both
question and answer. The network of relationships between Saul, Jonathan
and David is characteristically tragic and the collisions between Saul as
father and Jonathan as son, and between Saul as father and David as son,
point to an interpretation of Jonathan's motivations within the tragic
matrix. Jonathan's love for David and the resulting conflicts with Saul are
more than simply a technique for legitimizing David's succession: they are
functions of the tragic vision. A further question which is raised by Exum
and Gunn is the possibility of a more calculating aspect to Jonathan's
motivation. Gunn has not developed this possibility within his work,[46] but
Exum draws attention to two remarks Jonathan makes which point to what
she terms a 'complication' in Jonathan's character: 20.13 ('May Yhwh be
with you [David] as he was with my father') and 20.16 ('May Yhwh
requite the enemies of David'). Exum asks, 'is Jonathan, knowingly or
unintentionally, calling down divine wrath upon his own father?'[47] Furthermore, Exum points out that Jonathan acknowledges David's future
succession and plans to be his second in command (23.16-18). On this
basis one might well imagine that Jonathan's position as second to David
might be more agreeable than his position as Saul's son. This interpretation fits with Saul's complaint that 'No one discloses to me when my son
makes a league with the son of Jesse; none of you mourns for me or
discloses to me that my son has stirred up my servants against me to lie
in wait for me as this day' (22.8). Saul's fears concerning his subjects'
loyalty often verge on paranoia, but are rarely politically groundless.[48]
Thus Niels Peter Lemche's assessment of Jonathan's behaviour may be
precipitate. Lemche contends that 'Jonathan is obviously very naive and
acting against his own interest and out of personal affection when he tries
to save his most dangerous rival'.[49] This makes sense if one accepts
Lemche's view that Saul's insanity was invented by the author of 'David's
Rise' (i.e. involving a perspective of historical reconstruction), but from a
literary-synchronic perspective such a conclusion draws attention to the
disparity between David's treatment of Jonathan and Saul's. Perhaps this

---

46. Gunn, *Fate*, p. 10.
47. Exum, *Arrows*, p. 80.
48. Cf. the women's song. See below, pp. 68-70.
49. Lemche, 'David's Rise', pp. 2-25 (8).

disparity might provide grounds for new position on the historical reconstruction of this material.

Tragic Mechanics

1 Samuel has long been considered a work whose compiler had access to
several sources and included as many as possible. This notion provides one
solution to the problem of multiple accounts of Saul's accession, his rejection, and his pursuit of David, among others. The identities of the sources
lying behind the final work are debated and renamed by the scholars, for
example: Fabrizio Foresti posits an original account (the ancient Saul-Uber-
lieferung), an account of David's rise (Aufstiegsgeschichte), and three
editors known as DtrP, DtrH and DtrN according to each deuteronomist's
agenda. Hans Wilhelm Hertzberg recognizes a Mizpah tradition, a Gilgal
tradition (probably corresponding to Foresti's DtrN) and a Philistine tradition. William McKane mentions a J source which is thought to be coexten-
sive within the book and refers to the theory that the book was written by
Abiathar, Ahimaaz or Zadok. There are almost as many theories about the
diverse origins of these narratives as there are source-critical scholars of 1
Samuel, and the five main approaches are neatly summarized by Moshe
Garsiel (pp. 13-14), who then states that none of them have ever arrived at
clear conclusions, though he does acknowledge a consensus in principle. He
goes on to say,

> But the author of Samuel, so it seems to me, reworked his material with
> such genuine creative artistry that he cannot be regarded as an 'editor' in
> the restricted technical sense of collecting and arranging together material
> and providing editorial links and glosses; rather he seems to have been a
> skilled creative artist—an author in the full meaning of the word.[50]

It is this skilled creativity in which lies the solution not so much to the
existence of juxtaposed multiple accounts as to the *significance* of their
juxtaposition.

It was Aage Bentzen who drew attention early on to the unusually high
number of multiple accounts in 1 Samuel,[51] and indeed if one examines
the repetitions at a linguistic and thematic level the sheer number is aston-
ishing. A careful reading of some of these may point to a stylistic device
central to the tragic reading of the Saul narratives. Exum is correct when

---

50. Garsiel, *I Samuel*, p.15.

51. Aage Bentzen, *Introduction to the Old Testament* (Copenhagen: G.E.C. Gads
Forlag, vol. II, 1949), p. 93.

she comments that 'each repeated weakness, each instance of vacillation, each violent and unstable action adds to the case against [Saul]',[52] but there is more to the repetitions than this. Miscall sees the repetitions as an expression of the author's anti-monarchical sentiments.[53] He contends that the doubles exude ambiguity, such as when the text 'presents us with at least two different views or versions of a given event or character'.[54] Comparing 1 Samuel 1–17 with mythic material in the story of Moses, Miscall argues that the doubles and repetitions in Samuel are not due to redaction but that this is a deliberate stylistic device, designed to present kingship in a negative light, although he does not touch on the tragic perspective. Lemche's approach differs somewhat: he views the repetitive structure as a function of the author's 'interest in the glorification of his hero David'.[55] Correspondingly Saul is thus portrayed as fully responsible for the break with David.

Robert Alter has noted the importance of examining typescenes and repetitions in order to determine not only their similarities but also their differences.[56] Meir Sternberg has done some extensive work on categorizing repetitions in biblical narrative[57] and concludes,

> In each case, then, the repetition and/or variation opens a gap concerning the reteller's state of mind. And the reader fills in the gap through a hypothesis that assigns to this retelling character some form of deliberateness or non-deliberateness in transmission, according to the factors and pointers available in context—including the nature of the retold object.[58]

Thus, while Saul's errors have a cumulative effect (so Exum), it is crucial to compare and contrast the repeated features. Crucially, we are not concerned here only with Saul's fall; some of the repeated material relates to Saul's rise and thus takes on a subtler colouring than a 'cumulative effect'

---

52. Exum, *Arrows*, p. 30.

53. Peter D. Miscall, 'Moses and David: Myth and Monarchy', in Exum and Clines (eds.), *Literary Criticism*, pp. 184-200 (185).

54. Miscall, 'Moses and David', p. 189.

55. Lemche, 'David's Rise', p. 5.

56. Robert Alter, *The Art of Biblical Narrative* (London: George Allen & Unwin, 1981) chs. 3, 5, 7. Kort considers Alter's assertions 'controversial' in that he 'takes the juxtaposition of two stories concerning a single set of events to be intentional' (Wesley A. Kort, *Story, Text, and Scripture: Literary Interests in Biblical Narrative* [University Park: Pennsylvania State University Press, 1988], p. 93), but most critics accept Alter's conclusions.

57. Sternberg, *Poetics*, ch. 11.

58. Sternberg, *Poetics*, p. 410.

will allow for. Following models such as those of Alter and Sternberg I will examine some of the repetitions. This is not intended to be an exhaustive list of all the repetitions or type-scenes in 1 Samuel, but it will include the most prominent examples. I discuss gap-filling by means of the same hypothesis in each occurrence in order to make my case that the multiples function as the workings of the tragic vision. Rather than dividing them into categories, I shall deal with them as far as possible in the order in which they appear in the text, to preserve any sense of thematic development. Since in most cases there are large sections of unrelated narrative between the first account and the second (and in some cases third or fourth), the order will be most conveniently determined by the second occurrence of the material.

Saul Becomes King (10.1-16 and 10.17-27)
It is often asserted that there are two accounts of Saul's becoming king, and so I will begin by addressing this claim. In 10.1-16 Saul is anointed by Samuel and on his way home God's spirit comes upon him. The second account is taken to be 10.17-27, in which Samuel calls the people together and Saul is chosen by lot. The spirit of God comes upon Saul in 11.6, and after a battle against the Ammonites the kingdom is renewed. Although these are often purported to be the result of discrete sources, the narrative flows so easily from 9.1 to 11.15 that it is difficult to tell at first glance where one source ends and another begins. Nevertheless, there is an account of a private confirmation of Saul's kingship and another account of a public confirmation of Saul's kingship, though I am not alone in contending that the two accounts represent a process rather than a problem. V. Philips Long puts the case for narrative coherence in 1 Samuel 9–11 and points out that

> The pessimism regarding the possibility of reconstructing a history of Saul's rise reflects two convictions of a literary nature about the section 1 Sam 8–12: 1) that it is not in any but the most artificial sense a literary unity, and 2) that even in its final redaction it does not present a very coherent sequence of events. Both these convictions are based on perceived difficulties within the texts—tensions, contradictions, repetitions and the like.[59]

Long investigates an accession process in Israelite ideology and historiography and tackles the issues that source critics have considered problematic. He concludes that these issues 'can be explained satisfactorily in literary, narrative terms'.[60] If there are two accounts of the manner in

---

59. Long, *Reign and Rejection*, p. 174.
60. Long, *Reign and Rejection*, p. 233.

which Saul becomes king (though I believe the two accounts should be read as two parts of a process), the similarity between them is Samuel's authority in announcing Yhwh's choice, and also Saul's reluctance to make his identity known. The difference is that after the account of the anointing, Saul's new status is unknown except to Samuel and Saul, due to the private nature of the anointing and Saul's silence when questioned, whereas after the account of the lot Saul's new status is a matter of general knowledge, due to the public nature of the process and despite his attempt to hide among the baggage. The combined effect of the similarities and differences is to depict a two-step process by which Saul becomes king. Saul's apparent reticence is explicable in the first account, but in the second account it appears somewhat unexpected and may be seen to foreshadow the problems that Saul's personality will cause in the course of his kingship.

Saul Goes to Gilgal (11.15 and 13.4)

As Saul leaves Samuel after his anointing, Samuel tells him to go to Gilgal where he is to wait seven days until Samuel comes to make offerings (10.8). Peter Ackroyd believes that this verse has been added to harmonize with ch. 13 and to point forward to Saul's rejection: 'the compiler is fully aware of the tragedy of Saul'.[61] In 11.14 Saul has just defeated the Ammonites and the people have called upon Samuel to put to death those who had opposed Saul's kingship (10.27), but Saul refuses to have anyone put to death. Samuel then tells the people to go to Gilgal to renew the kingdom, and they go and make offerings and rejoice. Thus Saul is at Gilgal, but no further mention has been made of waiting seven days. Therefore an aware reader may anticipate a recurrence of Samuel and Saul's meeting at Gilgal in view of 10.8. It comes eventually in 13.4. Saul had been at Michmash with his troops and after Jonathan's success against the Philistine garrison he calls the people to join him at Gilgal in preparation for his first battle against the Philistine army. He waits the prescribed seven days while he watches his army desert him, and when Samuel does not arrive he makes the offerings himself. Immediately he has done this Samuel arrives with words of rebuke and rejection. At his first meeting with Samuel in Gilgal his kingship is joyfully affirmed; at the second meeting his kingship is undermined. In between the two references to Saul's waiting seven days for Samuel at Gilgal, Samuel has spoken extensively to the people, berating them for requesting a

---

61. Peter R. Ackroyd, *The First Book of Samuel* (Cambridge: Cambridge University Press, 1971), p. 84.

king. He has called upon Yhwh to send rain and thunder at the wheat harvest and the people have acknowledged their sin in asking for a king. Samuel has charged them to fear Yhwh and warned that if they do wickedly they and their king shall be swept away. This ambivalent attitude to kingship between ch. 11 and ch. 13, together with the circumstances surrounding the connection between the original charge to wait seven days and the circumstances surrounding Saul's actions in ch. 13 has the effect of raising questions concerning Saul's fate and the continuance of his kingship. The first suggestions of the tragic vision are being developed through this doublet.

Saul's Errors (13.8-15 and 15.1-34)

Crucial to the development of this technique of multiple accounts emphasizing the tragic vision, there are two accounts of the errors leading to Saul's rejection, in ch. 13 and ch. 15. In ch. 13 there are a number of viewpoints. Saul offers the sacrifice when he sees that Samuel has not come within the time appointed. Samuel considers that Saul's action constitutes a breaking of the divine commandment; however if Saul has broken a commandment, it was that of Samuel, who did not say in 10.8 that the necessity of waiting seven days was a commandment of Yhwh. Samuel has not mentioned the word of God since 9.27, before the narrative of the anointing. In fact, Samuel does not stress that the waiting time is actually a matter of such great importance that Saul's sovereignty depends upon it, and does not give any details concerning what it is he wants to show Saul how to do. Saul has been told in 10.7 that he should do what his hand finds for him to do. Yhwh's viewpoint, if it is represented here, is on the lips of Samuel: because Saul sacrifices without Samuel present Yhwh will not establish Saul's kingdom and in fact has already found a man 'after his own heart' who will be prince. Saul at this point might wonder what has happened to the new heart that God gave him in 10.9.

By contrast, in ch. 15 Saul clearly has not kept the commandment of Yhwh as explained to him by Samuel. However, there is no indication in the text that he is being deliberately disobedient. He pauses to allow the Kenites to escape before his army attacks the Amalekites (in another quasi-doublet at 27.10 David tells Achish that he has slaughtered all the Kenites—this, then, is the sort of man who is after Yhwh's own heart) and Saul and the people spare Agag and some of the animals for sacrifice. Hertzberg points out that the difference between killing by putting to the ban and killing by sacrifice is that with sacrifice the people get a portion as well,[62] though Gunn (citing Gottwald) contests the notion that the 'holy war' was ever as formulated a practice in ancient Israel as von Rad suggests. On Hertzberg's reading it appears that in listening to the people Saul really has disobeyed Yhwh's commandment given to him by Samuel. Gunn, however, emphasizes Saul's response to Samuel's charge and argues that 'it is not the 'facts' which are in dispute but their interpretation vis-à-vis the instruction'.[63] Yhwh's response, that he has repented of making Saul king, stands in stark contrast to Samuel's words to Saul at 15.29: 'the Glory of Israel will not lie or repent, for he is not a man that he should repent'.

The difference in Samuel's estimation of Saul's culpability, and in the degree to which Saul has transgressed Yhwh's codes of practice, between these two accounts emphasizes Saul's weaknesses and also the tragic elements in his story. Furthermore, there is a further direct reference to the events of ch. 15 during Saul's consultation with Samuel's ghost in ch. 28, but there is no mention later in the narrative of the events of ch. 13. The account in ch. 15 is much longer and much more detailed than that of ch. 13. Clearly in ch. 15 Saul has not understood what Samuel has known intuitively: that keeping to the exact letter of Yhwh's commandment is necessary if one wants to retain Yhwh's favour. What Saul has failed to grasp is that Samuel's instructions are not open to interpretation. Crucially, for the first time since before the anointing of Saul, Yhwh speaks within the narrative, though he has been active at many points in between. At 9.16 Yhwh had chosen Saul to reign over Israel and told Samuel that the Benjaminite should be a prince over Israel and would save Yhwh's people from the hand of the Philistines. The language used is that of mercy. Now at 15.11 the words are of rejection: 'I have repented that I have made Saul king; for he has turned back from following me, and has not performed my commandments'.

The causes, effects and meanings of Saul's errors and rejection have been discussed at length by many scholars. A lengthy discussion of these is not possible here since my hypothesis depends merely on comparing and contrasting the two accounts with reference to evidence of the tragic vision. I find that the second account contains similar thematic elements to the first: Samuel tells Saul what to do, Saul acts, Samuel interprets his actions as contrary to the divine commandment, Samuel pronounces

62. Hans Wilhelm Hertzberg, *I & II Samuel: A Commentary* (trans. J.S. Bowden from the German 2nd revised edn; London: SCM Press., 1964), p. 127.
63. Gunn, *Fate*, p. 48.

Yhwh's rejection of Saul. However, the emphasis on all of these elements is heightened in the second account: Samuel explicitly tells Saul that the required action is the commandment of Yhwh, Saul's action unambiguously contravenes this commandment, Samuel is told by Yhwh that Saul had acted in a manner contrary to the divine commandment, Samuel pronounces Saul's rejection at length and the narrator provides confirmation that Yhwh has indeed rejected Saul. The tragic elements of Saul's hamartia and rejection are therefore also heightened in the second account, as is the involvement of Yhwh, who is off stage in ch. 13. It is significant, furthermore, that after Yhwh has announced to Samuel his rejection of Saul, and Samuel tells Saul that he will relate Yhwh's words (15.16), Samuel does not relate what Yhwh said to him that night. When he eventually comes to tell Saul of his rejection he does not even quote Yhwh; in fact what Samuel says is almost the reverse of what Yhwh has said. Yhwh has told Samuel he has repented of making Saul king, for he has turned back from him and has not performed his commandments. However, Samuel tells Saul that Yhwh has *rejected* him from being king over Israel and that Yhwh *will not repent*. Since repenting is exactly what Yhwh has done, it is curious that Samuel claims that he will not repent.[64] Saul's conflict with Yhwh is constantly conducted through Samuel, yet Samuel does not make accurate representations. This serves to highlight Saul's isolation from Yhwh and precludes reconciliation. Furthermore, the tragic reversal that is evident in ch. 13 is confirmed and embellished in ch. 15.

64. Angelo Tosato argues very persuasively that Saul's real sin is idolatry, taking 15.23ab as a gloss together with 15.29 and connecting these with the episode between Balaam and Balak in Num. 23. Thus the reason that Yhwh will not repent is because of Saul's idolatry. Of the purpose of the gloss he writes, 'Si tratta...di chiarire attraverso il caso di Saul, rispiegato nell'ambito della fede tradizionale ma secondo le formulazioni di Num 23,18-24, il caso molto più grave (e vivo nell'ambiente del glossatore) dell'inopinata rovina del Regno di Israele' (Angelo Tosato, 'La Colpa di Saul (1 Sam 15,22-23)', *Biblica* 59 [1978], pp. 251-59 [259]). [Translation: It is about... clarifying through the case of Saul, explained again in the sphere of traditional belief but according to the formulations of Num. 23,18-24, the much more serious (and living in the milieu of the glossator) case of the undisputed ruin of the King of Israel.] In other words, the gloss serves to explain Saul's fall intertextually by appeal to a traditional formula. Persuasive though this argument is, it is not ultimately convincing as the reason for Saul's downfall because there are no other references in the narrative to idolatry on Saul's part. There is no reason to suppose that Saul is sacrificing to other gods in 1 Sam. 13 (in fact, Yhwh is specifically mentioned in v. 12) or at any other point. Saul's enquiries of the deity are likewise properly addressed.

Chapter 15 marks the turning point in Saul's fortunes: despite the reversal
of ch. 13 he is able to continue to function adequately both as a king and
as a human being, notwithstanding his flaws. From this point onwards he
is in a constant state of decline. Furthermore, there is tragedy in Yhwh's
rejection and in Saul's alienation from both Yhwh and Samuel (15.35)
because it is a greater punishment than he deserves. However, Sternberg
contends that

> Saul must go because he is a liar and coward as well as a violator of God's
> ordinance; David deserves to keep his throne, after all, because he is an
> admirable as well as a pious king.[65]

This sort of general statement does not do justice to the circumstances
either of Saul's kingship or of David's, and it is surprising in the work of a
scholar usually so attentive to detail. More appropriate to Saul's story, in
the light of the tragic reversal which he undergoes as a result of the events
of these two chapters, is Sternberg's comment that

> The passage from ignorance to knowledge, one of the great archetypes of
> literature, is another Hebraic invention, for which the Greeks got all the
> credit.[66]

Saul's Two Daughters (18.17-19 and 18.20-29)

On two occasions Saul promises a daughter in marriage to David, and both
times his hope is to see David killed in battle. Both times David speaks of
his unworthiness to be the king's son-in-law. Hertzberg and others consider that there may be a reference in 18.17 to 17.25, in which David is
told that the man who kills Goliath will be given the king's daughter,
though others see no allusion here to ch. 17, and not all MSS contain the
Merab story. Codex Vaticanus lacks both 18.17-19 and 17.25, which may
suggest their interdependence. The two daughter stories placed together
here are to be understood in relation to each other.

The first episode is related briefly and concludes when Saul arranges
Merab's marriage to another man, and it is not related whether David did
indeed go into battle in order to win her hand. The second episode is much
more detailed and follows immediately from the first. Michal loves David;
Saul finds this convenient (following McKane, 'it was plain sailing'[67]), as

65. Sternberg, *Poetics*, p. 158.

66. Sternberg, *Poetics*, p. 176.

67. William McKane, *I & II Samuel: Introduction and Commentary* (London: SCM
Press, 1963), p. 116.

it gives him the opportunity to set a trap for David. Saul's servants intercede between Saul and David: previously David has expressed a concern that his background is too humble; this time his concern is lack of wealth. Both remarks are reminiscent of 17.25, where the soldiers told David that Saul had promised the hero who would kill Goliath not only his daughter, but also great riches and freedom to the hero's father's house. While Saul cannot alter David's background, he can provide a solution to David's financial concerns by requiring a bride price of one hundred Philistine foreskins. David finds this convenient (וישר הדבר בעיני cf. v. 20) and kills two hundred Philistines, bringing back their foreskins to count out to Saul.

Fokkelman sees in this matter of the foreskins a certain Freudian undertone, in which Saul's desire to strike the enemy in its potency is combined with Saul's fear of David's potency:

> Beside himself with rage and jealousy he threw the phallic weapon in a desperate attempt once again to be the only loved one at the top. Now he continues destruction in incorporating into his strategy the woman, first hesitantly (Merab), and then clearly developed (Michal as the snare).[68]

Furthermore, Fokkelman states that the quest would be unpleasant and painful for David,

> The first reaction of an Israelite required to think of the foreskin of a Philistine is, of course, one of disgust towards the uncircumcised; the foreskins primarily conjure up rejection of the unclean… [B]y this condition Saul really wishes to contaminate David, make him unclean.[69]

Now perhaps a reading of phallic symbolism is perfectly legitimate, were it not for the fact that a foreskin is utterly unnecessary for potency, while its lack, in the context of 1 Samuel, is a symbol of Yahwism. Therefore one might perhaps read this as Saul's asking David to prove his loyalty to the cult of Yahwism and thereby to its political operations, that is to Saul as it's anointed king. In any case, Saul wishes to strike at the enemies of God, at those whose destruction is supposed to be Saul's destiny (9.16). Only the Philistines among the enemies of the Israelites in 1 Samuel are described as uncircumcised, and therefore they occupy a special position against Israel and Yahwism.[70] As for these particular foreskins, surely the David who was offended at the words of the uncircumcised Goliath would have few qualms about removing a few of the offending objects from their

68. Fokkelman, *Narrative Art*, p. 245.
69. Fokkelman, *Narrative Art*, p. 245.
70. Cf. McKane, *Samuel*, p. 162.

original owners? In fact, so enthusiastic is he that he brings back twice the number required. There is a textual problem with v. 27: Codex Vaticanus and the Lucianic LXX read 'one hundred' instead of 'two hundred', as does 2 Sam. 3.14 MT. Most scholars prefer the MT here. If, with Hertzberg, we understand the original tradition to have represented Saul's wish to have David join his house, we may infer that Saul's desire for Philistine fore-skins as a bride price is related to a wish to have David join his destiny as well as his dynasty. A discourse- (rather than source-) oriented reading such as is my concern might ask whether David thought Michal was worth twice what Saul offered her for (though there is no evidence that David returned her love), or whether David was paying as well for the daughter Saul had denied him, in order to make a gesture concerning Saul's broken word, or, as is most probable, whether David's doubling the bride price is a sneer at Saul's attempt to get him killed. After all, the daughter episodes follow immediately from Saul's first direct attempt on David's life. These questions all arise from the fact that Saul's attempt to rid himself of David has failed, and that, moreover, David has survived twice as many Philis-tines as the number Saul hoped would overpower him.

The Merab episode demonstrates Saul's intention to be rid of David, but Saul ultimately forgoes this course of action by giving Merab to another man. When Saul perceives a second opportunity with Michal he carefully sets up a new scenario, but this time David with shrewd political acumen outwits Saul's plan. David's concern for his economic position, which is different from his previous concern, forces Saul to name a price, which David easily meets, ridiculing and at the same time challenging Saul by doubling the amount and causing Saul to fear him more acutely. In this way Saul abdicates from his God-given Philistine-killing destiny, too easily manipulated by David's superior political talent. Thus while Saul had appeared to be controlling the situation with respect to Merab, the second episode with Michal demonstrates that Saul cannot win in his conflict with David, and there is tragic irony for Saul in David's doubling his success.

Saul's Attacks on David (18.10 and 19.9) and Jonathan (20.33)
Saul makes two direct attacks on David's life. The first, at 18.10, comes after the account of the women's victory song. An evil spirit from God has come upon Saul, and David's lyre-playing is this time to no avail. In fact it appears as though David is playing the lyre not to soothe Saul, as was the original intention, but as a matter of daily habit. It is not clear whether Saul actually throws the spear, though that is certainly his intention. The

MT's punctuation is from the root טול (cast) but Targum points as from נטל (take up).[71] Either way, David is aware that Saul intends him harm and manages to get out of the way.

The second occasion is at 19.9, again involving an evil spirit from Yhwh, and again David is playing the lyre. The sense is virtually identical to the previous account, with a slightly different conclusion: Saul's spear sticks in the wall, David flees and escapes that night. The effect on Saul of the evil divine spirit has become more of a menace to David than his musicianship can compensate for and he must do more than simply evade Saul on this occasion. The conclusion of this pericope forms the background for Michal's help with David's escape from the court of Saul. Thus Saul's second attack on David is more threatening than his first and the action that David must take is more drastic.

There is a further event concerning Saul and his spear: his attack on Jonathan in 20.33. The attempt here is not to pin Jonathan to a wall, but to smite him. There is no mention here of an evil divine spirit, though the attack arises during an outburst of anger at Jonathan's loyalty to David, and Jonathan perceives that the object of Saul's murderous intentions is ultimately David: he knows that his father is determined to put David to death. By this point in the narrative Saul's visitations by the evil divine spirit are a habitual event (this will receive fuller attention in Chapter 2), and we might ask tentatively whether we may infer the influence of Yhwh in this further step towards Saul's decline. But the narrator's omission of reference to the evil spirit directs us to look for a different inference, and we may conclude that the habit which has been formed is Saul's throwing his spear. There are several conclusions to be drawn from the similarities and differences between these three accounts. First, David's music ceases to drive away the evil spirit from Yhwh, but the spirit continues to torment Saul and therefore Yhwh is complicit in Saul's attacks on David. Second, Saul's attacks become progressively more desperate. Third, Yhwh is not directly complicit in Saul's attack on Jonathan. The significance of this third conclusion is that prior to the evil spirit's torment of Saul, the king displayed no signs of the jealousy and paranoia he is increasingly feeling. After sustained torment, Saul's responses have altered, whether or not the evil spirit is directly affecting him. His behaviour towards Jonathan is

---

71. So S.R. Driver, *Notes on the Hebrew Text and the Topography of the Books of Samuel, with an Introduction on Hebrew Palaeography and the Ancient Versions, and Facsimiles of Inscriptions and Maps* (Oxford: Clarendon Press, 2nd edn revised and enlarged, 1913), p. 152.

characteristic of his behaviour under the influence of the evil spirit, yet no evil spirit is mentioned. Saul is becoming a victim of his fate.

Is Saul also among the Prophets? (10.11 and 19.24)

Two explanations are given for the origin of a proverb which links Saul with prophecy. On both occasions the spirit of God comes upon him, (ותצלח עליו רוח אלהים and ותהי עליו גם־הוא רוח אלהים), and he prophesies (ויתנבא). The first occurrence is in the context of the story of his anointing, and it is one of the signs Samuel tells him to expect which offers confirmation of his new status as king and as a new man, and that Yhwh is with him. It is the only one of the signs that Samuel mentions that is described in detail in the narrative; that simply 'came to pass that day'. The proverb has been understood to imply that Saul's behaviour was not fitting for a man of his background, or that Saul was regarded as a member of (Samuel's?) prophetic order. A second explanation of how the proverb came about is found in 19.24. On this occasion, David has just escaped Saul's murderous intentions with Michal's help, Michal has deceived Saul with the lie that David threatened to kill her, and David has fled to Samuel. Saul's messengers follow to capture him, but they fall into prophetic ecstasy and eventually Saul himself goes and he too prophesies.

Alter attributes the two contexts of the quotation of the proverb to a 'folkloric function'. He contends that 'the pressure of competing etiologies for the enigmatic folk-saying determined the repetition more than any artful treatment of character and theme'.[72] However, there are two important features of this second pericope. First, at 16.14 we were told that the spirit of Yhwh departed from Saul, and since then he has been tormented by an evil spirit from Yhwh. The passage 19.18-24 is the only occasion after the anointing of David where a divine spirit comes on Saul which is not described as an evil spirit. However, unlike Saul's previous prophetic ecstasy, this divine spirit causes Saul to lose control to the extent of taking off his clothes and lying naked before Samuel. Verse 19.24's גם suggests that the three sets of messengers he sent ahead of him were also naked. Under the influence of this divine spirit Saul makes himself vulnerable and is unable to do what his hand finds to do (10.7), viz. capturing David. The divine spirit limits him and the mention of the proverb recalls a happier time in Saul's life, his anointing, thus emphasizing Saul's degeneration.

Second, the presence of Saul in Samuel's company is significant, since 15.35 states that Samuel did not see Saul again until the day of his death.

72. Alter, *Biblical Narrative*, p. 89.

Fokkelman claims that Saul does not see Samuel in this narrative because he is not *compos mentis*;[73] however, there seems little reason to suppose that he and the messengers were blind in their ecstasy. (Fokkelman here is flaunting his argument for delving into 'subjective, capricious, associative, fanciful, arbitrary and chaotic readings'.[74]) Throughout the earlier narratives it is Samuel who communicates to Saul the words and intentions of God, and Samuel's absence after ch. 15 is indicative of God's rejection of Saul. Samuel's anointing of David coincides with the onset of Saul's anguish under the influence of the evil divine spirit (16.13-14), and it is only here, in Samuel's presence, that Saul experiences a different kind of divine spirit, one which prevents him from carrying out his murderous intentions rather than driving him to homicide. The presence of Samuel provides momentary relief from Saul's alienation from God, yet at the same time affirms his rejection. Fokkelman sees Saul's pursuit of David to Ramah as an indication that Saul has not learned from past experience:

> One of the effects of the series *gam hemma* (3×), which merges into the series *gam hu* (4×), is the demonstration of Saul's inability to learn. This becomes all the clearer if we think back to Ch. 10. There, as a sign of his vocation, Saul had already experienced once that a band of prophets in exaltation was irresistible. Here in Ch. 19, therefore, he negates his own experience—until he falls down. He should have known that when Tom, Dick and Harry are without exception drawn in by energies around the prophet, he himself will be seized by the divine force a fortiori.[75]

This seems a little harsh, since Tom, Dick and Harry were not present in ch. 10: Saul apparently had only his (unnamed!) servant with him and there is no account of the servant prophesying.[76] The repeated גַּם־הוּא

73. Fokkelman, *Narrative Art*, p. 278.
74. Fokkelman, *Narrative Art*, p. 9.
75. Fokkelman, *Narrative Art*, p. 278.
76. Adele Reinhartz draws attention to the function of anonymous characters in the narrative. She notes that servants, among others, 'shed light on the characters of their masters' (Adele Reinhartz, 'Anonymity and Character in the Books of Samuel', *Semeia* 63 [1993], pp. 117-41 [125]); she cites 16.16 but the two prophesying incidents would be just as appropriate: Saul is shown at these two points to be particularly susceptible to the divine spirit. The woman of Endor fulfils a similar function, and, in addition to the other unnamed women in 1 and 2 Sam., her function is primarily communicative. Reinhartz writes that the woman of Endor 'shows [Saul] to be a desperate man, who must break the laws that he himself promulgated in order to obtain the information that his usual sources —the Lord, the Urim, or the prophets (1 Sam 28.6)—have denied him' (p. 135).

aligns Saul with his messengers, who are controlled by a divine spirit, over against Samuel and David, who generally interact with the deity and who are not depicted in the narrative as having succumbed to the ecstasy; indeed, David is not mentioned at all in these verses. Hertzberg is more generous, 'We can see elsewhere that Saul is particularly affected by all that is holy',[77] though he adds that the description here is not written in praise of the king.

To summarize, then, in the first episode Saul's ecstasy is associated with his anointing and his change of status. Along with the throne, Saul is given charismatic gifts. At the repetition of the proverb, however, Saul's ecstasy is associated with his downfall and his charismatic gifts have degenerated into madness.[78] The presence of Samuel in the second episode highlights this, since Samuel was so closely connected with the first episode. The role of the divine spirit is crucial to the comparison between the two episodes, since in the course of events between the two quotations of the proverb David has been anointed and is the recipient of a divine spirit, while Saul has been the victim of torment by an evil divine spirit. We may understand this passage as an incidence of God's using the divine spirit to manipulate Saul and his messengers not only to keep David safe, but to bring the king and his servants into disrepute, as suggested by the pejorative interpretation of the proverb. The very long gap between the two references to the proverb serves to emphasize the extent of Saul's decline by 19.24 and the tragic reversal that has occurred since the reference to the proverb in 10.11.

Letting David Go (19.17 and 20.29)
On two occasions Saul's designs on David's life are thwarted by his offspring who let the latter go. In ch. 19, as a result of an attack of the evil divine spirit, Saul sends messengers to watch David's house and capture him in the morning. But Michal apparently knows of Saul's plans and helps David to escape. In v. 17 Saul asks Michal, וַתְּשַׁלְּחִי אֶת־אֹיְבִי וַיִּמָּלֵט לָמָה כָּכָה רִמִּיתִנִי 'why have you let my enemy go and he has escaped?' Michal tells Saul a lie: that David said, שַׁלְּחִנִי לָמָה אֲמִיתֵךְ 'let me go, why should I kill you?' This episode is followed in the narrative by David's flight to Samuel at Naioth, Saul's attempt to capture him there, Saul's prophetic ecstasy, David's flight back to Jonathan, and David's attempt to convince Jonathan that the king is trying to kill him. They hatch the plot

77. Hertzberg, *Samuel*, p. 168.
78. Cf. Humphreys, *Tragedy*, p. 25.

that Jonathan should tell Saul that David cannot be at the new moon feast because of family commitments. The first day of his absence Saul thinks David may be unclean, but when he is absent a second day Saul asks Jonathan where he is. Jonathan tells Saul a lie: that David said, שלחני 'let me go'. There is no evidence to indicate that Saul suspected either of them was lying. Saul makes no sustained display of rage against Michal despite his anger, which is understandable if he believes her story. However, even if he believes Jonathan, he sees that Jonathan has no interest in succeeding him, and he insults him, at the same time appealing to him to claim his throne for himself. Ackroyd comments that Saul's anger at Michal is parallel to his anger at Jonathan's behaviour in 20.30-31.[79] Fokkelman believes Saul's anger is centred in his belief that David's first loyalty should have been to his king,[80] but McKane asserts that 'kin obligations were among the most primary and urgent'.[81] There is no reason to suppose that Saul temporarily forgot this, or that there is any feeling of status infringement in his anger. The most probable reason for Saul's anger in 20.30-31 is that it is indeed parallel to his anger in 19.17 and that the reason is not that he believes David has been disloyal (so Fokkelman) but that he believes Jonathan has been disloyal, just as he initially believes Michal has deceived him.

Michal's disloyalty may be regarded by her father as to some extent justifiable, as it is at the same time loyalty to her husband. However, Jonathan's disloyalty to his father is seen by Saul to be incomprehensible. Taking together the imputed insult to Jonathan's mother (against Hertzberg, p. 172) and the parallel with Michal's disloyalty, there is an implicit attack on Jonathan's masculinity in Saul's outburst. Jonathan has chosen David just as Michal has chosen David, but Saul seems to consider it an inappropriate choice for a man, especially for a man whose duty is to succeed his father. Berlin has examined the characterization of Michal and noted that Michal has masculine traits and Jonathan has feminine traits, particularly in respect of their relationships with David, which supports this reading.[82] The difference between Saul's estimation of Jonathan's disloyalty in comparison to Michal's is even more pronounced at v. 33, where Saul casts his spear at Jonathan, just as he had done at David

79. Ackroyd, *Samuel*, p. 158.
80. Fokkelman, *Narrative Art*, p. 332.
81. McKane, *Samuel*, p. 129.
82. See Adele Berlin, *Poetics and Interpretation of Biblical Narrative* (Sheffield: Almond Press, 1983), p. 24.

(18.10; 19.9). Thus the similarities between the episodes, which both point to Saul's increasing isolation from his offspring, engage the tragic vision, but it is the differences which are even more tragic. Saul begins in both episodes with the intention of killing David. In the first David escapes and Michal's deceit is accepted, but in the second David escapes and Jonathan's deceit endangers his life. Saul is thereby shown to be progressively more unstable.

The Women's Song (18.7; 18.8-9. and 21.12 [ET 21.11]; 29.5)
Words used in one context and repeated in another take on particular significance when used on the lips of different characters. A good example of this is the song of the celebrating women in 18.7, 'Saul has slain his thousands and David his ten thousands'. The song appears for a second time immediately: Saul quotes it angrily in the following verse, reversing the order, 'They have ascribed to David ten thousands and to me they have ascribed thousands', and as a result Saul fears for his kingdom. Alfons Schulz takes the verse as a simple indication that David's bravery exceeds Saul's.[83] Fokkelman, following Gevirtz,[84] claims that the verse sung by the women is simply synonymous parallelism and that Saul misunderstands, hearing 'but' rather than 'and'. He thinks it incredible that the welcoming party should insult their king and therefore questions whether Saul does justice to the women.[85] Hertzberg agrees that the verse is not meant to disparage Saul, but that 'within the general framework of the material, his perception is correct'.[86] Whether or not the women intended to insult Saul, his anger is justifiable, since after all, Saul really has killed thousands and up until this point in the narrative (18.7) David has killed just one man, albeit a giant (hence Schulz's conclusion is unreliable, and moreover, he misquotes the song). The question should be, do the women do justice to Saul? The repetition of the words on the lips of Saul, with no gap and no other events between statement and repetition, points to an immediate interpretation in the exact context of the original statement. The reversal of

83. Alfons Schulz, 'Narrative Art in the Books of Samuel', in David M. Gunn (ed.), *Narrative and Novella in Samuel: Studies by Hugo Gressman and Other Scholars 1906–1923* (trans. David E. Orton; JSOTSup, 116; Sheffield: Almond Press, 1991), pp. 119-70 (163).

84. Stanley Gevirtz, *Patterns in the Early Poetry of Israel* (Chicago: University of Chicago Press, 1963).

85. Fokkelman, *Narrative Art*, pp. 214-15.

86. Hertzberg, *Samuel* p. 157.

the order encapsulates Saul's fear. Saul's fear for his kingdom is another example of the tragic irony in 1 Samuel, since Saul does not know what the narrator has imparted: that David will indeed have the kingdom. Since Yhwh has rejected Saul and chosen David in his place, there is nothing that Saul will be able to do to prevent David from having the kingdom.

The words of the women's song appear twice more, both times on the lips of the Philistines. In 21.12 (ET 21.11) the Philistine court describes David to Achish as 'king of the land' and they quote the verse, stating that it is a song, which prompts David to feign madness in order to escape. Thus the words are interpreted as implying that David is a threat to the Philistines, which is, after all, their original context. Then in 29.5 Achish's generals refuse to include David in their campaign against the Hebrews on the grounds that David might change sides, and they quote the women's song, again stating that it is a song. Fokkelman points out that

> the courtiers… appear to have the same perspective of David as Saul, because *just like Saul they extrapolate David's kingship from the victory song*… [Saul's] interpretation of it was both objectively and politically correct,[87]

which seems to conflict with his earlier assessment of Saul's interpretation. By ch. 29 David has acquired Achish's support during his residence among the Philistines, although Achish must heed his military commanders. David has no fear of the Philistines in ch. 29, in contrast to ch. 21, and protests the decision, stressing his reputation of loyalty to Achish.[88] The implication on both these occasions is that the ten thousands David has killed are Philistines; indeed the song arose after the slaying of Goliath, so on the lips of Philistines the words represent a threat to David rather than to Saul. McKane comments that David was a fugitive because of his designs on Saul's throne, 'and a leopard does not change its spots. David knew that this was how Achish would react'.[89]

At their first occurrence the words are intended as praise of David, but at the second (Saul's quotation) they constitute a threat, since this is the first appearance of Saul's jealousy. The third iteration, in ch. 21, is also a threat to David, this time from the Philistines, and the fourth, in ch. 29, while representing a threat, precludes David from participation in the

87. Fokkelman, *Narrative Art*, p. 365.

88. This is based on deliberate misrepresentation, as David has told Achish that he has slaughtered the enemies of the Philistines whereas in fact he has actually slaughtered the enemies of Israel (27.8-12).

89. McKane, *Samuel*, p. 133.

battle between Saul's army and that of Achish. This is also Saul's last battle, and David as a result succeeds to the throne that Saul begrudges him in 18.8. By this means David is completely absent when Saul meets his fate. This of course not only absolves David of any guilt with respect to Saul's death, but also precludes the possibility of his changing sides and engineering a win for Israel and thus Saul. The fact that the Philistines explicitly cite the source of the words is also significant, since this points to the verse as a legend concerning David within the narrative and not simply a single instance of cause for Saul's jealousy. The repetition of the women's song is differently treated in the three different contexts, and on each reiteration perception of David's power is increased, while conversely Saul's tragic fate is more emphatically foreshadowed.

The Tearing of the Robe (15.27 and 24.5 [ET 24.4])
The two accounts of robe-tearing are not similar linguistically, but they are significant symbolically. In 15.27 Samuel has just told Saul of his rejection and as he turns to go, ויחזק בכנף־מעילו ויקרע 'and he took hold of the edge of his robe and it tore'. Many commentators assume that it is Saul who takes hold of Samuel's robe as he turns to go. This is Prouser's position in his monograph on symbolic use of clothing, and he contends that

> Saul, in reaching for Samuel's cloak is reaching for everything he lacks, namely power, faith and authority... Saul intended only to grasp the hem as a gesture of supplication or submission.[90]

But McKane points out that the subject of ויחזק could be either Samuel or Saul. He prefers Samuel because Samuel was the subject of the previous verb and of v. 28, and furthermore Samuel's words in v. 28 have more force with this reading.[91] Ackroyd also prefers this reading[92] while Hertzberg does not commit himself, emphasizing the symbolism of the tearing away of Saul's kingdom rather than the identity of the cloak-tearer. Despite the fact that Saul eventually understands his rejection by Yhwh, he wants Samuel to return with him to honour him before the elders and before Israel, and this Samuel (eventually) does. So Saul still displays the image of kingship to his subjects, even if he has lost his kingship's endorsement from Yhwh.

The symbolism is reintroduced in 24.5 (ET 24.4) with the account of Saul's relieving himself in the cave where David's men are hiding. This

---

90. Ora Horn Prouser, 'Suited to the Throne: Symbolic Use of Clothing in the David and Saul Narratives', *JSOT* 71 (1996), pp. 27-37 (29).

91. McKane, *Samuel*, pp. 102-103.

92. Ackroyd, *Samuel*, p. 128.

time it is David who tears the cloak, after his men suggest killing Saul. David cannot let Saul leave the cave without making some kind of gesture, even though he will not kill him. As soon as he has cut off a piece of Saul's cloak, we are told that 'his heart smote him'. Fokkelman interprets this as palpitations, and goes on to point out that David leaves out this detail when he relates the event to Saul, but the fragment of cloak is represented as a sign or statement of his power over Saul. The symbolism of ch. 15 is used here with added effect: not only is Saul's kingdom to be torn away, but David has succeeded in effecting it. Hence McKane:

> It should perhaps be understood there [ch. 15] and here not as a mere symbol, but as a symbol having the power to bring about the event which it represents, so that it is as if the event were already fulfilled.[93]

Fokkelman says something similar when he writes that 'the act of cutting and its symbolism mediate between life and death'.[94] McKane points out that Saul has brought three thousand men with him, which is of course a very large number against David's band, and Fokkelman suggests that the six hundred men of David's are the same six hundred men that constituted Saul's shrunken army in ch. 13,[95] though there is no reason to suppose that this is the case. Although David invites capture, instead Saul makes an apology for his behaviour; Saul has the power and keeps it while David goes back into hiding at the end of the chapter.[96] This is yet another indication that Saul struggles on against the inevitability of his fate: David already has the kingship and Yhwh's sanction. Saul here, as in ch. 15, keeps political control of a country whose spiritual king (i.e. that sanctioned by Yhwh) is unable to thwart his power. It is also in this account that Saul acknowledges David's destined succession. It seems that on the basis of this parallel symbolism there is a case for following McKane and Ackroyd and reading Samuel tearing Saul's cloak in chapter 15. Thus there is a very strong connection between this passage and Yhwh's rejection of Saul in ch. 15, which once more demonstrates the tragic vision.

Saul Falls into David's Hands (24.1-22 and 26.1-25)
On two occasions during David's exile Saul falls into his hands. David has the opportunity to kill Saul, yet both times he refrains. In chapter 24, Saul accidentally chooses the cave where David and his men are hiding to

93. McKane, *Samuel*, p. 148.
94. Fokkelman, *Narrative Art*, p. 459.
95. Fokkelman, *Narrative Art*, p. 531.
96. McKane, *Samuel*, p. 147.

'cover his feet'. David's men refer to a saying of Yhwh (24.5 [ET 24.4])
which has no corroboration anywhere in the entire work: 'Behold, I am
giving your enemy into your hand and you shall do to him as it shall seem
good to you'. S.R. Driver considers the use of אשר here as pointing to the
interpretation by David's men that this is 'an indication of Yahweh's
purpose to deliver Saul into his hands'.[97] Instead of killing Saul, David
cuts off the skirt of his robe, his heart smites him, he refuses to let his men
attack Saul, and he holds the piece of cloth up to Saul shortly afterwards as
a sign that he has had Saul in his power. There is a textual issue here:
many scholars (Ackroyd, Driver, McKane *et al.*) believe that the verses
are in the wrong order, on the basis that David's heart's smiting him (24.5
[ET 24.4]) offers a different interpretation of his action to that David gives
Saul in 24.12 (ET 24.11). David asks in his speech that Yhwh may judge
between them, but insists that he himself will not do harm to Saul. Saul's
response is to weep—Fokkelman contrasts this with ch. 11, where Saul
was the only person not to weep[98]—and to place himself in a father–son
relationship to David ('Is this your voice, my son David?'), and also to
acknowledge that David will be king. This itself is a kind of repetition
echoing 23.17 where Jonathan tells David that Saul knows David will be
king. Saul then asks David to swear that he will not cut off his descendants, and David complies. Yet any notion of reconciliation is undermined
when Saul returns home while David returns to his men. McKane suggests
that 'because of his madness, Saul's constancy of purpose could no longer
be relied on and reconciliation might soon turn again to hatred'.[99] Hertzberg, however, finds the lack of sequel remarkable: 'A novelist would
have had David return to Saul's court to take up his old position again'.[100]
Perhaps, however, the composer of a tragic novel might have the two men
go their separate ways in ambiguous reconciliation so that the unresolved
conflict would surface once more in a similar manner.

In ch. 26 Saul is again told of David's whereabouts. A diachronic reading might contend that this story is an alternative to that in ch. 24, with the
absence of the water jar from v. 22 used as evidence. However, it is the
spear that Saul needs most, since he cannot defend himself with water.
Fokkelman believes that the spear is a symbol of death, while the water is

---

97. Driver, *Hebrew Text*, p. 192
98. Fokkelman, *Narrative Art*, p. 468.
99. McKane, *Samuel*, p. 147.
100. Hertzberg, *Samuel*, p. 198. For an example of what a novelist actually did, see
below, p. 239.

a symbol of life, and David's omission of reference to it in v. 22 is an indication that figuratively David no longer wishes to refresh Saul.[101] A synchronic reading, however, might recognize that in between these two episodes David has taken two wives and consolidated his position. When he becomes aware of Saul's pursuit, he and one of his men (Abishai) sneak into Saul's camp at night and steal Saul's spear and a water jug. Abishai believes that God has provided David with an opportunity to kill Saul (26.8, cf. 24.4 [ET 24.3]). Saul and his men do not stir because 'a deep sleep from Yhwh had fallen upon them' (v. 12). David gets away and stands at the top of a mountain and wakes them all up by calling to Abner and criticizing his failure to protect the king. Saul recognizes David's voice and asks, as at 24.17 (ET 24.16), 'Is this your voice, my son David?' David advises Saul to sacrifice to Yhwh if it is Yhwh who has stirred Saul up against him, 'or if it is men, let them be cursed' (26.19). One of David's concerns may be that if he is driven away he will be outside the jurisdiction of the practice of Yahwism. This is generally understood in the light of the important connection between the political and the religious in ancient Semitic religion. In any case, if Saul believes it is either Yhwh or men who are to blame, he does not act on David's advice. He admits once again his culpability and blesses David. This time the lack of reconciliation is emphasized further by 27.1, where David recognizes that he is not safe from Saul and so decides to go over to the Philistines.

In the first account David is hiding in a cave, clearly an outlaw. In the second account David has more power and is more daring. His encounter with Saul is not an accident, even one of divine devising (if indeed the first one was). David deliberately goes to Saul's camp to make a point, whereas in ch. 24 the meeting appears to be a coincidence despite the words of David's men. While Saul's life is under threat in ch. 24, the threat in ch. 26 is the demonstration that God is siding with David, and Saul might as well give up, since although David himself will never touch Saul, he has expressed the expectation that divine retribution will come to the king (24.9). In the first episode David asks that Yhwh will deliver him from the hand of Saul; in the second he asks that Yhwh will deliver him from all tribulation. One might make a case that 24.11a (ET 24.10a) הנה היום הזה ראו עיניך את אשר־נתנך יהוה היום בידי במערה ואמר להרגך might be translated 'Behold this day your eyes have seen how Yhwh gave you today into my hand in the cave and he *kept saying* to kill you' (my italics); however, Driver rejects the idea here of a W.C. (waw consecutive) perfect

101. Fokkelman, *Narrative Art*, pp. 537, 549

used to express reiteration. Nevertheless, I suspect that continuing to interpret Yhwh as the subject of the verb is what he is really objecting to, and it may be that this is what David is suggesting to Saul (i.e. that Yhwh has said David should kill Saul), even if this is not consistent with the events narrated in 24.5-23 (ET 24.4-22). A further textual problem is found in 24.20b (ET 24.19b), which McKane translates literally 'in return for this day with respect to which you have done to me', and he remarks that this hardly makes sense.[102] Perhaps, however, this incoherence is an indication that Saul is overcome with emotion. A similar solution to a garbled text is found in Willey's study of the woman of Tekoa: she argues that the difficulty in translation of 2 Sam. 14.13 is due to the narrator's stylistic technique and complains that the English translations 'all revamp the grammar on the rather large assumption that the author meant to write a sentence'.[103] It is reasonable to assume that something similar is evident in this case.

The difference between the two episodes is that by ch. 26 David has gained enough power that he no longer needs an accidental meeting to demonstrate it. The ambiguity of reconciliation at the end of the first episode becomes an impossibility of reconciliation at the end of the second. In the first, David responds to Saul's 'my son' with 'my father'; in ch. 26 to the same words David responds with 'my lord the king', thus establishing greater distance between them, which serves to isolate Saul, who, it must be recalled, has already been distanced from Jonathan and Michal. The greater distance is also stressed in the narrative. In ch. 24, Saul and David are face to face (24.8 [ET 24.7]), whereas in ch. 26 David is so far away he has to shout loudly enough to wake the whole camp: 'David went over to the other side and he stood on the top of the mountain far away, a great space between them' (26.13). Saul makes no further appeal for the future of his line, but prophesies success for David. Saul is coming to realize that he cannot escape his fate, and that his tragic destiny is in the hands of the deity.

Summary
There is an extraordinary number of multiple accounts in the narrative of the story of Saul, and I have not been able to address all of them here. There are two anointing scenes, two accounts of David's introduction to

102. McKane, *Samuel*, pp. 145-46.
103. Willey, 'Importunate Woman', p. 120.

Saul,[104] and two accounts of Saul's death (the latter comes in 2 Samuel). I have omitted these primarily for reasons of space, though the third is outside the scope of my admittedly arbitrary frame of reference. Of the many examples I have investigated, some may be regarded as typescenes, some are repetitions of phrases, some have been attributed to alternative sources. Whatever the origins of the diverse accounts, they have been juxtaposed by the author of the work we have received. Most have been separated from each other by other material, with the effect that they have taken on the dynamics of plot development and characterization. One of the crucial effects of this use of the material, whatever its origins, is that it leads to comparison on both the level of plot and the level of characterization. Alter points to Gros Louis's proposal that the two introductions of David to Saul 'correspond to two different aspects of the future king which are reflected in his relationship with Saul'. Alter adds that we need to consider also matters of style and narrative approach.[105] The comparisons between each set of these doubles point in the same general direction: evidence of a tragic vision in the story of Saul and an understanding of the ambivalence of the deity in the fate of the king.[106] In each example the complicity of God is strengthened and Saul's decline is heightened. In each example we find that the second of the pair portrays a heightened tragic depiction of Saul. Thus we may conclude that the author or compiler of 1 Samuel uses a technique of multiple accounts and repetitions to express the tragic vision.

Conclusions

I have discussed the approaches to the interpretation of the tragic vision in 1 Samuel that have been put forward by various scholars and I have

104. Good points out the extension of the irony of Yhwh's secret choice of David through the two accounts of David's introduction to Saul (*Irony*, p. 73): the second account features Saul's successor fighting his battles for him. This concurs with Exum's remark (quoted above) that there is a cumulative effect to these multiple accounts.

105. Alter , *Biblical Narrative*, p. 148.

106. George Nicol draws a similar conclusion from his examination of story patterning in Genesis: God's jealousy is exposed through the parallels between Gen. 3 and 11—the Garden of Eden and the Tower of Babel. See George G. Nicol, 'Story-Patterning in Genesis' in Robert P. Carroll (ed.), *Text as Pretext: Essays in Honour of Robert Davidson* (JSOTSup, 138; Sheffield: Almond Press, 1992), pp. 215-33 (226-28).

outlined their pros and cons. From this point I have outlined briefly the tragic events and circumstances in 1 Samuel. I have then looked at one example of a tragic collision in more detail. Finally and most substantially I have explored the mechanics by which the tragic vision works in 1 Samuel, namely the use of repetitions, type-scenes and other multiple accounts. I have found that although several scholars have asserted the existence of the tragic vision in 1 Samuel, there are still many aspects that would benefit from further work, one of which has been the mechanics of the tragic vision, which I have addressed. The conclusions that I have drawn from this investigation point in a new direction: the ambivalent role of the deity in the tragic vision.

Chapter 2

AN UNSYMPATHETIC FIRST CAUSE:
DIVINE AMBIVALENCE IN BIBLICAL TRAGEDY

Introduction

In Chapter 1 I examined the mechanics of the tragic vision in 1 Samuel. In this chapter I will explore the consequences for the portrayal of the deity in that tragic vision. Despite Exum's focus on the hostility of God, and Gunn's focus on the deity's role in the concept of Saul's fate, this is a matter that has barely been touched upon in many previous studies of 1 Samuel's tragic vision,[1] and since it is crucial to the understanding of Saul's tragedy I intend to examine it in detail. I have already concluded in Chapter 1 that Yhwh is portrayed as ambivalent towards Saul (and to some extent towards his people and towards David) and I will now investigate these claims in a careful reading of those passages in which Yhwh's agency is portrayed. I will begin, as in Chapter 1, with an overview of the events, this time beginning where I left off in Chapter 1, at 1 Samuel 15. I will then proceed with my investigation of ambivalence in divine agency and I will continue by addressing briefly the questions that this hypothesis raises concerning the problem of evil.

Overview of Divine Ambivalence

Rather than remove Saul from the throne, Yhwh gradually destroys his integrity and his authority by visiting insanity upon him. The connection

---

1.   V.P. Long responds at length to Gunn, and argues that it is the people rather than Yhwh or Samuel who are '*ultimately* responsible for the situation' (*Reign and Rejection*, p. 240). Long does not tackle the issue of the tragic vision, however, and he admits that there may be a 'punitive element in the appointment of Saul' by Yhwh. This undermines his argument that there is 'no cause to question the 'moral basis of Yahweh's action'' in the 'direct relationship between Saul's misdeeds and the failure of his kingship' (p. 239).

between David's new-found favour in his anointing and Saul's loss of
reason is not only consequential but also literary. The narrator tells us in
16.13 that 'the spirit of Yhwh came mightily upon David from that day
forward' and then in the following verse we learn that 'the spirit of Yhwh
departed from Saul and an evil spirit from Yhwh terrified him'. That the
relief from this torment is provided by David in his capacity as musician is
a dark twist to the plot, and the reader may naturally be inclined to suspect
that Yhwh has contrived these circumstances. Saul has no inkling of
David's anointing; the only possible hint is in the counsel of his servants
that Yhwh is with David. Not surprisingly, Saul is grateful for David's
assistance in alleviating his symptoms, and before he comes to suspect
him of treachery he feels a great love for him and he makes David his
armour bearer. This relationship provides the framework for Saul's ago-
nizing decline, for if David were simply a perfidious villain it would be
simple for Saul to have him killed. However, one may infer that Yhwh has
engineered a situation that guarantees intense confusion and distress for
Saul, and which serves not only to undermine Saul's hold on his kingship,
but also to place David in an better position from which to make his claim
on the throne.

The role of the divine spirit is crucial within the narrative. It is used to
signify Yhwh's disposition towards those on whom he sends it. Yhwh's
spirit appears at points of import, usually to show that the individual it
possesses is the happy recipient of divine predilection, and Saul's prophetic frenzy in ch. 10 is a particularly vivid example. Saul's behaviour
here makes such an impression that a proverb actually arises: 'Is Saul also
among the prophets?' It appears that Saul's reaction to the divine spirit is
spectacularly intense. In a similar vein, Saul's distress under the influence
of the evil spirit from Yhwh has dramatic consequences. Humphreys expresses it vividly: Saul's charismatic gifts deteriorate into madness.[2]

Closely associated with the role of the evil spirit is the question of
divine intervention; Yhwh's actions and motives appear to conflict with
one another. Throughout the narrative Yhwh's intervention in Saul's life
threatens the success of Yhwh's intention that David should become king.
The narrator presents us with an interventionist deity, a deity who not only
determines the success of battles, but who manipulates individuals by
supernatural means. Yet, where one might expect Yhwh to step in to
rescue those who incur the divinely initiated wrath of Saul, one encounters
a passive streak in Yhwh's character. The evil spirit from Yhwh is the

---

2.   Humphreys, 'Tragedy', p. 25.

origin of murder and destruction among the people for whom Yhwh claims to have a particular sympathy (e.g. David, the man 'after [Yhwh's] heart'), and the question arises whether Saul must bear the entire responsibility for this. Exum affirms Saul's guilt, commenting that 'he is not really wicked'.[3] Kaufmann insists on a distinction between tragic guilt and moral fault, although he then says this does not go far enough. He maintains,

> 'Guilt' is not the right world where guilt feelings are not appropriate; and we do not really admire those who harbour such feelings in a situation in which they are not to be blamed. The *mot juste* is not tragic guilt but tragic *responsibility*; for responsibility, like pride, is something one can *take*.[4]

Thus, while Saul may be required to take responsibility for his actions, I would contend the moral fault is not his.

The first sign of Saul's derangement is his jealousy of David's military success. When the troops return home following David's extraordinary defeat of Goliath, Saul imagines that the people's admiration for David is a threat to his sovereignty. In the women's song, 'Saul has killed his thousands and David his ten thousands' (18.7), Saul perceives an attack on his kingship. Knowing as he does that Yhwh intends to demolish his kingdom and set up another king in his place, he is highly sensitive to the threat of David. The narrator tells us that this incident is the origin of the increasing conflict between Saul and David: 'And Saul eyed David from that day on' (18.8). In fact, the next day, when the evil spirit from Yhwh comes on Saul and terrifies him, David is no longer able to alleviate Saul's misery, with startling results. Saul makes his first attempt on David's life, throwing his spear at him, but David manages to dodge him. Saul becomes obsessed with the idea that David intends to take control from him; he is afraid of David because he knows that Yhwh is with David, though he does not appear to know of David's anointing, nor of the covenant between Jonathan and David. This is the first of a series of assaults on David, assaults which become increasingly desperate the further David's success and popularity extend, and as Saul's affliction by the evil spirit becomes yet more pronounced.[5]

---

3. Exum, *Arrows*, p. 40.

4. Kaufmann, *Tragedy*, p. 246.

5. Saul's torment under the evil divine spirit has been variously interpreted by some scholars who wish to draw a comparison with the symptoms of mental illness, such as manic depression or schizophrenia. Thomas Preston suggests melancholia or 'very agitated depression' (Thomas R. Preston, 'The Heroism of Saul: Patterns of Meaning in the Narrative of the Early Kingship', *JSOT* 24 [1982], pp. 27-46 [35]).

Saul is keenly aware of Yhwh's absence; it cannot escape his notice that divine favour now rests with David, and his feeling of powerlessness against Yhwh causes him to fear David. He is loath to take direct action against David, but is unable to tolerate David's presence, and so he appoints him commander of an army in the hope that David will fall in battle. However, David is remarkably successful, due, the narrator tells us, to the fact that Yhwh is with him. This makes Saul even more afraid to kill David outright, though nevertheless more determined to be rid of him. His next scheme is to use his daughters as pawns: first he promises Merab in marriage to David on the condition that David fight many battles, but instead marries her off to another man. Then, to Saul's delight, it tran-spires that his younger daughter Michal loves David, and he promises her to David, still hoping that the Philistines will serve as the instrument of David's demise. He requests of his prospective son-in-law a rather gory marriage present of one hundred Philistine foreskins, but this stratagem, like the others, only serves to augment Saul's failure. When David returns alive and counts out two hundred foreskins, Saul perceives not only that Yhwh is still with David, but also that Michal admires and loves him, and that he has acquired an enemy as a son-in-law. Never an astute politician, Saul's rashness in his attempt to thwart Yhwh has only served to bring his adversary into an improved position.

Saul is undoubtedly confused. In his more reasonable moments he holds a great affection for David, and admires David's military prowess, yet he becomes more openly determined to have David put to death. In David's defence, Jonathan comments on Saul's rejoicing at David's success against the Philistines (19.5), and Saul admits that his plotting against David is criminal. He swears that he will desist (19.6). However, Yhwh will not indulge Saul's goodwill towards David, and at David's next military victory the evil spirit from Yhwh comes on Saul again, and for a second time Saul attempts to murder David by casting his spear at him. Again David escapes,

Robert Gordon has suggested another possible medical interpretation of Saul's divine possession: meningitis (referring not to the evil spirit but to the spirit which causes Saul to prophesy in 19.24). The Targum translates עְרַם with the word בְּרָשִׁין which is translated by Harrington and Saldarini as 'he fell *under those having power*' (Robert P. Gordon, 'Saul's Meningitis According to Targum 1 Samuel XIX 24', *VT* 37:1 [1987], pp. 39-49 [39]), although they note that the meaning is uncertain. Gordon suggests that the word is related to the Arabic *birsam*, which 'denotes a disease often associated with delerium' (p. 41). There were contemporary Arabic medical texts in which the word was used to render the Greek 'frenitis' which was considered contagious (cf. 19.18-24). Gordon therefore posits meningitis.

but Saul is resolute, and plans to kill him the following morning. David is saved by Michal, who can no longer remain loyal to her increasingly deranged father. She warns David of Saul's intentions and David escapes into the night, leaving Michal to arrange a trick for Saul's men and then to lie to her father to protect herself.

Saul's behaviour becomes so irrational that eventually he even attempts to murder Jonathan. Already Michal has been forced to take perfidious action in order to protect David from her father, and now Jonathan has encouraged David to become a fugitive. Saul's fury is centred in fear for his kingship, and in his desire to safeguard Jonathan's succession. He cannot comprehend Jonathan's loyalty to David and finds it shameful. Indeed, he seems to find in Jonathan's devotion something unmanly, and calls him a 'son of a perverse, rebellious woman', stressing a certain feminine quality to Jonathan's guilt, as though it were innately feminine to yield one's rights.[6] Jonathan's denial of his legitimate claim appears feminine and weak to Saul, to the extent that Saul for the first time calls openly for David's death. When Jonathan continues to defend David, Saul is enraged to the point of throwing his spear at his son, just as he has thrown his spear at David. The effect of this is to emphasize the profound deviation in Saul's tortured mind. In his frantic endeavours to keep hold of his kingdom, he risks destroying his dearest subjects. There is a parallel here with Euripides' *Heracles*, who is manipulated by divine forces outside his control with the result that in his madness he slaughters his children.

Once David has become a fugitive, Saul neglects his battles with Israel's enemies to search for David. This course of action results in Saul's realizing with greater certainty his subjects' growing support for David. When Saul learns that Ahimelech and the priests of Nob have harboured David, he views it as conspiracy.[7] Not only has Ahimelech given David shelter and

---

6. See also above, p. 68.

7. Pamela Reis terms it 'collusion'. She argues that David does not deceive Ahimelech, but rather that Ahimelech and David are 'partners in intrigue' (Pamela Tamarkin Reis, 'Collusion at Nob: A New Reading of 1 Samuel 21–22', *JSOT* 61 [1994], pp. 59-73 [59]). Ahimelech's trembling is thus a sign of fear that David, not knowing of Doeg's presence, may incriminate them both, and David's request for bread is 'a pretext before Doeg to account for his approach to Ahimelech', while his request for a weapon is based on the need to defend himself against any attack by Doeg. David's subsequent flight to Gath is an attempt to shake off any pursuit, and Doeg feels he has been played for a fool which is why he accuses Ahimelech of enquiring of Yhwh on David's behalf. On this reading Saul is correct to suspect that David has the support of the priests at Nob.

food, he has also given him the sword of Goliath, symbol of victory against the Philistines, of David's first triumph, and of the origin of the women's song implying David's superior military genius, which is quoted again in ch. 21 by Achish, king of the Philistines. Saul's chief accusation is that Ahimelech has enquired of Yhwh for David. Saul questions Ahimelech and reveals that he fears David intends to rise against him, and that Ahimelech's assistance to David has strengthened his position. Ahimelech protests that David is loyal to Saul and that he had no idea that David might be planning to usurp the throne. But Saul shows no mercy towards him and sentences him and all the priests to death. However, Saul is faced with mutiny: his men refuse to murder the priests. It is left to Doeg the Edomite, from whom Saul has heard of David's encounter with Ahimelech, to slaughter not only the priests, but all the inhabitants of Nob, and to destroy all their livestock. The treatment that Saul ought to have meted out to the Amalekites, the enemies of Yhwh, in ch. 15, he now apportions to Nob, the city of the priests. One again perceives ambivalence in a deity whose action leads to violence and whose inaction results in the slaughter of his priests.

The tension between the human and the divine is acute in this episode; Saul's murder of the priests is a demonstration not only of his hubris, but also of the inevitability of catastrophe in a situation where he is intermittently manipulated by forces outside his control. His conduct flies in the face of the heroic potential accorded him at the start of his story. Saul is ruined by his circumstances and is powerless to master them. As he becomes increasingly frantic at David's rise, he tries harder and harder to maintain his hold on the kingdom. With each endeavour his violence becomes more extreme and his failure more pronounced, to the extent that he breaks cultural taboos and destroys the very people he ought to protect. This downward spiral leads him to his darkest moment yet: his encounter with the Samuel's ghost through the woman of Endor.

Yhwh's destruction of Saul has proved very effective, and Saul's final days are desperate. In an unbalanced and frantic state of mind, and in a wretched attempt to regain control of his life and his sanity, Saul turns to the one figure who has given him advice: Samuel. He is facing the most terrifying battle yet against the Philistines and seeks Yhwh's counsel, but Yhwh remains silent and will not communicate with him by any of the conventional methods. As a last resort he turns to a necromancer (since Samuel is dead), a woman who has had to keep her trade secret because of Saul's previous efforts in driving every medium and wizard out of the land. He goes at night, disguised, reflecting the dark and dissembled state of his mind. What he learns from the sarcastic ghost of Samuel is that Yhwh is more hostile than ever: Yhwh has turned from him and become his enemy. Not only has Yhwh torn the kingdom from him and given it to David, but Saul is to die in battle the following day, along with his sons and a large number of the Israelite soldiers. The lengths to which Yhwh is prepared to go to destroy Saul are extreme, and it is remarkable that Yhwh should sacrifice a whole Israelite army to the purpose of achieving revenge against Saul.

And Saul does indeed die in battle the following day, not an honourable death, but in the shame and humiliation of suicide. Having pursued his fate to the extent of turning to necromancy in his acute compulsion to know his destiny, his last action is a final attempt to conquer the forces that have subjugated him. Even in this he cannot succeed: his armour bearer is afraid to take his life and Saul must fall on his own sword. His body is then mutilated and displayed by the Philistines, and later burned (a practice prohibited in Israel) by his own men. Again here we see evidence of divine ambivalence—Yhwh had declared that Saul would deliver Israel from the hand of the Philistines, yet instead the Philistines become the instrument of Saul's demise.

The plot of 1 Samuel is constructed in such a way as to emphasize the incongruity of Yhwh's attitudes and behaviour. As the plot develops, Saul comes to know that David, whom he genuinely loves, is the man Yhwh has chosen to replace him, and this knowledge comes as a direct consequence of divinely generated insanity. Saul continues to turn to Yhwh for direction in his kingly function, and Yhwh abandons him to the extent of refusing to answer, yet Yhwh continues to take an interest in him. Rather than communicating with Yhwh directly, Saul is forced to encounter the deity through fate, and the fate Yhwh has ordained for him is a tortured progression into madness. Saul's perception of David as a threat is reasonable, and his desire to rid himself of this usurper is rational; giving his daughter in marriage to David is ill-conceived; threatening Jonathan's life and slaughtering a community of priests is insane. Yet from the attempts on David's life to the murder of the people of Nob these incidents have their origin in divinely generated distraction. Yhwh's conduct exhibits contradictory motives, and the question that now arises is that of the extent to which Yhwh may be considered culpable in the face of Saul's maniacal excesses.

Divine Agency

In order to test the hypothesis of divine ambivalence it will be necessary to examine closely the accounts of divine agency. There are three different manners of divine agency:

1. Episodes in which Yhwh intervenes by speaking or acting. Each of the instances where Yhwh intrudes in the narrative by speaking or acting shows Yhwh's response to the circumstances in which the human story finds itself.

2. Episodes in which Yhwh answers enquiries. The chief significance of this category is how the accounts of Yhwh's answers relate to the two accounts in which Yhwh does not answer Saul, and the occasions where Yhwh answers David's enquiries are also connected to Yhwh's dealings with Saul.

3. Episodes in which Yhwh sends a spirit on someone. Of the many accounts of a divine spirit coming on a human being, all but one concern Saul. The exception is the spirit which comes on David at his anointing and the similarities and differences between the accounts are indicative of the constitution of the divine will.

a. *Yhwh Intervenes*

Yhwh Feels Rejected (8.7-9). Yhwh speaks to Samuel when Samuel prays in response to the elders' demand for a king, which displeases Samuel. The request is made on the basis that Samuel's sons are not fit to govern, being perverters of justice, and the context is one of war, cf. vv. 19-20. McKane argues that the issue is nothing to do with the lack of integrity in Samuel's sons, 'although the leaders make this the immediate occasion of their demand'[8] and goes on to say that it may be 'the intention of the writer to convey that the elders were disingenuous in the reason which they gave'. However, the narrator confirms the people's assessment of Samuel's sons (8.3). Certainly the central thrust of the people's request appears to be a desire to be governed like 'the nations'. The only time that Yhwh speaks directly in 1 Samuel prior to this is when he calls to the child Samuel and tells him of the judgment against Eli's house for the wickedness of Eli's sons and Eli's failure to restrain them (3.3-18). Therefore we know that Samuel is aware of the consequences of having wicked sons. However, there is no mention here of divine judgment on Samuel's house. Yhwh tells Samuel that it is not Samuel who has been rejected but Yhwh himself, but in the same breath tells him that all the [wicked] deeds the people have done[9] from the day he brought them up out of Egypt they have committed against Samuel too. Yhwh then tells Samuel to warn the people of the ways of the king who shall reign over them. Yhwh here is

8.   McKane, *Samuel*, p. 65.
9.   LXX adds 'to me' (i.e. Yhwh) at this point.

portrayed as jealous of the people's desire for a king. Hertzberg writes, 'Yahweh…interprets the people's request to mean that they wish to forsake him, the real king…Here one of the basic features of world history emerges: the struggle of man against God.'[10] This is also, of course, one of the basic features of the tragic vision.

Yhwh Concedes (8.22a). Samuel warns the people of the likely outcome of their insistence on a king, but they persist and Yhwh tells Samuel to listen to them and make them a king. It seems here that Yhwh has resigned himself to the people's request. He could have chosen instead to smite them as he did when they forsook him from the day he brought them out of Egypt and served other gods (cf. v. 8[11]), but instead Yhwh concedes their desires. This concession, in view of the feelings of jealousy that Yhwh has previously expressed, leaves the way open for tragic consequences.

Yhwh Tells Samuel to Expect the Future King (9.16). During the narrative concerning Saul's search for his father's lost asses, we are told that the previous day Yhwh has spoken to Samuel to tell him that he will send him a Benjaminite man and Samuel is to anoint him prince over the people. This man is to save Yhwh's people from the hand of the Philistines, for Yhwh has seen the affliction of[12] his people and heard their cry. It seems that Yhwh has decided to make the best of an uncomfortable situation by using this anointed prince as an instrument to give these people who have rejected Yhwh relief from their struggle against their oppressors despite their forsaking him and serving other gods. Perhaps Yhwh hopes that a prince anointed by Samuel who is victorious against the Philistines will make the people grateful and cause them to perceive that it is Yhwh's instrument who has delivered them. This speech of Yhwh's engenders hope, both for Saul and for the people, and the reader may be satisfied that Yhwh has resolved to use the people's demand for his own purposes. Yet the background of Yhwh's jealousy may indicate that those purposes are not entirely benevolent.

Jonathan Attacks the Philistine Garrison (14.8-15). The narrator does not explicitly relate much action of Yhwh in this episode, yet most scholars

---

10. Hertzberg, *Samuel*, p. 72.

11. In Exod. 32.35 Yhwh sends a plague on the people because they have made the golden calf.

12. LXX reads 'the affliction of'; omitted by MT.

have understood Yhwh's involvement from the outcome. Jonathan pronounces a test of a sign from Yhwh; if the Philistines make the appropriate
response then Jonathan and his armour bearer will attack. The Philistines
do make the appropriate response and Jonathan and his companion are
successful against the garrison, which is followed by a battle on a larger
scale, and it is related that Yhwh delivered Israel that day (14.23). Thus, as
Long expresses it, 'The ultimate attribution of [the Philistines'] 'panic' to
divine agency…is consistent with Jonathan's own perspective that Yahweh
alone gives victory'.[13] The account relates the first battle with the Philistines after Saul's error in ch. 13, and demonstrates that despite Samuel's
assertion of Saul's rejection Yhwh still tolerates Saul's status as military
leader and causes Israel to conquer under his government. There is, therefore, a great ambiguity concerning Saul's fate: how can he have been
rejected by Yhwh from being king and yet his kingly function still be
tolerated by Yhwh?

The Commandment to Annihilate the Amalekites (15.2-3). Yhwh never
speaks directly to Saul: he always makes things known to Saul through
Samuel, and ch. 15 contains the only two occasions where Samuel claims
to quote Yhwh directly to Saul. No speech is attributed to Yhwh by the narrator in ch. 13; Samuel claims to be speaking with divine authority, yet
there is no mention in the narrative that Yhwh has made these statements.
However, in 15.2-3 Samuel, apparently quoting Yhwh, tells Saul of Yhwh's
commandment to annihilate the Amalekites. He gives the reason that the
Amalekites opposed Israel on the way up from Egypt, thus continuing the
theme of 9.16 that the anointed person is to deliver Israel from her enemies.
Despite the fact that the Amalekites do not appear to be posing Israel any
problems at this time, nevertheless Yhwh has decided to punish them for
the deeds of their ancestors. The instructions are quite clear: Saul is to
destroy all that they have and to spare nothing, not even the vulnerable
members of the Amalekite population, nor their animals. This Saul utterly
fails to do.

Yhwh's Repentance (15.11). When Saul fails to perform to the letter the
divine commandment that Samuel has communicated to him, Yhwh
speaks to Samuel, saying that he repents of making Saul king. Hertzberg
comments,

13. Long, *Reign and Rejection*, p. 111

Here we have the theologically important concept of the repentance of God: God is not slavishly bound by his own decisions, but is almighty to such an extent that he is Lord even of them. Just as he takes the action of men into consideration in his decisions, so that omnipotence never means that man is deprived of his responsibility, so, too, the election of a king is not irrevocable. God can at any time lay aside the instrument which he is using if it appears to him to be neither tried nor suitable. Here it is remarkable that Samuel is painfully distressed and evidently does not agree.[14]

Samuel is angry, but despite this Yhwh does not appear to change his mind. Fokkelman considers that Samuel is also angry at Saul and comes to several startling conclusions:

I re-read the beginning of I Sam. 15 in favour of this interpretation. In that case it is striking that the order to Samuel is verbalized as if nothing has happened (in this particular case I Sam. 13-14) and the king is not doomed. Is it perhaps God's intention to make a new start with Saul or at least offer him one last chance?…Samuel's judgement on Saul in 13 is *not* introduced by the prophet himself with a 'thus speaks Yahweh' nor is it characterized as the 'word of the Lord' in any other way… [T]he difference [in ch. 15] warns us as readers against thinking too readily that Yahweh's attitude is completely and entirely covered by the prophet's position. At various places in the OT the God of Israel is…sufficiently flexible to go back on a prophecy of disaster. Perhaps he has therefore done so after rejecting Saul in the first instance, and to the prophet's surprise to boot.[15]

If Fokkelman is correct, these conclusions only serve to emphasize Yhwh's ambivalent attitude to Saul.

After Samuel's display of anger, he goes to Saul (and has difficulty finding him since Saul has made a detour to set up a monument to himself) and says he will tell him what Yhwh said to him during the night. He does not quote Yhwh at this point, but berates Saul for failing to obey the voice of Yhwh, adding that Saul should have obeyed because Yhwh anointed him king over Israel. Samuel's scolding takes the form of several questions: though Saul is little in his own eyes, is he not head over the tribes of Israel? Why did Saul not obey the voice of Yhwh? Why did he swoop on the spoil and do what was evil in the sight of Yhwh? Saul attempts to defend his actions, Samuel rules his defence inadmissible, tells Saul that Yhwh has rejected him, that today the kingdom has been torn from him and given to one who is better than Saul and finally in v. 29 gets around to

14. Hertzberg, *Samuel*, p. 126.
15. Fokkelman, *Narrative Art*, pp. 93-94.

saying something that relates linguistically to Yhwh's words to Samuel during the night (although in v. 26 the use of דבר, שוב and מלך relates to v. 11). However, rather than telling Saul that Yhwh has repented of making him king, he says 'the Glory of Israel will not lie or repent, for he is not a man that he should repent'. But this is exactly what Yhwh *has* done! McKane suggests that this verse was either added by a later writer who disliked the anthropopathism of v. 11 or that the writer 'is telling us that he is perfectly aware that his anthropopathism should not be pushed too far'.[16] Sternberg contends that

> Even if Samuel literally meant what he says—and his own conduct suggests that he knows better—then his claim would just expose his own unreli-ability. To guide our expectations, we look to the lord of history and the master of narrative, rather than to any creature of theirs, however eminent; and these two speak here with one voice.[17]

Sternberg is attempting to align Samuel with Jonah in opposition to the concept 'that God often forgives', but the tragedy for Saul is that Yhwh does not forgive him, neither on this occasion nor at any other point, despite Saul's confession of sin. One of Sternberg's greatest weaknesses, despite his highly insightful commentary and concern for accuracy, is his assumption of divine inspiration and authorial intention, for which he provides no concrete evidence. Furthermore, for Sternberg 'the reader' is identified with Sternberg's own conception of ideal reader, which under-mines his argument.[18] The appeal to a 'lord of history' is surprising in a discussion of a narrative that shows no inclination towards a twentieth-century philosophical conception of history.

The general understanding of 15.29 is that having repented once Yhwh will not repent again and change his mind. But Saul has not been told of Yhwh's repentance concerning his kingship; only of Yhwh's rejection. Is Samuel misrepresenting Yhwh? Why does Samuel embellish Yhwh's words to such a great extent? The answer is to be derived from the emphasis of Samuel's words. Samuel is concerned with Saul's status as anointed king of Israel, a status that Samuel conferred upon him both by

16. McKane, *Samuel*, p. 103.
17. Sternberg, *Poetics*, p. 502.
18. For example, Sternberg assumes that all readers respond as he believes the narrator intends them to; thus he comments that the reader cannot help condemning Jacob's sons for the 'shocking disproportionateness of their reaction' to the humbling of their sister (*Poetics*, p. 445). In fact, some readers may condone at least some of their actions.

anointing him and by drawing lots in his favour. Samuel upbraids Saul for listening to the people, but Samuel himself appears to be concerned with his own reputation.

I would contend that Samuel is indeed misrepresenting Yhwh, since the concept of Yhwh's repentance is stressed by the narrator a few verses later. The chapter closes with the only occasion in 1 Samuel where the narrator provides a window into Yhwh's mind: 'And Yhwh repented that he had made Saul king over Israel' (v. 35). There are several consequences of this reading: Yhwh's repentance rather than rejection is most emphatically stressed by the narrator, but to Saul Samuel stresses Yhwh's rejection. It seems that for the narrator repentance and rejection are not the same thing, but Saul has no knowledge that there is a distinction between what Samuel tells him and what Yhwh feels. Samuel is Saul's link to Yhwh, yet by Samuel's misrepresentation Saul loses this link's efficacy. Samuel is therefore instrumental in attenuating Saul's tragic isolation from Yhwh. Moreover, if McKane is right about the symbolism of the tearing of the robe 'having the power to bring about the event which it represents, so that it is as if the event were already fulfilled',[19] and if he is right that Samuel tears Saul's robe, then Samuel is attempting to force Yhwh's hand and tear Saul's kingdom from him immediately. The narrator tells us that Samuel grieves over Saul (v. 35); perhaps in the space between Yhwh's ambivalent repentance and Samuel's conception of rejection is the possibility for the evasion of tragedy. However, Samuel's grief for Saul is futile in the face of Yhwh's determination, as becomes evident at Yhwh's next intervention in the plot.

God Sends Samuel to Bethlehem (16.1). Immediately following this look into Yhwh's mind, we are told that Yhwh says to Samuel 'How long will you grieve over Saul, and[20] I have rejected him from being king over Israel? Fill your horn and go; I will send you to Jesse the Bethlehemite, for I have provided for myself a king among his sons'. Samuel resists, saying that Saul will kill him if he goes. So Yhwh tells him, 'Take a heifer with you, and say, 'I have come to sacrifice to Yhwh'. And invite Jesse to the sacrifice, and I will show you what you shall do; and you shall anoint for me him whom I name to you'. No sooner has Yhwh repented of making Saul king than he puts into operation his plan to anoint another king despite the continuance of Saul's reign. Yhwh's language here is of rejection

19. McKane, *Samuel*, p. 148.
20. Or 'when…'., cf. Driver, *Hebrew Text*, p. 132.

rather than repentance and echoes Samuel's words in 15.26. This change is undoubtedly a further indication of ambivalence on the part of Yhwh. We might ask ourselves, how can two men both be anointed king? Surely Yhwh will somehow have to dispose of Saul, if it is in fact David whom he has now chosen. Hertzberg states, 'The Lord is…concerned not to let the kingdom fall with the 'rejected' king, but, on the contrary, to take care that it is preserved'.[21] However, what Yhwh actually does in this situation is to create a situation of political instability, which has the potential to lead to division of the kingdom.[22] Many commentators (e.g. McKane, Hertzberg) point to Samuel's fear as an example of political realities, yet it is hard to tell whether Samuel really believes Saul will kill him; Saul has not yet tried to kill anyone except the enemies of Israel, and he has acquired a reputation for sparing some of those. Perhaps Samuel is making an excuse because he is grieving over Saul and is reluctant to anoint another king. We should not make assumptions based on how we think Samuel ought to feel, or on Saul's later behaviour. This reading would concur with Samuel's behaviour in chapter 15, where he appears to be concerned for his reputation, and where he is possibly attempting to avert Saul's tragedy.

Yhwh Looks at Men's Hearts and has David Anointed (16.7, 12). Samuel comes to Jesse's house and invites him and his sons to the sacrifice. When he sees Eliab, the eldest, he assumes this is the man whom Yhwh has chosen. But Yhwh tells Samuel, 'Do not look on his appearance or on the height of his stature, because I have rejected him; for [Yhwh sees] not as man sees; man looks on the outward appearance, but Yhwh looks on the heart'. The words 'Yhwh sees' are absent from MT but are in LXX, which is the sense of the phrase. As seven of Jesse's sons go by Yhwh rejects them all. When the physically attractive David enters, Yhwh, perhaps unexpectedly, says, 'Arise, anoint him; for this is he'. Sternberg contends that physical attractiveness in the books of Samuel is a motif which signals that the

---

21. Hertzberg, *Samuel*, p. 136.

22. Some centuries later in Israel's history it is just this type of fragmented political situation, coming about as a result of the division of the empire of Alexander the Great in 323 BCE, which led to the Hasmonean revolt and the establishing of an independent Jewish state before the advent of the Roman Empire. Viktor Tcherikover writes, 'the Jewish state was not the product of the inner strength of the Jews, but was rendered possible by the weakness of the Seleucids' (Viktor Tcherikover, *Hellenistic Civilization and the Jews* [trans. S. Applebaum; New York: Atheneum, 1976], p. 241).

reader's expectations of good character will be unfulfilled, and Saul is the model, with his homicidal rages and loss of sanity. Therefore David's good looks bode ill for the future, as witnessed in his adultery with Bathsheba and murder of Uriah in 2 Samuel. The theme is then continued with Absalom.[23] Certainly it appears that Yhwh is leading Samuel a merry dance, perhaps, as Sternberg suggests, in order to manipulate him because of his grieving over Saul.

Yhwh rejects (מאס) seven of Jesse's sons, the same word Samuel uses to Saul in 15.26 and Yhwh uses of Saul in 16.1. The reason appears to be that the hearts of these sons fail to impress him, and there is an implicit comparison of Saul and David. Fokkelman mentions the significance of the word 'heart' in connection with Saul's election but does not pursue the idea far enough. The question must be asked, what has gone wrong with the new heart that God gave to Saul (10.9) following his anointing? Lyle Eslinger argues that God found Saul's heart deficient, and that this is the reason he gives Saul a new heart, 'to ensure that Saul has the divinely approved psychological profile'.[24] Has God in fact deliberately given Saul a heart that is inadequate? Again, God appears to have been complicit in Saul's fate from the very beginning of his kingship. The twofold connection between the attributes of Saul and David—heart and good looks—points once again to the ambivalence of the deity.

God Does not Give David into Saul's Hand (23.14). The first half of ch. 23 is concerned with events at Keilah: David rescues the town from the Philistines and Saul pursues David there. It is significant that it is David rather than Saul who goes into battle against the Philistines, since delivering the people from the hands of the Philistines is Saul's calling. It is yet more significant that Saul only approaches Keilah in order to pursue David, and that he believes that 'God has given him into my hand' (v. 7). It is Yhwh's answer to David's inquiry that delivers David from Saul's hand at Keilah and after David has escaped: 'Saul looked for him every day but God did not give him into his hand' (v. 14). Notwithstanding the danger to David when Saul was being tormented by the evil divine spirit, it appears that God is now prepared to protect David from Saul's homicidal inclinations. Saul's decline is now advanced and his fantasy that God

---

23. Sternberg, *Poetics*, pp. 354-64.

24. Eslinger, '"A Change of Heart": 1 Samuel 16', in Lyle Eslinger and Glen Taylor (eds.), *Ascribe to the Lord: Biblical and Other Studies in Memory of Peter C. Craigie* (JSOTSup, 67; Sheffield: JSOT Press, 1988), pp. 341-61 (345).

will support his cause against that of David is chilling, particularly as it comes only a chapter after the slaughter of the priests. It is important to recognize that v. 6 stresses Saul's lack of contact with God: his fantasy can be neither confirmed nor denied since he has no ephod. The one priest who escaped Nob has taken the ephod to David.

Saul and his Men Sleep through David's Infiltration (26.12). In the second account in which Saul falls into David's hands, David discovers Saul's camp, steals into it, and makes off with Saul's spear and water jug. His companion, Abishai, intends to kill Saul, believing that Yhwh has pro-vided David with an opportunity, but David refuses and asserts, 'Yhwh will smite him, or his day will come and he will die, or he shall go down to battle and he shall perish'. One way or another, then, Saul is mortal. In fact, in the event Saul does die in battle, but by his own hand rather than in the usual manner. So has Yhwh provided David with an opportunity? The reason David and Abishai are able to creep into the camp and remove Saul's spear is that Saul and all his men are unable to wake, because 'a deep sleep from Yhwh had fallen upon them' (v. 12). If David is right, then the opportunity with which Yhwh has provided him is the opportunity to engage the king rather than to kill him in order to establish his own kingdom. There is a sense of tension when David calls to the camp and mocks Abner: has David's intention been one of ridicule and derision, or has it been merely to seek a safe audience with Saul? The balance of David's words is very careful and Saul admits his guilt. Nevertheless, just as reconciliation with David is impossible, Yhwh's forgiveness is not forthcoming. David's words, that 'Yhwh gave [Saul] into [his] hand this day' (v. 23) echo those of Saul in 23.7, and the contrasting outcomes of the two events signal once more the ambivalence of the deity.

b. *Yhwh Answers Inquiries*
God Answers Saul with Silence but Chooses Jonathan in the Lot (14.37, 41-42). During Saul's first protracted battle against the Philistines, in which he has already apparently offended God, according to Samuel's words at least (in chapter 13), Saul inquires of God concerning the coming clash, but God does not answer him. The reason for this is understood to be that sin has silenced the oracle. Fokkelman sets himself against Saul, and contends that

> God's silence cannot cause the critical spectator any real surprise. To Saul, the fact of being ignored is so humiliating and so painful that he at once provides an 'explanation': a 'sin' must be the cause of God's silence. Once

again he moves on the ritual plane and once again forgets to search his own heart. He places the blame outside himself. Thus this incident, the sequence vv. 36-37, becomes the detonation mechanism of the bomb that Saul has up his sleeve.[25]

However, Fokkelman does not specify what dark thing lurks in Saul's heart/mind/sleeve that might have prompted God's silence, although he does consider Saul's order to build an altar to be hypocritical, inasmuch as Saul by proclaiming a fast himself bears the full responsibility for the men's hunger, and is therefore a contributory cause of their sinning in haste.[26]

The fact that Saul gets an answer from God in the drawing of lots demonstrates that in fact he is right: a sin has been committed. God breaks his silence in v. 41 with the answer to the casting of lots, where Jonathan is eventually chosen. The LXX has an addition which makes the procedure of drawing lots less abrupt, and there is a general consensus of accepting it.[27] Furthermore, it is arguably not Saul who bears the full responsibility for the sin. Saul's behaviour has changed since his rejection in ch. 13. Craig draws attention to this change: in 11.13 Saul 'boldly proclaims' that Yhwh has brought deliverance; by ch. 14 'the king is portrayed as one who is too anxious to assume responsibility, one who is too eager to assert power'.[28] In between Saul's confidence has been knocked by Samuel's unexpected assertion of rejection by Yhwh, and in view of Yhwh's ambivalence towards Saul, it might not be too extreme to ask whether in ch. 14 God bears some of the responsibility for the men's hunger.

There are two possible interpretations of the sin: one is that someone may have broken Saul's oath that no one may eat (we are told that Jonathan, in innocence of his father's oath, has eaten some honey, v. 27) and the other possibility may be that it is the sin against God committed by the people who have eaten meat with blood in it (v. 33). When Saul enquires as to the identity of the one having sinned, he now gets answers: it is Jonathan who is guilty. The punishment, it seems, must be death, but the people do not allow Saul to put Jonathan to death because of the latter's remarkable success (with Yhwh's help) against the Philistine garrison, which Jonathan achieved without his father's prior knowledge and which

25. Fokkelman, *Narrative Art*, p. 71.
26. Fokkelman, *Narrative Art*, p. 69.
27. See particularly Driver, *Hebrew Text*, p. 117.
28. Kenneth M. Craig Jr, 'Rhetorical Aspects of Questions Answered with Silence', *CBQ* 56 (1994), pp. 221-39 (222).

enabled Saul's army to attack in the midst of the Philistines' divinely
induced confusion. There are a number of important motifs here. There is
an implied disagreement between Saul and Jonathan over military strategy
and procedure. This tension is characteristic of their relationship throughout 1 Samuel, as I have already asserted. God's involvement stirs the tension between the two men, so that eventually it becomes a matter of public
debate, which Saul loses when the people ransom Jonathan. Hertzberg
writes, 'The action is described with the utmost brevity. Only the absolute
essentials are given, so that there is an uncanny tension about the nocturnal
proceedings'.[29]

The reader might wonder whether God is silent in v. 37 just to see what
Saul will do, since there is no indication that God requires Jonathan's
death.[30] Perhaps it is Saul who sets up the situation by tempting fate with
the statement that whoever is guilty will die, even if it be 'Jonathan my
son' (v. 39). Saul requires the death of the guilty party in the hope of
preserving his reputation; he needs to be observed to be doing what is right
in the context of Yahwism. Saul's attitude here is the reverse of his gener-
osity in sparing life in ch. 11. It looks at first glance as if the sin should
really have been the people's sin of eating meat with blood in it. How did
it come to be Jonathan's action of eating honey which silenced God, rather
than a cultic infringement? How is Saul supposed to second guess God's
whims? There seems to be a dynamic here in which God's ambivalence
and Saul's difficulties in maintaining control come together to Saul's dis-
advantage. Hertzberg writes, 'The way in which [Jonathan] acknowledges
his guilt shows that he does not consider his conduct to have been so
serious'.[31] However, Jonathan knows that God has refused to answer the
enquiry because of sin, so surely he must consider it serious. But when
Jonathan is sentenced to death it is the people who do not answer Saul
(v. 39).

Kenneth Craig points to two occasions in 1 Samuel where 'it is clear
that the Lord does not respond to Saul's enquiry because the Lord chooses
not to respond'.[32] He goes on to suggest that in the reference to 'this sin'
in v. 38 Saul refers exclusively to the breaking of the oath. Craig concludes that ch. 14 and ch. 28 (the second occasion where Saul's enquiry of
the deity is answered with silence) form an inclusio, and comments,

---

29. Hertzberg, *Samuel*, p. 117.
30. But cf. Jephthah's oath which led to the execution of his daughter.
31. Hertzberg, *Samuel*, p. 117.
32. Craig, 'Rhetorical Aspects', p. 221.

> The multiple effects of the picture of a king unable to get answers combine to support the theme of decline, and the near duplication of images signals a distinct rhetorical strategy… [T]he reported questions in the two chapters play an important rhetorical function because they reveal the intentions of the speakers and, through them, their positive and negative attributes.[33]

Craig does not discuss any positive or negative attributes of God revealed by this rhetorical function, despite his assertion of Saul's 'tragic condition'. However, following his model, we may conclude that God is characterized by analogy through his silence: the theme of decline of which Craig writes is engineered by a deity whose every command and contrivance serves to precipitate Saul's downfall. That Saul is on the verge of taking his son's life as a result of the drawing of lots demonstrates a feature that anyone in his position ought to know instinctively: the answer one gets to a question will depend on the wording of the question itself. Saul's deficiency in political skill nearly costs him his son, and it is this same deficiency which ultimately saves Jonathan from death by the mutiny of the people.

Yhwh Answers David's Inquiries (23.2-4). There is a long gap in Yhwh's involvement in answering enquiries between 16.12 and 23.2. Yhwh's agency in the intervening material involves sending his spirit and will be dealt with below. He speaks again in response to an enquiry from David as to whether to deliver Keilah from the Philistines; David's men would prefer to remain in safety. This episode comes immediately after Saul has had the priests of Nob put to death; all but Abiathar, who escapes to David's camp in 22.20. David enquires twice and Yhwh answers twice, the first time telling David to save Keilah, and the second time assuring David that he will give the Philistines into David's hand. After the account of the battle, the narrator adds that when Abiathar came to David he brought with him the ephod. Thus we understand that David can enquire of Yhwh via the ephod, and perhaps we can assume that this is how the preceding enquiry took place. Hertzberg writes,

> The special character of David's undertaking is further underlined by a twofold inquiry made of the Lord…in this case [the *vox populi*] does not coincide with the *vox Dei*; it is merely an expression of fearfulness.[34]

---

33. Craig, 'Rhetorical Aspects', p. 239.
34. Hertzberg, *Samuel*, p. 190.

Yhwh Answers Further Inquiries (23.9-12). Immediately following from the preceding account, Saul is planning to besiege David at Keilah, and David knows that Saul is plotting evil against him. Saul believes that Yhwh has given David into his hand, but of course he cannot enquire of Yhwh since the last priest with the last ephod is Abiathar and he is with David. On hearing the news of Saul's plans, David again enquires of Yhwh twice, asking whether Saul will come down and whether the men of Keilah will surrender David to him. Yhwh answers that Saul will come down (v. 11) and the men of Keilah will surrender him (v. 12). Hertzberg contends that

> David appears here in a particularly attractive light. It is purposely said that he is ready to go to the aid of the city and that he is equally ready to depart, not because of his own uncertain position, but also because Keilah could incur new misfortunes on his account. Not once does he reprove the citizens for their attitude.[35]

However, this is merely David's interpretation of what may happen if Saul arrived at Keilah while David is still there. Saul himself is not said to have the intention of attacking Keilah *except* as means of getting his hands on David. It is to besiege David and his men that Saul plans to go down (23.8). If Keilah were to surrender David to Saul the city would escape unharmed. Hence David really is only trying to save himself and is not as concerned about the lords of Keilah as Hertzberg claims. This is another example of the phenomenon that I touched on earlier: a good politician knows that the answer to a question will depend on the way it is framed. In this case it is David who asks a question that determines its own answer.

These two sets of enquiries, coming together just after the slaughter of all but one of the priests, serve to emphasize David's power and Yhwh's true colours. Although Saul still wields considerable political power, as is evident from the attitude of the men of Keilah, David has the power to enquire of Yhwh what he should do, and this is a power Saul will never have again. David's survival in exile is made possible by the possession of the ephod. Driver remarks that the word בעלי used to describe the lords or citizens of a city is rare.[36] It occurs only four other times in MT. Notably, one of those is Judg. 9.22-57, with reference to Shechem: the city whose lords dealt treacherously with Abimelech after God sent an evil spirit between them and the king.[37]

35. Hertzberg, *Samuel*, p. 191.
36. Driver, *Hebrew Text*, p. 185.
37. On the parallels with Judg. 9, see below, pp. 101-102.

Yhwh Will not Answer Saul (28.6). Saul's inability to enquire of Yhwh is highlighted in ch. 28, when he sees the army of the Philistines and is terrified. He enquires of Yhwh but receives no answer by any of the various conventional methods. This silence drives him to take drastic action, action that is out of character, since it contradicts a measure he has taken in order to comply with the tenets of Yahwism according to Samuel. His driving of all the wizards from the land is related to Samuel's words to him at 15.23, that rebellion is as the sin of divination. These two passages are the only occurrences of this motif, so at this point it is useful for the reader to remember that Saul's state of mind is so desperate that he is willing to neutralize his previous work in service of Yahwism, willing to defy Samuel's portrait of divine rejection, all in the hope of getting an answer to his fears concerning the forthcoming battle. If he has no priests on his side (and after all, he has slaughtered most of them) then presumably he has no ephod, but Yhwh could have answered him at least by dreams. This Yhwh refrains from doing. There is no forgiveness and no move toward reconciliation on Yhwh's part. Saul's earlier mistake in his very first battle against the Philistines has never been forgiven, and now, as he approaches what will be his final battle against the enemies whom it was his destiny to defeat, Yhwh will not answer his inquiries. Fokkelman states, 'God has long given up answering Saul via the oracle (14.37), for Saul knows best (14.36) and He persists in that silence (28.6) to the end'.[38] In fact, only once in the narrative has God answered Saul: by lot in ch. 14, and the answer demanded the death of Saul's son. So to speak of God giving up answering Saul is to overstate the case. Despite Fokkelman's generalization, it is evident that the silence in 28.6 represents a terrible isolation for Saul.

Samuel Answers Saul (28.17). This is not, strictly speaking, an answer from Yhwh, but the answer Saul receives is the answer to his enquiry of Yhwh. Since Yhwh will not answer Saul, Saul induces the medium to bring up the ghost of Samuel, the 'man of God' or 'seer' who, it seems, even in death knows God's plans. Hertzberg notes,

> On being asked why he has disturbed the rest of the dead, Saul describes his straitened position and in particular points out that the Lord has turned from him. The omission here is the possibility of a decision by the holy lot ('Urim and Thummim'), mentioned earlier, may be intentional, so as to

---

38. Fokkelman, *Narrative Art*, p. 430.

> make it unnecessary to mention to Samuel the circumstances under which
> Saul lost possession of the oracle.[39]

Samuel emphasizes that Saul's enquiry is pointless, informs Saul that Yhwh has become his enemy, reminds Saul of his failure to destroy Amalek, and predicts that Saul and his sons will fall in the battle. The language of Yhwh's attitude towards Saul has become progressively stronger throughout the story: God repented of making Saul king, he rejected Saul, he has become Saul's enemy. Now that the word 'enemy' has been used, Saul cannot hope ever to achieve reconciliation with Yhwh. It seems his sin cannot be forgiven and Yhwh has now arrived at the point of causing Saul's death.

There is, however, a semantic problem with the word עָרֶךָ used to convey the idea of 'your enemy'. Driver notes that there is a Hebrew word צר from the root צרר, which is a cognate of an Arabic word meaning 'to harm', and this צר corresponds to the Aramaic ער. However, he rejects on philological grounds the assumption of a Hebrew word ער as the equivalent of צר. In a discussion of alternative cognates he mentions an Arabic word for 'rival' but argues 'there is no other trace of this word in Hebrew, nor would the idea of Yahweh's becoming Saul's *rival* be probable or suitable'.[40] He prefers to read it either as an error of transcription for חרך or to read with LXX and Peshitta ויהי עם־רעך 'and is become on the side of your neighbour'. Driver seems to prefer the latter, though this necessitates taking the LXX[41] sense לך in v. 17 (Yhwh has done to you as he spoke...) rather than MT לו (Yhwh has done for himself as he spoke...), otherwise the לו would naturally refer to David rather than to Saul, and it is God's actions concerning Saul that are under discussion here. If עָרֶךָ in v. 16 is an error of transcription, however, which is my preference, MT v. 17 may stand (thus reading 'Yhwh has become your enemy and Yhwh has done for himself as he spoke...'). McKane argues the converse:

> If G and S are followed in v. 16, it is possible to defend MT, although the effort is perhaps a little forced. 'Him' of v. 17 will refer back to neighbour of v. 16, i.e. the word of Yahweh, communicated by Samuel to David, has been fulfilled.[42]

But there is no evidence that Samuel communicated any such thing to David, whereas he has twice communicated to Saul that his kingdom shall

---

39. Hertzberg, *Samuel*, p. 219.
40. Driver, *Hebrew Text*, p. 217.
41. LXX, Vulgate and five Hebrew MSS.
42. McKane, *Samuel*, p. 162. For McKane, G is LXX and S is Peshitta.

be taken from him (13.14 and 15.28) and the latter contains reference to the neighbour whose kingdom it has become (cf. v. 17). Mine is the more difficult reading and it seems to me (against Driver) that the versions may have read לך in order to maintain the sense of v. 16. Furthermore, the Hebrew word for neighbour occurs in v. 17, which makes the versions more likely to have imported the sense into v.16. Driver also prefers to omit v. 19a and take the LXX reading of v. 19b 'tomorrow you and your sons with you will be fallen'. Again, the MT has the more difficult reading with the repetition of two virtually identical clauses and should in my opinion be preferred, as Martin Noth advises.[43] Fokkelman deals with the matter with a perfunctory statement: 'The last word, an Aramaicizing variant of sar, is chosen for the sake of 17c.'[44]

Yhwh Answers David's Inquiries (30.8). Yhwh speaks once more in 1 Samuel: David asks Abiathar to bring him the ephod, and he inquires of Yhwh whether to pursue after the Amalekites who have taken their women and children. Yhwh answers, 'Pursue, for you shall indeed overtake and you shall indeed rescue'. This leads David to rescue those who were taken and to smite all but four hundred of the Amalekites and capture their flocks and herds as spoil. There is no mention of putting them to the ban, but the reader may sense that here David is finishing the work that Saul left undone. This is the last appearance of Yhwh before Saul's death and it recalls ch. 15 and the crisis of kingship there, thus also foreshadowing the events of ch. 31.

c. *The Divine Spirit*
Fredrik Lindström has analysed the passages in the Hebrew Bible that have been the focus of claims concerning God as the author of evil, and one of the texts he examines is the set of narratives relating the possession of Saul by a divinely sent evil spirit. Indeed, the key to Saul's decline is his affliction by this evil divine spirit; however Lindström does not discuss in detail all of the passages relating to Saul and the spirit of Yhwh, and these others are crucial to an understanding of Saul's relationship to the deity, and of his rise and fall. As it is therefore necessary to investigate this in detail, I intend to look closely at each episode where Saul comes into contact with a divine spirit in order to determine the pattern of events.

At the very beginning of Saul's kingship, before he has been instituted

43. See Noth, *Old Testament World*, on versions and the *lectio difficilior*, pp. 360-61.
44. Fokkelman, *Narrative Art*, p. 611.

king by the people but after his anointing, Samuel tells him he will be given
three signs, one of which is that the spirit of Yhwh will come upon him and
he will prophesy in the presence of a band of prophets. As he turns to leave
Samuel, God gives him another heart and when he arrives in Gibeah he is
met by a band of prophets, ותצלח עליו רוח אלהים ויתנבא בתוכם
'and a spirit of God came mightily upon him and he prophesied among
them' (10.10).[45] This gives rise to a proverb concerning Saul and prophesy.
The spirit is apparently connected with the heart that God has given him
and with the legitimacy of the kingship for which God has chosen him.

The second occurrence of a divine spirit in Saul's life comes after Saul's
election by lot, and after acceptance from some whose hearts God had
touched and criticism from some 'worthless fellows'. The immediate
context is the Ammonite threat to Jabesh-gilead. When Saul hears of the
matter, ותצלח רוח־אלהים על־שאול 'the spirit of God came mightily
upon Saul' (11.6) and he becomes angry, cuts up a pair of oxen and sends
them throughout the land (גבול) as a message of conscription. This
occurrence of the divine spirit places Saul in the tradition of the Judges,
who experienced the spirit of God as a prelude to leading their people to
war (Othniel: Judg. 3.10; Gideon: Judg. 6.34; Samson: Judg. 13.25;
14.6,19, though Samson tends to fight single-handedly).

Saul's action with the oxen has a parallel in Judg. 19.29, in which the
Levite divides up his concubine and sends pieces of her throughout the
land (גבול) as a gesture of anger against the actions of the men of Gibeah,
with far-reaching consequences such as civil war among the tribes of
Israel, the killing of all Benjaminite women and eventually peace between
the tribes and intermarriage between Benjaminite men and women from
Shiloh achieved by carrying the women off from a dance, which was
deemed to be preferable to killing the men of Shiloh for their women. The
entire account spans three chapters and is enveloped by the inclusio that in
those days there was no king in Israel. This parallel is significant since
Saul is a Benjaminite with Gibeah connections whose first action as king
is to protect the people of Jabesh-gilead, the city that had not taken part in
the battle against the Benjaminites and who consequently forfeited all their
virgins in a fresh outbreak of civil war. The new king of Israel is therefore
rejoining the breaches between the groups that had fought one another
before Israel had a king. Crucially, Saul enters into this rejoining of
breaches at the prompting of the spirit of God, and after his victory against

---

45. V.P. Long notes that the spirit that overcomes Saul is the רוח אלהים whereas
Samuel had predicted the רוח יהוה (*Reign and Rejection*, p. 207).

the Ammonites Saul refuses to have his opponents put to death, for on that day 'Yhwh has wrought deliverance in Israel' (11.13).

The parallel between Saul and the judges has been noted by McKane, Ackroyd, Hertzberg and others, and has been more closely examined by Garsiel, who understands it as criticism of Saul. He points to comparative structures between Saul's kingship and the Gideon stories, which 'continue to form a background for antithetical comparison',[46] and also the kingship of Abimelech:

> the author sets up an analogy between Saul's degeneration and the story of Gideon's son and opposite, Abimelech, whom Saul is shown to resemble. Various opportunities are exploited to suggest this analogy, and in this way again to enrich the perspective within which the author brings to bear the antimonarchical stance which forms the central focus of the book.[47]

One feature of the parallel with Abimelech is that Abimelech's fall is attributed by the author to an evil spirit in Judg. 9.23: וישלח אלהים רוח רעה, 'God sent an evil spirit' between Abimelech and the lords of Shechem and the lords of Shechem dealt treacherously with Abimelech. Garsiel points out that Abimelech was actually the first king in Israel. The parallels are numerous: the razing of a whole city (Shechem/Nob), the survival of one son (Jotham/Abiathar), the king's instruction to the armour bearer to kill him when death is inevitable at the hand of the enemy (Thebez/Philistines) are but a few. Garsiel argues, against Gunn, that these comparative structures are evidence of an author who used earlier written texts rather than orally transmitted literature; either way one must draw this parallel for a richer understanding of the tragic elements of Saul's story. Garsiel states,

> The analogy developed by the author or redactor of Samuel between Saul and Abimelech sharpens the condemnation of Saul, who changes from a modest person (like Gideon) to a despot pursued by an evil spirit, who— like Abimelech—casts everyone about him into terror.[48]

What Garsiel neglects to mention is that Saul changes back again into a modest person (cf. 1 Sam. 26.21-25), that the effects of the evil spirit are intermittent, and that their divine origin ricochets away from any antimonarchical tendencies of the author or redactor, leaving ultimate moral responsibility for the carnage at the feet of Yhwh. If the text has an

---

46. Garsiel, *I Samuel*, p. 94.
47. Garsiel, *I Samuel*, p. 94.
48. Garsiel, *I Samuel*, p. 99.

antimonarchical thrust, it undermines itself through the evil divine spirit, which may evoke sympathy for the rejected king.

The next mention of a divine spirit is in the context of David's anointing, when 'the spirit of Yhwh came mightily to David from that day forward' (16.13). The syntax is not identical to that of Saul's two early experiences, since this spirit is described as from Yhwh rather than from God, and this account substitutes אל for על and adds מהיום ההוא which alters the sense. David undergoes neither Saul's intermittent charismatic experiences nor his terrors. The sense is rather one of a constant divine presence. It is significant, therefore, that this is the only account of a divine spirit coming on David, and will contrast sharply with the following verse.

Saul's first experience of an evil divine spirit comes in 16.14, immediately after the narrative of David's anointing: שאול ורוח יהוה סרה מעם ובעתתו רוח־רעה מאת יהוה 'the spirit of Yhwh departed from Saul and an evil spirit from Yhwh terrified him'. Driver comments that ובעתתו is a strong word which occurs in prose only in this passage; elsewhere it is found in poetry, chiefly in the Book of Job.[49] Saul's servants perceive the cause of his distress, רוח־אלהים רעה מבעתך 'an evil spirit from God is terrifying you' (v. 15) and they suggest finding a musician so that when והיה בהיות עליך רוח־אלהים רעה 'the evil spirit from God will terrify you', the musician will play and Saul will be well (v. 16). One of Saul's servants has seen a suitable musician, David, who is brought to the court and Saul loves him. So והיה בהות רוח־אלהים אל־שאול, 'whenever[50] the evil spirit from God was upon Saul' David played, and Saul was well, וסרה מעליו רוח הרעה 'and the evil spirit departed from him' (v. 23).

The language used concerning this evil divine spirit is not the highly repetitive formulaic language one might find in the narrative style of other parts of the Hebrew Bible. At first the spirit is described as being from Yhwh (v. 16) and thereafter from God until ch. 19. The spirit that departs from Saul in v. 16 is Yhwh's spirit, and the evil spirit that departs from Saul in v. 23 is simply the 'evil spirit'. The action upon Saul of the evil divine spirit is the same, however: it terrifies him (בעת). Ackroyd remarks 'what comes to a man, good or ill, is seen as from God'[51] and Hertzberg comments that:

---

49. Driver, *Hebrew Text*, p. 134.
50. Driver remarks that a series of perfects with W.C. (waw consecutive) is used to express what happens habitually. (*Hebrew Text*, p. 137.)
51. Ackroyd, *Samuel*, p. 135.

> Saul's suffering is described theologically, not psychopathetically or psychologically. And rightly so, for in an obscure way the hand of God invades the life of this man who, as can be seen often, exerts himself so much for Yahweh.[52]

Fokkelman's assessment of the situation is that God is responsible for Saul's misfortune: 'It is Yahweh who holds Saul captive',[53] and this is a poignant way of expressing the cause of Saul's terror.

The evil divine spirit is reported to afflict Saul twice more in the narrative. At 18.10 ותצלח רוח אלהים רעה אל־שאול ויתנבא בתוך־הבית, 'an evil spirit from God came mightily to Saul and he prophesied within the palace' while David plays the lyre. Hertzberg suggests that in the general context it looks as if the women's song has brought on the attack.[54] This spirit comes upon Saul in the same manner as in 10.10 (ותצלח) and causes in Saul the same response (ויתנבא). Driver translates it as '*played the prophet*, viz. by gestures and demeanour, as 10, 5'.[55] Ackroyd remarks that 'the external effect of possession is the same whether the spirit is thought to be good or evil'.[56] However, there is a rather different outcome: Saul's attempt on David's life, which corresponds to the only difference in language: the fact that the spirit is evil.

The next appearance of the evil spirit is at 19.9. David has slaughtered many Philistines, and afterwards as Saul sits in his house with his spear in his hand, ותהי רוח יהוה רעה אל־שאול, 'an evil spirit from Yhwh was upon Saul' while David plays the lyre. It is significant that the evil spirit comes again while David is playing.

The final manifestation of a divine spirit comes at 19.23, when Saul has pursued David to Naioth in Ramah and all three sets of messengers he has sent have succumbed to prophecy. Saul follows them, ותהי עליו גם־הוא רוח אלהים 'and the spirit of God was upon him also' and as he went ויתנבא 'he prophesied' until he arrived at Naioth. Driver notes that this word is irregular: one would expect והתנבא in this context.[57] However, in this form it recalls 10.10 and in its narrative context it gives rise to the second explanation of the proverb concerning Saul's prophetic inclinations. After this there are no further reports of Saul's terror under the

---

52. Hertzberg, *Samuel*, p. 141.
53. Fokkelman, *Narrative Art*, p. 134.
54. Hertzberg, *Samuel*, p. 157.
55. Driver, *Hebrew Text*, p. 152.
56. Ackroyd, *Samuel*, p. 150.
57. Driver, *Hebrew Text*, p. 160.

influence of an evil divine spirit; perhaps, however unlikely, this prophe-sying before Samuel has somehow exorcized it. However, Saul's behav-iour becomes increasingly disturbed, as do his relations with those who are closely connected with Yhwh (Samuel, David and the priests). He has the priests of Nob slaughtered, and his final encounter with Samuel is the recognition of his fate, at Endor.

Since Lindström deals chiefly with the passages concerning the evil spirit (omitting other spirits of Yhwh) in 1 Samuel, he locates them within 'what will once have been an independent work, usually termed the History of David's Rise to Power',[58] that is 1 Samuel 15–2 Samuel 5. Of course the second explanation of the proverb concerning Saul's prophetic behaviour comes within this block as well, yet Lindström does not men-tion it. Lindström attempts to reconstruct the original traditions and then discuss their reinterpretation by the author of 1 Samuel, concluding that 'the author is fitting his concept of the negative effects of the divine charisma to the tradition of Saul's agony'.[59] He maintains that in the origi-nal tradition the 'spirit' designates Saul's mood, and that the function of God/Yhwh as sender of the spirit is the creation of the author of the later work, hence there is 'no reason to suppose that Saul's agony was ever understood to have been caused by supernatural powers'[60] by which he implies demonic forces, neglecting the possibility of an understanding of God as a supernatural power. He attributes Saul's attempts on David's life in 18.10-11 and 19.9-10 as later than the original tradition, in which

> Saul is refreshed with the aid of David's playing on the lyre. The lyre-play recurs in all three passages, even if the expected result is omitted in 18,10f. and 19,9f.[61]

Lindström does not take account here of the possibility of artistic design. The reason the expected result is omitted is because the result is unexpected. In 18.10-11 Saul intends to pin David to the wall; in 19.9-10 Saul actually throws his spear at David, who then has to escape during the night. This is not the behaviour of a man who has been soothed by some pleasant lyre music; it is the behaviour of a man who finds the music an additional torment. As Lindström points out, there are some passages in the context where Saul will not lay a hand on David (e.g. 18.17, 25). The

58. Fredrik Lindström, *God and the Origin of Evil: A Contextual Analysis of Alleged Monistic Evidence in the Old Testament* (Lund: C.W.K. Gleerup, 1983), p. 78.

59. Lindström, *Origin of Evil*, p. 82.

60. Lindström, *Origin of Evil*, p. 80.

61. Lindström, *Origin of Evil*, p. 80.

evil spirit and the music in combination in chs. 18 and 19 are what cause Saul to lose his self-control. As Fokkelman remarks, 'Saul this time has guessed who is his rival and…he has the misfortune that it is the same person as his musical therapist'.[62] In his comment on ch. 19 he hints that David may not be trying his best to cure Saul: 'We may also ask whether David is playing inspiredly. Can music still have a curative action if it is not played with curative intent?'[63] S.D. Walters, apparently in a desperate attempt to force a Christian notion of divine grace onto the text,[64] suggests that David's playing is intended to show that

> grace operates on the personal level even in Saul's rejection from office. The fact that Saul was unable to accept the boons of David's service does not change the text's implication that gracious benefits are in the new king's gift.[65]

Walters can draw this conclusion only because he sidesteps the issue of the origin of the evil spirit.

Lindström makes much of the omission of the deity in 18.23:

> a close reading of the passage reveals that there is no sign that it is *God's* evil spirit that abandons Saul because of the lyre music. The striking distinction between 'the spirit of God' and 'the evil spirit' which is made in 16,23 may well suggest that the author attempted to avoid an unintended consequence of his new interpretation [of God's evil spirit as a negatively effective charisma].[66]

Are we to assume, then, that an evil spirit from Yhwh came upon Saul and terrified him but when David played to him it was another evil spirit that departed from him? The most plausible conclusion is that which Lindström is quite candidly attempting to avoid: that the author of this passage believed the spirit of God could be influenced by the sound of a lyre.

62. Fokkelman, *Narrative Art*, p. 222.
63. Fokkelman, *Narrative Art*, p. 260.
64. Cf. Walters's use of the terms 'light' and 'dark', terms that are foreign to the text, to describe the characterization of David and Saul, and his conclusion that 'our work, in a world where Saul is still king' must continue 'until the antinomy of light and dark disappears, and we come to where there is no dark, because the Lamb is the light'. See S.D. Walters, 'The Light and the Dark', in Eslinger andn Taylor (eds.), *Ascribe to the Lord*, pp. 567-89 (589).
65. Walters, 'Light and Dark', p. 579.
66. Lindström, *Origin of Evil*, p. 82.

Lindström's deconstruction (in a broad sense) of the text and ascription of verses to original traditions or to the later author of the book, without reference to the work of those scholars who have concentrated on the details of questions of source in 1 Samuel, is not convincing; his argument depends on his own arbitrary methodology. For instance, McKane suggests that 18.10 and 19.9 may originally have been two variant accounts, a possibility that Lindström has not acknowledged. Nevertheless, I agree with his conclusion that 'there is no indication in these texts that Saul's anguish was understood as the result of demonic influence'[67] unless one may define 'demonic' widely enough to include Yhwh.

Summary

When Yhwh speaks or acts in this narrative it is frequently in response to a cue from Saul. Yhwh's ambivalence towards Saul is clear. He seems at the same time to be in collision with Saul and to tolerate Saul. He repents of making Saul king, but it is initially Samuel who rejects Saul, although Samuel is also ambivalent concerning the king. Samuel as Saul's link with Yhwh expresses some of the deity's ambivalence. Yhwh does not punish Saul as he punishes the enemies of his people; he does not smite Saul in ch. 13, nor in ch. 15 when the divine command has more clearly been transgressed. Unlike the enemies of Israel he does not put Saul to the ban; however, he does utterly destroy Saul. Yhwh is ambivalent in that he allows two anointed kings to vie for power; to one he gives a new heart and the other is a man after his own heart. Despite his repentance, Yhwh does not actually tear away Saul's kingship for quite some time. Instead he tears away Saul's sanity. Perhaps even the deity himself is loath to put out his hand against Yhwh's anointed.

Yhwh answers only David's enquiries; he never answers Saul's, with the one exception of the lot that condemns Jonathan to death. All Saul's other enquiries are answered with silence, though Samuel eventually answers his final question, but only under duress, thus emphasizing Yhwh's deliberate separation from Saul. Yhwh tolerates Saul's sovereignty only up to a point, and as Saul loses his grip Yhwh torments him throughout his attempts to retain it.

It is without a doubt Yhwh/God who sends spirits on Saul and this demonstrates the deity's ambivalence. Sometimes the spirit is evil and sometimes not, and there is no pattern in relation to Saul's status as anointed

---

67. Lindström, *Origin of Evil*, p. 84.

king or rejected king. The divine spirits that come upon Saul contrast greatly with the divine spirit that Yhwh sends to David. There is also ambivalence in view of the consequences of the coming of spirits, for example, Saul's attempts on the life of the man after God's own heart. Eslinger, commenting on 1 Samuel 8–12, writes

> The reader is asked to step across the usual bounds of human understanding of God's motives, to cross over the theological barrier described by God in the well known passage from Isaiah (55.8-6[*sic*]). God's motives can be known and they are not always the most complimentary… For the biblical God, the end does justify almost any means.[68]

The implications of this remark could be extended to refer to the Saul narrative as a whole.

The Problem of Evil

Lindström writes in the preface to *God and the Origin of Evil* that the conclusion at which he ultimately arrived was one whose very possibility he had neglected when he started his study.[69] This conclusion is that none of the texts usually quoted in support of an idea of a demonic force being later identified with God in fact gives rise to any reason for such an identification. However, Lindström's arguments are largely circular and self-fulfilling. When he deals with the evil spirit from Yhwh in 1 Samuel, he concludes that there is no reason to suppose that this is a demonic force. Indeed it is not a demonic force: it is an evil spirit from Yhwh and the problems that this throws up are theological, at least in view of Sternberg's conception of the 'lord of history'.

First of all the terms of the problem must be set out: the problem of evil which theodicy aims to address is a (Judaeo-)Christian philsophical problem. Stephen Davis gives a useful summary:

> [I]f God is omnipotent…he must be *able* to prevent evil… And if God is perfectly good he must be *willing* to prevent evil. Both if God is both able and willing to prevent evil, why does evil exist?[70]

Davis outlines two common approaches: the logical approach, which tends (or intends) to criticize theism by stressing the logical incompatibility of

---

68. Lyle M. Eslinger, *Into the Hands of the Living God* (JSOTSup, 84; Sheffield: Almond Press, 1989), pp. 22-23.

69. Lindström, *Origin of Evil*, p. 7.

70. Stephen T. Davis (ed.), *Encountering Evil: Live Options in Theodicy* (Edinburgh: T. & T. Clark, 1981), p. 3.

the three terms of the problem; and the epistemological approach, which tends (or intends) to criticize theism by claiming that the existence of evil constitutes powerful evidence against the existence of such a God. M.B. Ahern is one scholar who approaches theodicy from a logical and a theistic perspective, and concludes, after a valuable discussion, that 'the only positive answer...is an indirect one, i.e. the answer that all actual evil is justified if God exists',[71] which seems to me as good a reason as any for becoming an atheist. Other theists (and non-theists) approach the problem from other perspectives and with arguments such as Free Will (Alvin Plantinga[72]), Platonic (David Griffin[73]) and Irenaean (John Hick[74]), with varying degrees of success and plausibility. To every approach objections are raised, and so ultimately there is no consensus and there is no straight-forward solution.

Each approach appears to operate by redefining and/or weakening one of the three terms: thus God's omnipotence falls down in front of free will, or evil does not really exist because God justifies it, hence it is only apparent evil. The term of God's perfect goodness can be weakened by a division of evil into moral evil and non-moral, or natural, evil, which accompanies a claim that God does not commit moral evil but does permit or commit natural evil. Once one law is weakened, the other two yield, rather like Asimov's positronic brains.

1 Samuel does not raise this specific philosophical problem because it precludes the conclusion that Yhwh is wholly good. The theological perspective here is not only that evil in the world comes from Yhwh, but that Yhwh may commit acts of moral evil (such as Saul's torment), against Ahern, for example, who argues that God, being wholly good, does not commit moral evil. The emphasis, then, is on Yhwh's omnipotence.

John Gibson has tackled the wider view of God in the Hebrew Bible with specific reference to the tragic vision. He argues that, despite figures such as Leviathan, the writers of the Hebrew Bible preferred 'to live with the thought of an ambivalence in the divine will than to envisage a force or creature that could be considered God's opposite'.[75] Thus he contends that

71. M.B. Ahern, *The Problem of Evil* (London: Routledge & Kegan Paul, 1971), p. 75.

72. See Michael L. Peterson (ed.), *The Problem of Evil: Selected Readings* (Notre Dame: University of Notre Dame Press, 1992).

73. See Davis (ed.), *Evil.*

74. See Davis (ed.), *Evil.*

75. John C.L. Gibson, 'Biblical Tragedy', *Reformed World* 36.7 (1981), pp. 291-98 (293).

the New Testament conception of Satan as an evil power is contrary to the perspectives of the Hebrew Bible. His views are certainly in accordance with the portrayal of the deity in 1 Samuel. A different perspective may be found in Rogerson's monograph 'Can a Doctrine of Providence be Based on the Old Testament' in which he argues that 'material dealing with the relation between God's purposes and human freedom' might be said 'to count against the idea'[76] of divine providence. On this he specifically cites the story of Saul, with reference to his rejection, and he later returns to the point, commenting,

> In narratives such as those about the obstinacy of Pharaoh and the fate of Saul, [the Old Testament writers] wrestled with the intractable problem of the relation between human freewill and the will of God.[77]

On this view, it is not Yhwh's goodness, but Yhwh's omnipotence that is called into question. R.N. Whybray, however, supports the first line of argument and draws attention to 'certain narratives in the Old Testament where God seems to have been intentionally depicted as behaving in an immoral or amoral way'.[78] He does not examine any passages in 1 Samuel, but he does draw attention to God's fear and jealousy in Genesis 2–3, God's injustice in Genesis 18, God's immorality in Job 1–2, and God's uncontrollable rages in Exodus 32 and Numbers 14. On the same kind of model, I have outlined Yhwh's ambivalence in 1 Samuel 8–31, and have argued, after Gibson, that this ambivalence is a feature of a tragic vision in the Hebrew Bible.

Gibson, in his later work 'On Evil in the Book of Job', while arguing that Job's suffering is undeserved (and there are few who would disagree), examines God's speeches from the whirlwind and complains that many lines of interpretation are 'too 'Christian' in their desire to denigrate Job's knowledge of God and their reluctance to admit that he deserved the acquittal which he is...to receive'.[79] He objects to interpretations of Leviathan and Behemoth which 'swallow up evil in mystery' and instead argues that

---

76. John Rogerson, 'Can a Doctrine of Providence Be Based on the Old Testament?', in Eslinger and Taylor (eds.), *Ascribe to the Lord*, pp. 529-43 (535).

77. Rogerson, 'Providence', p. 543.

78. R.N. Whybray, 'The Immorality of God: Reflections on some Passages in Genesis, Job, Exodus and Numbers', *JSOT* 72 (1996), pp. 89-121 (89).

79. John C.L. Gibson, 'On Evil in the Book of Job', in Eslinger and Taylor (eds.), *Ascribe to the Lord*, pp. 399-419 (403).

> Job is…being given an intimation…of the terrible reality of evil and…of
> the dangers it presents to men but, above all, of the frightening problem it
> poses to the God who in his wisdom—or should we say in his folly?—built
> it into the fabric of creation,[80]

which is an understanding of God as the author of moral evil. Even more
significantly, Gibson concludes by tackling the function of the Satan in the
Book of Job. The Satan represents 'that side of divinity which for whatever reason visits affliction on men' and the absence of this character from
the epilogue is on the grounds that 'it would not do if those for whom [the
folk tale] was intended were even remotely tempted to use the Satan's
presence in the heavenly court as a means of letting God escape his
responsibility'.[81]

In summary, then, the philosophical problem of evil to which theodicy
addresses itself does not arise from an honest reading of the portrayal of
Yhwh in 1 Samuel, since throughout the narrative Yhwh is depicted as
ambivalent and therefore outside the philosophical terms that denote God
as 'perfectly good'. Thus if a solution to the problem of the existence of
evil were to be advanced by appeal to 1 Samuel, it would be simply that
God may be the author of moral evil.

Conclusions

Elisabeth Schüssler Fiorenza, in a presidential address to the Society of
Biblical Literature raises methodological questions that relate to a decentring process in biblical scholarship. She argues,

> The…literary-hermeneutical paradigm seems presently in the process of
> decentering into a…paradigm that inaugurates a rhetorical–ethical turn.
> This…paradigm relies on the analytical and practical tradition of rhetoric in
> order to insist on the public-political responsibility of biblical scholarship.
> It seeks to utilize both theories of rhetoric and the rhetoric of theories in
> order to display how biblical texts and their contemporary interpretations
> involve authorial aims and strategies, as well as audience perceptions and
> constructions, as political and religious discursive practices.[82]

This, then, is the method. The aim is 'to engender a self-understanding of
biblical scholarship as a communicative praxis'. Although her notion of

---

80. Gibson, 'Evil', p. 417.
81. Gibson, 'Evil', p. 418.
82. Elisabeth Schüssler Fiorenza, 'The Ethics of Biblical Interpretation: Decentering Biblical Scholarship', *JBL* 107:1, 1988, pp. 3-17 (4).

'the rights of the text' seems a trifle trendy, Fiorenza's concern that the text 'may say something different from what one wants or expects it to say'[83] is crucial, and is not as highly developed in biblical studies as she asserts.

Fiorenza responds to the notion that biblical studies 'appears to have progressed in a political vacuum'[84] which she does not condone. She comments that 'The decentering of this rhetoric of disinterestedness and presupposition-free exegesis seeks to recover the political context of biblical scholarship and its public responsibility.'[85] Although I disagree with Fiorenza's assessment that the apolitical detachment in biblical studies has been presupposition-free, I believe that she is correct on the question of political context. Fiorenza discusses an 'ethics of historical reading' and remarks,

> The rhetorical character of biblical interpretations and historical reconstructions…requires an *ethics of accountability* that stands responsible not only for the choice of theoretical interpretive models but also for the ethical consequences of the biblical text and its meanings. If scriptural texts have served not only noble causes but also to legitimate war, to nurture anti-Judaism and misogynism, to justify the exploitation of slavery, and to promote colonial dehumanization, then biblical scholarship must take the responsibility not only to interpret biblical texts in their historical contexts but also to evaluate the construction of their historical worlds and symbolic universes in terms of a religious scale of values.[86]

At this point it will be pertinent to mention Tod Linafelt's work in using this idea of an 'ethics of accountability'. Linafelt explores the extended Samuel narrative with reference to the theme of the taking of women as a sign of male power, and discusses David's show of power in taking Abigail and Saul's parry of giving Michal, his daughter and David's wife, to another man. Later, after David has become king, it becomes apparent that God is involved in exactly the same activity, when he ordains that David's women shall be taken by a neighbour who shall lie with them, which culminates in a scene in which David's son Absalom, advised by divine oracle, publicly 'goes in to' his father's concubines in order to

---

83. J. Hillis Miller, 'Presidential Address 1986: The Triumph of Theory, the Resistance to Reading, and the Question of the Material Base', *PMLA* 102 (1987), pp. 281-91 (284). Quoted in Fiorenza, 'Ethics', p. 5.

84. Fiorenza, 'Ethics', p. 9.

85. Fiorenza, 'Ethics', p. 11.

86. Fiorenza, 'Ethics', p. 15.

shame David. The ethical outrage over God as the instigator of this crime against the women is almost equalled by the commentators whom Linafelt quotes:

> [Hertzberg] goes so far as to affirm the taking of David's wives as 'a fitting punishment' with no consideration of how fitting it is for the women who are taken as punishment for the actions of men. Mauchline…writes that 'the open shame which is to befall David's wives is fit penalty for the secret act of shame which he committed against Bathsheba'. How can one blindly affirm that the raping of women is 'fit penalty' for a man's sin? It seems that in so doing, Mauchline believes he has preserved a sense of YHWH's justice. But is this the kind of justice worth preserving? Hertzberg…goes on to write that in this passage, 'God's justice is not suspended even for the mightiest'. Unfortunately, justice *is* suspended for those without might.[87]

Linafelt suggests reading intertextually to cite God against God, in order to demand justice. I conclude with Linafelt that 'like Abraham, we must press the question, 'Shall not the judge of the earth do justice?' (Gen 18.25)'.[88] This is a vital question to ask of the deity portrayed in the story of Saul.

87. Tod Linafelt, 'Taking Women in Samuel: Readers/Responses/Responsibility', in Fewell (ed.), *Reading Between Texts*, pp. 99-113 (108). Linafelt quotes Hertzberg, *Samuel*, p. 314, and John Mauchline, *1 and 2 Samuel* (London: Oliphants, 1971), p. 254.
88. Linafelt, 'Taking Women', p. 111.

Face II

SAUL IN LAMARTINE'S SAÜL

Chapter 3

IF ALL WERE ONLY VANITY:
STRIVING AFTER THE BIBLICAL PLOT

Introduction

The definitions and understandings of intertextuality that exist in critical
debate are outlined in the introduction to the thesis. At this point the
primary concern is with the applications of intertextual principles. First of
all the texts that relate to this chapter must be declared. If, after Julia
Kristeva, all discourse may be regarded as textual, then the following
could be considered to be texts that have among them a network of
relationships relevant to this chapter:

1. the (MT) of 1 Samuel
2. various English translations of 1 Samuel, including my own
3. the text of my reading of 1 Samuel
4. the text of the foregoing chapters of this thesis which relate to 1 Samuel
5. de Cognets's critical text of Lamartine's Saül: Tragédie
6. the text of Lamartine's reading of 1 Samuel
7. the text of Alfieri's Saul
8. the text of Lamartine's reading of Alfieri
9. the text of my reading of Lamartine's drama
10. the text of this chapter
11. the text of my implied reader's reading of this chapter

(But this is not an exhaustive list of the texts which are juxtaposed with
one another; there are many more that play minor roles. Furthermore, a
reader of this chapter will add a new level of texts to the above list, and if
he or she discusses the chapter with another reader [or readers] then the
number of levels and texts will increase exponentially. In the above list
there are texts that have a place in the matrix but which are not available
for investigation: Lamartine's reading of 1 Samuel is not available, but
texts that depend on it are. Naturally Jean de Cognets's publication of *Saül*
is available, but it reproduces the text of ms. 40 of the Bibliothéque
Nationale, while the text of mss. 41 and 42 remain unpublished and in

practical terms unavailable [except perhaps to established Lamartine scholars]. Some of Lamartine's correspondence is available, which forms another text [and in published form has been edited: a new text]. Moreover, de Cognets has chosen some fragments of Lamartine's correspondence as explanation of his interpretation of 1 Samuel, which appear in the notes in the critical edition of the drama, and all these texts expand the range of the matrix and therefore it is necessary to consider Lamartine as reader and writer so that the text of *Saül* is not isolated from some of the texts in its network.)

The centre of the matrix is Lamartine himself. Alphonse of Lamartine came from a wealthy and educated family that had survived the revolutionary period of 1789 to 1799 retaining most of its influence and assets. From an early age his parents had introduced him to literature, and his mother's devout Catholicism had instilled in him a love and knowledge of the Bible. Indeed, the Bible 'came to exercise a very profound influence on Lamartine, providing him throughout his life with literary, intellectual and spiritual inspiration'.[1] J.C. Ireson cites Job as having had an intense effect on Lamartine's literary imagination, asserting that 'Lamartine finds in Job the universal blueprint for the philosophy of resignation which the two poles of existence—horror and doubt, wonder and belief—have brought into being in his own case'.[2] It was this literary perspective which led to the conception of *Saül*. De Cognets, in the introduction to his critical edition of *Saül*, writes, 'It was in order to write his tragedy that...Lamartine filled himself with the poetry of the Bible'.[3]

Lamartine is (and was during his lifetime) better known for his poetry than his other literary efforts, so his use of verse in alexandrine meter in *Saül* comes as no great surprise, though it is worth noting that this application is attributed to the influence of Voltaire by de Cognets[4] and less specifically by William Fortescue.[5] Significantly, de Cognets comments that 'The language and the poetry of the *Méditations* differs

1.   William Fortescue, *Alphonse de Lamartine: A Political Biography* (London: Croom Helm, 1983), p. 13.

2.   J.C. Ireson, *Lamartine: A Revaluation* (Hull: University of Hull, 1969), p. 23.

3.   Jean de Cognets, introduction in Alphonse de Lamartine, *Saül: Tragédie* (critical edition with an introduction and commeñary by Jean de Cognets; Paris: Librairie Hachette, 1918), p. vii.

4.   De Cognets in Lamartine, *Saül*, p. vii.

5.   Fortescue, *Lamartine*, p. 13.

little from that of *Saül*,[6] thus raising the question of the comparative reception of the two works: it was the *Meditations* which brought Lamartine fame if not fortune. It may be observed that Lamartine uses in *Saül* many of the themes and techniques found in his early poetic works, such as the instilling of memory into landscape, the human symbolism of nature and the use of elegaic metaphor.[7] These themes are worked into the handling of biblical material to effect a dynamic compound.

It is crucial to an understanding of Lamartine's work to remember that Lamartine was a notable, if ultimately unsuccessful, politician. At several points in his life Lamartine argued that his involvement in politics was of greater importance to him than his significance as a poet, yet if he had a fatal flaw it was his eagerness to appeal to all sides at once, which led to an abdication of responsibility for his political errors. In *Saül* one can distinguish political themes which de Cognets has suggested may be allegorical. The presence of this political motif provides a fresh perspective from which to engage the biblical narrative.

Lamartine began work on *Saül* in January 1818, at a turbulent point in his life. He had for some time been attempting to begin a political career by applying for various sub-prefectures, which had involved the raising and dashing of his hopes on several occasions. His family had opposed a number of romances, including two that resulted in illegitimate sons, and his most recent lover, a married woman named Julie Charles who profoundly affected his life and work, had died in December 1817. De Cognets remarks,

> If Lamartine, during this troubled period of his life, took such a strong interest in this work that it caused him to forget the pain of his bereavement in love, his physical sufferings, his career worries and the ceaselessly reborn troubles of a stormy heart, it is because he was able to pour out there all the feelings that suffocated him.[8]

That de Cognets is the only Lamartine scholar to have attached importance to this early drama remains somewhat scandalous.

Although in order to write this tragedy Lamartine became imbued with the Bible, it was not the Bible alone that influenced the young poet. The importance for Lamartine of Vittorio Alfieri's *Saul* must be stressed,

6.   De Cognets in Lamartine, *Saül*, p. viii.
7.   See Mary Ellen Birkett, *Lamartine and the Poetics of Landscape* (Lexington: French Forum, 1982), and Laurence M. Porter, *The Renaissance of the Lyric in French Romanticism: Elegie, 'Poëme' and Ode* (Lexington: French Forum, 1978).
8.   De Cognets in Lamartine, *Saül*, p. viii.

particularly with regard to an intertextual approach to Lamartine's drama. De Cognets remarks, 'Alfieri became his model: he wanted to imitate him'[9] and goes on to quote from Lamartine's *Correspondences*,

> Alfieri gave me the idea, but mine will have a progress which appears warmer to me and an intrigue a little more urgent than his.[10]

Certainly in comparison with Alfieri, Lamartine's *Saül* appears to have more plot twists, while in terms of characterization, Saül in particular is allowed more scope for warmth of sentiment. Furthermore, Lamartine's drama absorbs more of the biblical thematic material; for example, in Alfieri's *Saul* there is no scene with a Pythonisse to correspond to Saul's visit to the woman of Endor in 1 Samuel. Lamartine has to some extent modelled his characterization on Alfieri's work, for example Abner's interference, but it is the structure that points overwhelmingly to Alfieri's influence. The first few scenes of Alfieri compared with Lamartine are virtually identical in terms of structure:

Table 1. *Comparison of scene structures*

	Alfieri	Lamartine
Scene 1	David's monologue: he considers his position	David's monologue: he considers his position
Scene 2	Gionata enters: they discuss the plight of their people, Saul's suffering, and David's love for Micol	Jonathas enters: they discuss the plight of the people, Saül's suffering, and David's love for Micol
Scene 3	Micol reflects on her troubles, Gionata tells her David has returned	Micol reflects on her troubles, Jonathas tells her David has returned

This similarity continues throughout, though naturally there is no rigid adherence on Lamartine's part to Alfieri's structure, and in fact Lamartine's drama is noticeably longer in consequence of developments in a number of directions which depart from Alfieri's work. Alfieri himself had a number of reasons for his own reworking of the biblical material:

> Le modificazioni sono in parte determinate dalle regole cosi dette aristoteliche, seguite dall'Alfieri, che imponevano di contenere nelle ventiquattro ore l'azione rappresentata. Per questo e per animare l'azione

9.   De Cognets in Lamartine, *Saül*, p. xiv.
10.   *Corr.*, I, xcv, quoted by de Cognets, in Lamartine, *Saül*, p. xv.

l'autore—che di suo colora di tinte fosche il personaggio di Abner—
anticipa l'inimicizia fra David e il ministro, della quale the Bibbia parla
solo dopo the fine di Saul,[11]

and Lamartine worked with the consequences. I do not propose to deal
further with Alfieri's drama in its intertextual relation, since it's function is
chiefly as a structural model and, despite the significance of Alfieri's
characterization for Lamartine, *Saül* has a direct and primary relationship
to the biblical material. If *Saül* is to be considered on its own merits, then
the intertext with which we must be fundamentally concerned is that of 1
Samuel. Therefore we shall begin by considering the relationships
between these texts in plot and in characterization. The plot traces the
manner in which Saül's character flaw and his fate unfold, while the
characterization defines the nature of his flaw and the phenomena that
govern his fate. As these elements are the two that Aristotle considered
most important it seems a fitting place to begin.

Plot

One of the first things that may strike a reader of *Saül* who is also familiar
with 1 Samuel is the extent to which Lamartine has departed from the
order of events and the placing of events as found in the biblical narrative.
As we have seen, this modification derives from Lamartine's adoption of
Alfieri's structure, although not all of the modifications are identical to
Alfieri's. The seven acts cover only a few hours and take place entirely in
the narrative context of Saul's final conflict with the Philistines, in
accordance with Lamartine's (or Alfieri's) understanding of Aristotle.
Furthermore, David's role in the battle is markedly different from the
biblical account; in 1 Samuel David is faced with the possibility of
fighting in this battle on the side of the Philistines whereas in Lamartine's
drama he returns in the nick of time to fight with Saul's men. This is no
doubt the reason for the altered outcome of the battle: in 1 Samuel Saul's
army is crushed, but the help of David in *Saül* wins the battle for the

---

11. Vittorio Alfieri, *Saul e Filippo* (introduction and notes by Vittore Branca;
Milano: Biblioteca Universale Rizzoli, 1980), p. 157. Translation: 'The modifications
are in part determined by the rules as dictated by Aristotle, followed by Alfieri, which
imposed the containment of the represented action within twenty four hours. For this,
and in order to animate the action, the author—who himself coloured the personality of
Abner with dark shades—anticipated the animosity between David and the minister, of
which the Bible speaks only after the end of Saul.'

armies of Israel. Thus we find that the framework in which the battle is set also differs radically. In 1 Samuel this battle is Saul's first defeat, whereas in *Saül* the framework is one of Israelite despair at God's perceived abandonment of his people. In *Saül* the armies of the king depend on David for success, but in the biblical material the situation is more complex: Saul suffers no terrible defeats during David's exile but his actions in pursuing David are of questionable strategy. Lamartine's drama paints a far less subtle picture of the military fortunes of Israel, which in turn enhances his own distinct characterization. Most crucially of all, the absence in the drama of Saul's healthier and happier years brings the focal point forward to emphasize Saul's demise, yet with no anterior referent for contrast. Without an account of Saul's 'rise' there is no apex from which Saul has fallen, and his deterioration depends on an intertextual relation for meaning. This example is the most striking but by no means the only incidence of the drama's dependence on the reader's or audience's knowledge of the biblical material. Thus the remodelling of the biblical material that takes place in *Saül* effects and reflects Israel's dependence on David and also amplifies Saul's failures, but at the cost of the subtlety and intricacy of the biblical text. The subtleties of Lamartine's work lie elsewhere: in the use of overtly complex characterization and in the provision of the 'window into the mind' that is said to be so often absent in biblical narrative. To illustrate more precisely the effects of Lamartine's revision of the plot for the ends of characterization, there follow some examples.

Abner's Political Influence

Abner's role in *Saül* is much more central than in 1 Samuel, where he is named as the commander of Saul's army (14.50) and is addressed by David while Saul sleeps (26.14-16); he does not become more involved than to retort to David's insults. In Lamartine's work it is at Abner's suggestion that Saül speak with the medium. Abner speaks at length to Saül to put doubts in his mind over the loyalty of David and of the people, Abner tries to manipulate David into taking Saül's place in battle, Abner influences Saül in the face of Achimelech's religious fervour, and he finally kills the priest at Saül's command.

In Act 2 Abner plays the type of role at which David hints in 1 Sam. 24.9 ('Why do you listen to the words of men who say, "Behold, David seeks your hurt"?' [RSV]). He tells Saül he fears victory for the king:

> Yes, Lord, yes, tremble to be conqueror today

If David alone must have the honour of success.[12]

Saül is prepared to put the interests of the people ahead of his own, and Abner goes on to raise the question of what will happen if Saül dies. Saül is confident that his death will be glorious and that his son will succeed, but Abner puts a new doubt into his head:

> What? You count, Lord, on the gratitude
> Of this people famous for their cowardly fickleness.[13]

As Saül begins to weaken, he wishes to know his fate, and Abner seizes this opportunity to speak of corrupt priests who are responsible for the absence of the spirit of God, but assures Saül that there are some pious individuals who can read the future. Saul pleads to be able speak to such a person, and Abner tells him that there is a woman who wants to speak to him, who is waiting for him. De Cognets comments at this point,

> Quite improbable. When Saül goes to find the Pythonisse, in the Bible, she fears that he wishes to put her to death for her evil spells.[14]

But of course the plot trajectory connecting the woman with Samuel's reference to witchcraft in his speech concerning Saul's rejection in 1 Samuel 15 is absent from Lamartine's plot framework. Nevertheless, here it is not Saül's idea to consult a necromancer, but Abner's suggestion at the conclusion of a dialogue in which he has robbed Saül of every security. The notion of divine disapproval of necromancy is entirely absent. Abner's actions are central in the sequence of events, and he is portrayed as a political manipulator while Saül's confusion, insecurity and weaknesses are readily apparent in the face of Abner's cunning. The effect is a slur on the legitimacy of Saül's kingship, and on his qualities as a ruler: a leader should of course take note of his advisers, yet it seems that Saül is without good judgment in the face of Abner's politicking and is easily swayed by Abner's playing on his paranoia.

However, this perspective on Saül is challenged somewhat when Abner attempts to manipulate David in a similar manner in Act 3. Abner evidently finds it easy enough to manipulate the king who trusts him. How will he fare with a political opponent, with someone who does not trust him as Saül does? Surely the astute David will resist Abner's gnawing at his weaknesses? In Scene 2 David is about to depart, having announced

---

12. Lamartine, *Saül* (hereafter *Saül*), ll.439-40.
13. *Saül*, ll. 465-66.
14. De Cognets in *Saül*, p. 38, note on l. 517.

his intention as 'This last sacrifice for my unhappy King',[15] which Jonathas accepts as David's magnanimity. Abner arrives at the scene and sneers at his leaving before the battle:

> What! The son of Jesse, what! The messenger of heaven
> At the moment of battle abandons Israel?[16]

but David replies that he is only fleeing injustice and his enemies. Abner contests this: David is overreacting; he may have rivals but not enemies in 'the camp of God'.[17] David hints that he suspects Abner is his enemy, but Abner claims that

> in such moments, Abner must attend to
> Concerns more important than setting you straight.[18]

Abner then suggests that either he or David should take Saül's place in battle, since Saül is 'in funereal raptures'[19] but David's initial reaction is one of horror at the thought. Abner shifts his focus from this appeal to David's compassion for Saül and concentrates on bolstering David's ego, claiming that David is indispensable. He quickly suggests, as an alternative, that the two of them could share the honour, but David cannot think of taking Saül's place. Abner then asks him whether to defend one's country is a crime and maintains that they will be innocent if the people are saved. David is now weakening and so makes his strongest play in his defence: God has not authorized it. No prophet has spoken, no inspired hand has anointed them with sacred oil that they should take for themselves the authority of kings. Abner comes in for the kill: the only prophet is 'necessity': 'She is the voice of heaven which man must understand'.[20] Finally David capitulates, but agrees to fight only as a soldier of the king.

David's reasoning always makes reference to God's will, and whenever he is faced with a difficult decision he will use theological arguments as his motivations. However, in this scene he has been entirely turned around. He began with the intention to flee after hearing Jonathas tell how Saül in his madness has been behaving:

15. *Saül*, l. 796.
16. *Saül*, ll. 803-804.
17. *Saül*, l. 811.
18. *Saül*, ll. 827-28.
19. *Saül*, l. 833.
20. *Saül*, l. 878.

He believes he is striking David, he names him, he rushes
Twenty times, his arm deceived, pierces the air with his sword.[21]

David intended to leave the 'wife whom I adore'[22] which he expressed as a
last sacrifice for the king. Now, after discussion with the man he suspects
of being his enemy, he has been persuaded to stay and fight, convincing
himself despite Abner's rather untheological theology that it is God's will.
Will he really limit himself to the role of an ordinary soldier, or, now that
the idea has been placed in his head, will he aspire to lead Saül's army?

Abner is thus depicted as a master politician who can influence those
who trust his advice to the point of agreeing with his every word, and
those who mistrust him to the point of radically changing their plans.
Abner has played on Saül's political inclinations to cause Saül to change
his mind concerning David's loyalty, and has used David's theological
inclinations to persuade him to do the very thing that Abner has warned
Saül about. In both cases he has approached these inclinations as
weaknesses: Saül's political spectrum can easily extend as far as paranoia,
and David's insistence on having God's approval can be manipulated to
convince him that Abner's suggestion can be interpreted as God's will.
What Abner wishes to get out of these events for himself he never
explicitly states, and so, as with any spin doctor, one may speculate as to
his hidden agenda. Increasing his own power would seem to be a
reasonable assumption: if Saül is incapable of leading the army that Abner
commands, and David can be persuaded to fight with them, then there is a
good chance that they will defeat the Philistines and Abner will become
the recipient of the people's adoration of which he spoke to Saül. But if
this is Abner's plan, it all goes wrong when Achimelech becomes involved
in David's position.

In Scene 3, immediately after David is persuaded to fight, Achimelech
tells the army that 'David is your leader and King in battle',[23] a role that
David has little hesitation in playing. Saül discovers this when he emerges
from his bout of madness, but Achimelech insists that the whole party,
including Abner, should fall to their knees before David. Abner refuses but
Saül cannot help himself and afterwards is furious with Achimelech and
determines to have him killed. We already know that Abner has little
respect for representatives of God: he tells Saül that the priests are corrupt

21. *Saül*, ll. 769-70.
22. *Saül*, l. 793.
23. *Saül*, l. 902.

and he tells David that the only prophet is necessity. Despite the protests of Micol and Jonathas, Abner murders Achimelech but, after the people have seen David take the place of the king in battle and after the adoration of David, it is no longer possible for Abner to pursue any hopes of being Saül's successor. Abner's role in the drama raises several of the issues from 1 Samuel in a more explicit manner possible in drama: the human face of Saül's paranoia concerning David, the possibility of David's succession of Saül, and Saül's murder of priests (in 1 Samuel not only is Ahimelech murdered, but all the priests at Nob also). Thus Abner's character is a function of the transmission of the story from narrative to drama.

Fate and the Pythonisse
The account of Saül's visit to the woman of Endor is quite different to that found in 1 Samuel. Not only is she said (by Abner) to be anxious to speak to Saül, she claims to be 'the voice of the supreme God'.[24] Since it is the Pythonisse who has requested the meeting, Saül does not know what she will do. He only knows that he hopes to learn his fate, but he has not requested her to bring up the prophet, as in 1 Samuel. When she is afraid to speak, Saül becomes angry with her. She draws out the suspense by speaking of a terrible vision which Saül cannot see:

> But what bloody ray comes and strikes my eyelid?...
> What chaos of misfortunes, of virtues, of *forfaits*![25]

The images she uses are confused but terrible. She calls out names and Saül wants her to stop, but the vision becomes clearer and she sees David being crowned. Saül is furious but she continues, speaking of a young man who perishes and asking God to save him. Saül wants to hear no more but she will not be silenced and tells him that Jonathas has been rejected because of Saül's *forfaits*:

> From a condemned prince God turns away his face
> With a breath of his mouth he scatters his race.[26]

When Saül tries to silence her she tells him to listen to 'a God stronger than me'.[27] Saül says that God has promised him the throne 'and God does

24. *Saül*, l. 537.
25. *Saül*, ll. 557, 560. The word *forfaits* means 'hideous crimes'. As it is a *Leitwort* in the play, I shall leave it untranslated.
26. *Saül*, ll. 581-82.
27. *Saül*, l. 584.

not deceive',[28] which is one of only a few positive remarks Saül makes about God in the entire drama, and he says it to convince himself that what she has told him will not come about. However, the Pythonisse speaks of the fate in store for Saül, including his suicide. When he insists she identify his *forfaits* she tells him Samuel will explain. Saül doesn't understand, and she accuses him of Samuel's murder. Saül's response is the intention to kill her, and keeping to the theme of revelation of fate he asks her, 'Do you know what fate awaits you?'[29] But she is no longer intimidated and retorts, 'God will vindicate everything which God inspires in me!'[30] As he is about to strike her he sees Samuel's bloody ghost, confesses his murder, and invites Samuel to avenge himself. Samuel evaporates.

This all differs radically from 1 Samuel, where Saul is unable to get an answer from Yhwh and so turns to a necromancer. In the drama the priest Achimelech is still alive, and could in theory be consulted, but in 1 Samuel the priests have been slain at Saul's command. Here the Pythonisse, who has come looking for Saül, asserts that God insists Saül hear his fate. The only point of connection with 1 Samuel is that Saül learns that he and Jonathas will die, but he also learns that David will be crowned and that he will commit suicide. In *Saül* there is no time reference and no circumstantial details, unlike in 1 Samuel where death is to come in battle the following day. Since the first thing for him to consider is David's accession, Saül will not accept his fate, and unlike in 1 Samuel, where his reaction to the woman's intimation of his fate is a lack of energy, he responds to the news of David's crowning with fury, which informs all his following responses. He fluctuates between telling the woman to speak and telling her to be silent. In *Saül* the king is ready to kill the woman who brings him the answers for which he has been searching but is prevented by the sight of Samuel's ghost. We are thereby given the reason for Saül's rejection in the drama: the murder of Samuel. This, however, is problematic: Saül does not seem to admit to it when the Pythonisse accuses him, but only when he sees Samuel, so Saül's possible guilt is left ambiguous.[31] The effects on Saül of knowing his fate will be played out in the following acts, since this scene is so early in the drama. The characterization of Saül is therefore dependent on his attempts to escape

28. *Saül*, l. 595.
29. *Saül*, l. 599.
30. *Saül*, l. 602. In 1 Sam. 28.13 Samuel is described as אלהים.
31. See below, pp. 143-44.

the fate that he knows awaits him, rather than on the circumstances leading up to his attempt to discover his fate.

Micol's Care for Saül

Micol's role in taking care of Saül is peculiar to Lamartine's drama; there is no sign of it in 1 Samuel. Whenever Saül is raving and confined to his quarters she stays with him to try to ease his suffering. This was David's role in 1 Samuel until the point where Saul drives David away, but in 1 Samuel there is no one to step into this role. In Lamartine's drama David has already been driven away but Micol attempts to continue to care for Saül. One of the most indicative scenes is in Act 3 Scene 5, where Saül is without his reason to the extent that his army has gone to battle without him, with David in command. Micol attempts to restore him by reciting verses, and it is only during this scene that the established meter of the drama is changed to accommodate the verses. The content of her recitations is quotations from psalms, not whole psalms but rather lines from one and then another mixed together, though some verses are not quotations but nevertheless inspired by lines from psalms. A few lines she adds herself and are not related to psalms. Saül at first responds to her recitations as if delirious, wanting to crush Israel's enemies, recalling how he was once victorious, and he eventually becomes calm. At this point he mentions that

> It's just so that formerly David, David, my son,
> Told me of the assets that God had promised me.[32]

and expresses the wish that David might come back, but suddenly he hears cries of joy and the sound of the soldiers shouting 'David is our leader and King in battle!',[33] and immediately he inveighs once more against David's perfidy. There is nothing Micol can do except follow him out of the scene.

Micol's femininity has been constructed according to the cultural traditions appropriate to the culture of nineteenth-century France. The same process evidently occurs to some extent with the male characters in the drama,[34] yet we must ask whether in comparing Micol with Michal we are dealing with a different model of femininity or a different cultural

---

32. *Saül*, ll. 1120-21.

33. *Saül*, l. 1131.

34. De Cognets quotes a letter from Lamartine in which he comments on a similar point: in the scene between David and Abner he is concerned that perhaps David is too French. See *Saül*, p. 58, note on ll. 801-804.

model or simply a different characterization. The reason the question of models of femininity arises is that it is Micol in the drama who plays an originally male role, providing music to ease Saül's agony. The role of Saül's carer is central to Saül's characterization. Micol's own characterization is a function of this: she sees most closely Saül's *égarement*[35] and Saül's reasons for attributing it to God. Thus the scenes between Micol and Saül are fundamental to the tragic vision of the drama, since they draw out the characters' interpretations of their suffering. That Micol's recitation scene breaks the established meter of the drama draws attention to the scene, providing the only substantial account in it of the period that precedes the opening scene, a time before Saül's decline and the point from which Saül began to fall. Finding such a scene in the penultimate act of the drama blurs the boundaries of the tragic vision since the context is Saül's delirium. This is more than flashback: its position bends the time lines and locates Saül's activity within his destiny.

The Murder of Achimelech
Saul's slaughter of the priests at Nob in 1 Samuel is one of the features that directly feeds his decline. In Lamartine's drama, Saül has already consulted the Pythonisse and knows his fate, and also that David is destined to succeed him. Regaining his reason in Act 3, Saül has heard the people acknowledging David as their king in battle, and Jonathas has insisted that the victory is David's glory. Saül accuses David of exalting himself and in Act 4 Scene 3 attempts to kill him, having seen Goliath's sword in his possession. This scene has consequences that will seal the fates of most of the characters. Achimelech comes to David's defence, citing God (who he says condemns Saül) as his accomplice in elevating David, who he claims is a king, and encourages them all to fall down before him. Saül finds that 'Despite my hatred, a God forces me to adore him',[36] but immediately afterwards is furious and blames Achimelech for causing his fall and David's rise and intends to kill him. Micol and Jonathas are horrified and try to prevent Achimelech's murder, but Abner kills him on Saül's orders.

Achimelech has indeed given David the sword of Goliath, (cf. 1 Sam. 21.9), but this is not Saül's principal complaint against the priest, although this is the first action David has taken that could be construed as a direct attack on Saül's kingship. Achimelech, as a priest, has recognized David's

35. Like *forfaits*, *égarement* is a *Leitwort*. It means 'distraction'.
36. *Saül*, l. 1402.

proper destiny and has encouraged Saül and his family to recognize David. Saül thus holds Achimelech directly responsible for transferring sovereign power to David, and feels shamed by his own admission of David's claim on the throne. For the first time in the drama Saül has killed, though, recalling Samuel's appearance, he is now apparently guilty of the murder of both prophet and priest, and the shedding of Achimelech's blood appears to have given him a taste for more. The slaughter of the coming battle is what keeps him going:

> Despair finally restores power to my arm,
> I see floods of blood, I hear, I hear in advance
> The vain cries of the dying harvested by my sword.[37]

However, he recognizes that his real battle is with God, and from this point his attitude to the divine becomes one of combat. He is not content simply to suffer divine rejection any longer; if God has ordained that David be his successor, then he will fight against God:

> What pleasure! How fine it is for a simple mortal
> To do battle at once both with men and with heaven![38]

This modification of the plot line of the biblical material gives rise to a divergent development in characterization: Saül acquires a hostile attitude towards God.

Saül's Dialogues with Jonathas
Saül's relationship to Jonathas is developed in quite a different way in Lamartine's drama compared with 1 Samuel. This is particularly evident in Act 4 Scene 2, where the occasion of Saül's dialogue with his son is Jonathas's victory in his first battle. In 1 Samuel Jonathan goes into his first battle without telling his father, who, unlike here, is not in a mental state that leaves him unable to command an army. The tension between Saül and Jonathas over the latter's love for David reflects that of 1 Samuel; however, the relationship between Saül and Jonathas is characterized by their different attitudes to God.

Saül begins by congratulating Jonathas on his victory, but Jonathas insists that the glory belongs to David. Saül praises Jonathas for his modesty but is unwilling to accept his account, and tries to convince Jonathas that David is a perfidious enemy, asking whether Jonathas wants

---

37. *Saül*, ll. 1506-508.
38. *Saül*, ll. 1510-11.

to reign (cf. 1 Sam. 20.31). Jonathas at this point begins to speak of divine will: 'The throne will appear to me, if God has promised it to me',[39] but Saül argues 'God gives it, my son; but it is necessary to defend it'.[40] He tells Jonathas that David must die (cf. 1 Sam. 20.31) and Jonathas questions Saül's ambivalent attitude towards David. Saül admits now that he both fears and admires David: 'Absent, I regret him, and, present, I fear him',[41] and that he believes David to be the instrument of cruel priests, that the prophet has anointed his guilty head with the oil of kings. Jonathas comes back to the divine will which he believes must be respected and which cannot be thwarted: 'Ah well! if God wishes it, Lord, what can we do?'[42]

This scene develops the altercation between Saul and Jonathan found in 1 Samuel 20, and, while emphasizing Jonathas's abandonment of his succession rights, also gives him a theological motivation. Saül is out on a limb: the priests support David now that Achimelech has promoted him in battle, there are rumours that David has been anointed (there is no suggestion in 1 Samuel that Saul has any knowledge of this), and his own son is prepared to give up his throne to Saül's enemy. Furthermore, Jonathas believes that God has ordained this anomalous succession. Such development of this motif from 1 Samuel characterizes Saül as a man who is willing to defend his position against the deity who conferred it upon him, and Jonathas as a man who is willing to bend to the divine will that would deprive him of his political rights. This characterization proceeds from 1 Samuel but is accented by the theological dialogue between father and son and is crucial background for their next theological discussion at the occasion of Jonathas's death.

The differences between Saül and Jonathas do not cause Saül to act with hostility towards Jonathas (cf. 1 Sam. 22.8). In Scene 6 of Act 5, Saül is concerned for Jonathas's life during the battle: 'Despite heaven, still, preserve hope!'[43] He asks God to save Jonathas at least. Jonathas has been injured and is resting close to where Saül is standing and his father discovers him. Jonathas tells Saül that David has been chosen, and that he himself has been rejected. David's name on Jonathas's lips infuriates Saül. It is because God loves David that Saül hates him, and Saül goes on to rail

39. *Saül*, l. 1199.
40. *Saül*, l. 1200.
41. *Saül*, l. 1219.
42. *Saül*, l. 1258.
43. *Saül*, l. 1688.

against God: 'Your virtue is nothing but a name, your law nothing but a caprice.'[44] Jonathas tries to plead with God on behalf of his father, but the shock he feels at Saül's blasphemies places a separation between father and son at the crucial moment of Jonathas's death. As he expires he tells Saül of a great vision of light, but this does nothing to calm Saül's attitude to the divine. Even at the point of death the theological gulf between the two men widens as they consolidate their positions before Saül goes on to take his own life.

No related scene is found in 1 Samuel: Saul does not witness Jonathan's death. The theme of isolation at Saul's suicide is present in both stories, but here it is effected by emphasizing Saül's distance from Jonathas on a philosophical level rather than a material level, and also Saül's isolation from the divine as he denounces God. The light that Jonathas sees as he expires is a vision one does not expect for Saül's eyes. The dialogues between Saül and Jonathas increase dramatic tension and develop thematic material in a manner quite unlike that of 1 Samuel, yet the relationship between father and son in this drama is the relationship that is the most closely informed by the biblical material.

The Death of Saül

As Saül stands over the body of his son in Act 5 Scene 6, cursing false oracles that promised him an eternal destiny and wondering how

> Persecuting spirits, authors of my misery!
> What! you abandon me in my final hour?,[45]

he suddenly hears voices, the cries of victory, and, fearing discovery by the barbarous enemy, he takes his sword and pierces himself. The source of the voices arrives immediately on the scene: it is his own soldiers who have been victorious under David's command and they have defeated the Philistines. They see Saül fallen and then David arrives on scene and sees the king and his son. Saül recognizes David's voice, sees David weeping over Jonathas and in his last breath gasps, 'And my last glance sees David triumphant!'[46]

Immediately before his death Saül suddenly no longer feels persecuted by the shadows that have been tormenting him. Perhaps the fact that he recognizes his defeat and no longer seeks to evade his fate has caused

44. *Saül*, l. 1765.
45. *Saül*, ll. 1800-801.
46. *Saül*, l. 1819.

them to evaporate, or perhaps Jonathas's efforts on his behalf have persuaded God to desist. Certainly he gives no indication of any sense of reconciliation. It is tragic irony that Saül construes the cries of victory as those of the enemy and on hearing them commits suicide because despite all that he has experienced he is still blind to his fate. This tragic irony is made possible by the modification of the biblical material so that the outcome of the battle is victory rather than defeat. Further tragic irony is found in Saül's last words: David has been triumphant in battle, but at the moment Saül speaks David is weeping for Jonathas, so what Saül sees at the last is not a picture of a triumphant commander, but of a man in mourning. That Saül's last thought is informed by his jealousy and paranoia rather than his own loss of Jonathas or even of his life is truly the stuff of tragedy.

The techniques of plot in Lamartine's drama rarely echo those of the biblical material, although many of the events are incorporated, paralleled or alluded to. Where significant departures in the plot trajectory occur, they have the effect of complementing departures of characterization, or enhancing characterization, so that the dramatis personae take on attributes that are extrapolated from the biblical material, or, more frequently, absent in the biblical material.

Characterization

Lamartine has retained most of the central characters from 1 Samuel and has added some minor characters of his own. However, each of the biblical figures is characterized in a different manner and with some different traits and roles. The relationships between them differ substantially in almost all cases. Most strikingly, two major characters (Yhwh and Samuel) have been omitted and two minor characters (Abner and Ahimelech) are given major roles. Thus the dynamics between the rest are inevitably altered. The effect of this is to emphasize aspects of the story that are not stressed in the biblical material, and to construct a different kind of tragic vision in which the role of the deity is more ambiguous. The central question surrounding Saül's stature as a tragic hero in this drama is whether the deity indeed has a role at all.

Micol

Micol is torn between Saül and David. She spends most of her time looking after Saül, but pines for David. She holds God responsible for

Saül's misfortunes and therefore has an ambivalent attitude towards God, as her prayer at her first entry (Act 1 Scene 3) shows:

> You whom I invoke in vain...
> Regard with pity this people overwhelmed with misery,
> Regard with pity this King who pursues your anger...
> Restore power to Saül, and David to my heart![47]

When Jonathas tells her that God hears the cries of the innocent, she remarks that

> He has ravished my joy, and the tomb, today,
> Is the last blessing I await from him.[48]

Thus when David is returned to her, she takes a more positive stance: she believes that God must have protected him during his exile. In the following scene when Saül expresses horror at the dawn (Scene 4), she is cheerful, she has never seen the dawn look so lovely, and she tells him to put away such horrible thoughts, particularly his notion that 'The spirit of the living God has departed from me.'[49] Her change of mood has been brought about by David's return and her outlook moves away from her father's. This is no longer a woman overwhelmingly concerned with the suffering of her father and her people; her demeanour has been brightened by her good fortune and this occasions a distance between her and Saül.

Unknown to her, between Saül's first amicable meeting with David and her next encounter with Saül, her father has been speaking to Abner, who has put doubts into Saül's mind concerning David. Saül has also spoken with the Pythonisse, who has foretold his and Jonathas's deaths and David's accession. Micol is therefore concerned when she sees that Saül is once more plunged into despair because she now believes that

> the God of Israel, tired of his severities,
> Seems finally to be announcing an end to our misfortunes.[50]

But Saül believes she has been deceived by God, who has illuminated him via the Pythonisse. David's offer of help in battle (Act 2 Scene 4) is thus ill received, and Saül brandishes his spear in an attempt to kill him. When Micol and Jonathas shield David with their bodies, it is Jonathas whom Saül rebukes. At no point in the drama does Saül attack Micol for her

---

47. *Saül*, ll. 101, 113-14, 116.
48. *Saül*, ll. 147-48.
49. *Saül*, l. 252.
50. *Saül*, l. 647-48.

loyalty to David (cf. 1 Sam. 19.17); Jonathas is the heir and Micol is still David's wife. Saül does not give her to another man, as in 1 Samuel.

Micol's monologue in Act 3 Scene 4 depicts her again as a woman who despairs over her fate and that of her loved ones. David has just left for battle but Saül is too ill to go, and she thinks continually of death:

> Just like a victim escaped from the altar
> Who falls and gets up again and who, already struck,
> Carries away the knife of the sacrificer,
> So, living again, is death in my heart![51]

In the following scene she comforts Saül, whose distraction is severe. The role of dutiful daughter is something to which she has become accustomed, but she prays for divine inspiration and is able to recite some of David's psalms to calm Saül. Again she is depicted as fluctuating between a belief in a God who persecutes and praying in the hope of receiving God's pity and help. This accents her uniquely confused position: she is caught between Saül's fear and horror of the God who torments him, and David's hope and trust in the God who brings him success. Her own responses directly relate to the two most important men in her life, and when Saül comes around from his confusion to hear the voices of the soldiers honouring David her situation is at its most tense: she senses in Saül's face a new menace for her husband. When she recognizes the sword of Goliath in David's hand she fears the worst. With Saül's second attempt on David's life Micol again is forced to choose between her father and her husband, and she takes David's side, prepared to die herself rather than allow Saül to kill David, but Achimelech in the event is the one who is murdered, though Micol and Jonathas attempt to prevent this as well. Micol begs Saül, 'Die at least without crime',[52] and thus she has taken sides against her father not only with David but now with the priest. Symbolically she has chosen David's version of theology over her father's, and has rejected Saül in favour of those he considers his enemies, and now at this point he rebukes her: 'By your blindness my fury is revived'.[53] From the point of Achimelech's murder he leaves to prepare for battle, and Micol does not see him again.

While the army is at battle Micol remains in hiding with the priests and the other women, and in Act 5 Scene 1 they arrive at the camp in the dead

---

51. *Saül*, ll. 956-59.
52. *Saül*, l. 1465.
53. *Saül*, l. 1472.

of night to find it devastated. They can hear the battle and a warrior approaching, and David appears. He has heard of Israel's troubles and wants to know where the battle is taking place. Micol explains that the whole of Gelboë is a battlefield and the outcome is as yet unknown:

> ...the dark night
> Hides still our destinies in the horror of its shadow.[54]

As David departs, Micol imagines that he might die, and wishes to know what fate has in store, wishes the darkness and the shadows would disappear so that she might see her destiny, yet a moment later she and her companions must disappear into the shadows as the enemy soldiers come rushing towards them.

Micol is very close to Saül and indeed seems to resemble him. One can imagine her ranting at the skies just as her father does, but it is David's influence that stabilizes her. However, despite David she is obsessed with death. Her chthonic impulses are born of a certainty that her father's fate is inextricably linked with her own; that whatever is given to her will be taken away, and she is not quick to bless the name of the Lord as her brother is. Her moments of cheerfulness are short lived because her only joy is in relation to David, yet whenever he is present there is the constant threat that Saül will try to kill him.

Jonathas

The Jonathas of Lamartine's drama, as in 1 Samuel, is in constant conflict with his father. As in 1 Samuel, the content of this conflict largely concerns David; however, the drama emphasizes the theological differences between father and son and omits the military context that is the setting for the initial conflicts between Saul and Jonathan in 1 Samuel. Jonathas provides a crucial liaison between Saül and David, and, as with Micol, it is David who commands the greater loyalty in times of contention, although Jonathas's love for David is less emphatically expressed than in the biblical material. If there is a reason for this it is presumably because of the risk of homosexual interpretation. It is to Jonathas that David first appears, and at this stage Jonathas is as ambivalent as Micol about the divinely ordained fate that awaits Israël. He tells David that the battle on the next day will decide whether Israël will vanquish or perish, and that

---

54. *Saül*, ll. 1568-69.

God no longer remembers the people which adores him.
Israël, formerly the object of his love,
This day now appearing; is it your last day?[55]

David's confidence that he will turn the situation around and help to win
the battle convinces Jonathas that God has remembered his people. He
suggests to Micol that God may have altered his attitude towards Israël,

But if this God, my sister, tired of his anger,
Were to cast on Israel a less severe glance?[56]

From this point his confidence in David's ability to conquer for Israël
surpasses even Micol's and whenever he speaks of the fate that the
heavens have in store he remains certain that God's designs are for the
greater good of his people. His speech to Micol, combined with David's
appearance, convinces her that God may yet have some good things to
give to her. Therefore he argues with Saül in Act 1 Scene 4 when Saül
claims that God has abandoned him. Jonathas hopes that with David's
arrival the situation may be reversed to how it once was: Saül as Israël's
king, avenger and support, with God's help. He says Saül should

Ask of him, Lord, his power and his light,
Hope for everything from him.[57]

When Saül and David meet, Jonathas joins his father and sister in
honouring David, and gives him his helmet (cf. 1 Sam. 18.4). But at
Jonathas's next scene (Act 2 Scene 4) the situation is not so amicable,
since Saül has been convinced by Abner of David's claim on the throne
and by the Pythonisse of David's impending succession. Saül speaks in
veiled terms of the terrible thing that will happen, but Jonathas knows
nothing of the meeting and does not understand. He suggests that they
should put an end to the anxiety of not knowing and 'in the event let us
seek the truth'.[58] This comes from Jonathas's confidence in David's ability
to effect a victory, but Saül has received the revelation of the future, and
David's stated conviction of infallible divine assurance infuriates him.
Jonathas is put in a position where he must choose between his father and
his friend, and he chooses to protect David from Saül's attempt on his life.

The events of Act 3 Scene 1 are a parallel to the elements of 1 Samuel

55. *Saül*, ll. 70-72.
56. *Saül*, ll. 149-50.
57. *Saül*, ll. 289-90.
58. *Saül*, l. 660.

20, but incorporate elements from 1 Samuel 18 and 19. David must decide whether to stay or go, so Jonathas describes Saül's disturbed behaviour, his piercing of the air with his spear thinking he is striking David, his rantings to God, and Micol's devotion. He answers David's decision to flee and its accompanying language of sacrifice with words of admiration and support,

> I recognise David in this magnanimous deed…
> And, perilous day, count on Jonathas![59]

It is in Act 4 that Jonathas begins to confront the ongoing reality of the breakdown of the relationship between Saül and David, and is first faced with the question of whether he will ever succeed Saül, together with the notion that David is his enemy. His response is informed by his theological stance: if God has chosen David he will accept it; in fact he must accept it since it would be useless to pitch himself against God, which is what Saül is suggesting he do. Saül believes Jonathas is naïve in being able to see only what is written on human faces and not what is in their hearts,[60] but Jonathas remains loyal to David. Perhaps because he has seen his father's paranoia, and because he does not share his father's attitude towards God, he perceives Saül's arguments as flawed and does not wish to betray either his friend or the God whom he trusts.

His separation from Saül becomes even more apparent when at Achimelech's bidding he defies his father and falls down before David in Act 4 Scene 3, and when in the following scene he throws himself down before Saül to beg him, together with Micol, not to have Achimelech put to death. This leads to yet another theological argument: Saül believes that a God who is jealous of him inspires his son and daughter against him, 'And for my ruin my own blood also conspires',[61] but when Jonathas tries to convince him that to kill the priest would be a crime in God's eyes, his father's answer seems to him to be blasphemy. Nevertheless, despite Jonathas's horror at the murder of Achimelech, he prepares for battle with his father after the deed is done.

In his final scenes, Jonathas accepts his death and the fate which he believes God has decided for him. These scenes are highly sentimental, as

---

59. *Saül*, ll. 797, 800.

60. Cf. 1 Sam. 16.7; here it is Yhwh who sees into people's hearts. The context is the anointing of David. Saül's assessment of David's heart differs radically from Yhwh's.

61. *Saül*, l. 1469.

his equerry Esdras (invented for this scene) weeps over him, and Jonathas speaks his last wishes: that his father be told he died a glorious death, that Saül's clemency be asked for David, that God should avenge his innocence on Jonathas. The question of whose innocence is ambiguous: it could refer to God, to Saül or to David, but David is the obvious choice since Jonathas has recently pronounced his father guilty of the crime of Achimelech's murder. David, in Jonathas's eyes, will always be innocent since Jonathas believes his actions to be inextricably bound up with the divine will. But really it is Jonathas who is innocent, and who has been punished for his father's *forfaits*, and this innocence is portrayed in lines reminiscent of Job, 'The Lord wished it, blessed be the Lord!',[62] and 'May heaven be praised!'[63] When Saül discovers him on the point of death, Jonathas makes one last attempt to bring his father over to his point of view on the subject of divine design and the choice of David as successor, but a final bitter argument ensues and Jonathas prays that Saül's blasphemies will be treated with clemency. As he nears death he appears to experience some kind of theophany, and his death vision of lights depicts his innocence and his wisdom in accepting his fate. The man who at the beginning of the drama doubted God's fidelity has been converted by David and is rewarded at the end of his life.

David

The character of David is the one that perhaps Lamartine was most inclined to change, and yet at the same time the easiest to approach with a hermeneutic of suspicion. Many of his decisions and motivations can be ambiguously interpreted, and so it seems that the biblical characterization may have asserted itself despite Lamartine's efforts. Since it is impossible to be sure exactly what Lamartine really intended, the question may be an irrelevance (as it is to intertextual purists), yet nevertheless intriguing.

The aspect of change in David's characterization that one might notice most quickly in Lamartine's drama is David's profession of love for Micol. This is in stark contrast to 1 Samuel, where David never once speaks to Michal.[64] Since he cites this as a motivating factor in several of

---

62. *Saül*, l. 1650.

63. *Saül*, l. 1701.

64. See Exum, *Arrows*, p. 87. Lawton points to the possibility of a parallel between 1 Sam. 18 and Gen. 29 in which an elder and a younger daughter are offered in marriage to the same man. He contends that a reader aware of the parallel would expect to hear that David loves the younger Michal, but there is a silence here, and

his decisions, this factor affects the dynamics of relationship between all the major characters. In fact David's love for Micol is the reason he gives for coming to Saül's camp in the first place, although before he comes to mention her he remembers times past of happiness and glory. When Jonathas tells him of Israël's suffering he resolves to offer his help and mentions Micol only in passing as an absence he has regretted during his time of exile. His priority seems to be to offer his people his military aptitude, though when he is reunited with Micol he is overcome with emotion. He hopes that Saül's attitude will have changed during his time of exile, but Jonathas warns him to be careful in approaching Saül. From this we learn that Saül's instability has not faded during David's absence. The effect of beginning the drama with David's soliloquy is to delay the appearance of Saül, who does not enter until the fourth scene, and to build up a tension between the king and his son-in-law.

At David's reconciliation with Saül his demeanour is humble:

> Your slave comes forward trembling before you,
> And, heavily laden with the weight of your long anger,
> On his knees he begs for a less severe consideration.[65]

He is also wearing humble clothing, and Saül's response to his attitude and aspect is initially positive. When Saül gives David his spear (cf. 1 Sam. 17.38) and Jonathas gives him his helmet (cf. 1 Sam. 18.4), David prays that God will cause him to win the coming battle, thus abandoning to some extent the aspect of humility that he has been careful to adopt. However, there is no jealousy on Saül's part at this point, and the king hopes that the sight of David will give hope to the people.

The relationship between Saül and David starts to break down after Saül's conversation with Abner and consultation with the Pythonisse. Saül has been convinced that David represents a threat to the succession of his line. Saül's anguished utterances concerning the impending death of his son prompt a response from David which inevitably enrages Saül: David offers to fight in Jonathas's place, and claims his strength from God:

---

indeed it is Michal who loves David. Further support for a parallel here is the appearance of the household idol, which Michal uses to deceive Saul's men and Rachel conceals when Laban pursues Jacob and his wives. Lawton comments, '[Rachel] too is more devoted to her husband than to her father' (Robert B. Lawton, '1 Samuel 18: David, Merob, and Michal', *CBQ* 51 [1989], pp. 423-25 [425]).

65. *Saül*, ll. 344-46.

> This arm, which will support the arm of the Eternal,
> Will alone suffice to save Israel![66]

Not only does David claim superior strength, his remarks remind Saül of David's past actions and attitudes which led to Saül's wrath and David's exile. One must ask whether David is unaware that his words are likely to infuriate the king or whether he speaks with calculated conceit. At best it seems that his enthusiasm for the coming battle causes him to forget Saül's past jealousy and, now that his initial attitude of modesty is gone, his behaviour once more antagonizes the king. Each of David's replies irritates Saül still further to the point where Saül is ready to kill him. He protests, "God knows if I, Lord, have deserved this offence',[67] but in fact whether or not Saül's outburst is justified, it is inevitable in response to David's immodest behaviour towards Saül, who is, after all, his king. This marks another departure from the biblical material, in which David is consistently humble in his dialogues with Saül and thereby succeeds in effecting a semblance of reconciliation, at least temporarily, on each occasion (cf. 1 Sam. 24 and 1 Sam. 26). Furthermore, David's immodesty is given as the reason for Saül's previous anger leading to David's exile:

> It is thus that formerly you were heard to speak,
> When your exploits dared to equal mine,[68]

and thus the conflict is strictly between David and Saül; David's popularity with the people as a catalyst for Saul's jealousy (1 Sam. 18.7-9) is not reflected here.

Having escaped Saül's spear with Jonathas's and Micol's assistance, David learns from Jonathas that Saül's distraction has not abated (cf. 1 Sam. 20.35-39). In his delirium Saül pierces the air with his spear thinking that he is striking David (cf. 1 Sam. 18.11; 19.10). David decides to leave (cf. 1 Sam. 19.18–20.1), claiming that he owes this last sacrifice to his king. It is curious that having returned with the purpose of being reunited with Micol he is now prepared to leave her behind, especially since she has declared a desire to die with him or to follow him (l. 168), and perhaps the real sacrifice for David is having to abandon his hopes of joining the battle.

It is this latter consequence of his decision that Abner remarks upon in the following scene (Act 3 Scene 2), and by means of Abner's political skills David is persuaded to stay and fight. Abner plants the idea in

66. *Saül*, ll. 683-84.
67. *Saül*, l. 709.
68. *Saül*, ll. 687-88.

David's head that he should lead Saül's troops into battle, and, although David initially rejects such a suggestion, it is not long before Achimelech the priest persuades him that it is God's command, and furthermore that it is God's will that David take the sword of Goliath, which David initially refuses on the grounds that only Saül has the right to carry it.

After the battle, in which the army of Israël has been victorious, David announces to Saül his intention to return into exile (Act 4 Scene 3). Saül questions his loyalty, David asserts it, but Saül is convinced that 'above Saül you have chosen your place!'[69] Although David protests that he is 'Second after you and nothing before heaven',[70] Saül is stung by this reference to the heavens, and Abner comments that 'He is deliberately feigning this wild language'.[71] Saül insists that David knows how God has dealt with him and asks whether David intends to enrage him, but David claims a higher purpose: he speaks thus to render homage to God. Once again, David's retorts bring Saül to the point of attempting to kill him, especially once he spies Goliath's sword (cf. 1 Sam. 22.9-13). Achimelech defuses the situation by encouraging the company to pay homage to David, which David resists, although none too strongly, and once Saül has given way to the force that compels him to kneel before David, David simply exits the scene, making no comment on any of the eulogies spoken concerning him.

Although it seemed that David would return to his exile, he reappears in Act 5 Scene 2 having foreseen the perils of the battle. He speaks with Micol, promises that if he falls he will be reunited with her in death, and exits to fight with Israël's troops. He alters the course of the battle, and brings victory to his people. In the final scene of the drama, as he weeps over the body of Jonathas and as Saül expires, he mourns the king and vows to avenge his friend.

Saül

From his very first scene (Act 1 Scene 4) Saül is depicted as a tragic figure. Immediately we learn that his fortunes have changed and that he attributes this change of fortune to abandonment by God. We know already from the foregoing scenes that his army faces defeat at the hands of the Philistines, but we learn now that he believes he has been personally rejected by the deity, and he cites as evidence his terror of the dawn and of

---

69. *Saül*, l. 1289.
70. *Saül*, l. 1291.
71. *Saül*, l. 1293.

the darkness. Nature seems to him to reflect his melancholy. He has become a shadow of himself, an object of pity, and he wants the successes of his youth returned to him. He cannot understand the forces at work on him and he doesn't know what error he has committed to cause this persecution from the heavens, but he knows what mechanism causes his despair: 'The spirit of the living God has parted from me!'[72] Nothing Jonathas and Micol say to him can cheer him: he has lost all hope in God, who a long time ago ceased giving him answers, and his best soldiers have been killed in battle. He recognizes that his only hope is David, because God walks with him, but

> David is no longer my son, I have offended him too much;
> If my misfortune avenges him, he is avenged enough![73]

Saül knows that he needs David if he is to have any chance of conquering the Philistines, though when Jonathas announces that David has returned, Saül's feelings are mixed. He finds the notion painful, yet approaches the meeting with purposeful resolve and, when they come face to face, Saül's heroic qualities are plainly in evidence: he is able to admit his past misdeeds and to credit David with the commendation due to him for his loyalty to his king and country, even to the point of recognizing his courage in battle. David's reciprocal humility ensures an ambience of mutual respect and amiability, and Saül looks forward now to the coming battle, believing that the sight of David will encourage his soldiers. There is no sign here of any jealousy on Saül's part concerning David's superior ability as a warrior and the two men part as friends.

This state of relief, however, cannot last long. Immediately Saül has made his peace with David, his trusted adviser Abner casts doubt on the people's loyalty to Saül and to Jonathas's succession rights. Saül is tired of awaiting his fate in the fear and perplexity that envelop his days, and in true tragic tradition he must pursue his fate:

> In the face of my fate I intend to rush out,
> And, diving boldly into these funereal shadows
> Snatch my destiny from the heart of their gloom![74]

Abner encourages Saül's audacity by advising him that

---

72. *Saül*, l. 252.
73. *Saül*, ll. 315-16.
74. *Saül*, ll. 487-89.

Ah! prince, our destinies are made only by us;
It is in foreseeing them that we can ward off their blows.[75]

After this Saül is easily persuaded to receive the Pythonisse who has been waiting for him in order to reveal his fate and that of Jonathas and David. Saül is under no illusions concerning his own fate; he expects to hear misfortune for himself. Unlike the biblical material, where Saul consults the woman at Endor in order to receive instructions for the coming battle, the purpose of the consultation is that Saül might know in advance what awaits him. He hopes that this knowledge will enable him to take steps to ward off fate's blows.

The similarity to the biblical material is that during his encounter with the woman of Endor he receives more information than he anticipates. As the Pythonisse begins to untangle the threads of her confused and disturbing vision she calls out the names of David and Jonathas, describing David's coronation and Jonathas's death. It is almost as an afterthought that she mentions Saül's suicide. Saül seems to be particularly confused over the matter of his *forfaits*. As in the biblical material, it appears that the king is not aware of having committed any act that could have brought about God's rejection. However, there are no elements in the drama's plot, nor in its dialogue, which point to the nature of Saül's errors, and no hint of Saül's sacrificing against Samuel's will (cf. 1 Sam. 13) or failing to carry out God's commandment (cf. 1 Sam. 15). The conclusion of the scene provides a reason for divine rejection: Saül has murdered the prophet Samuel; however, the appearance of Samuel's bloody ghost, although supremely dramatic, is highly problematic. Saül claims not to know his error; surely he would remember killing Samuel? Perhaps it might be possible to read the dialogue between Saül and the Pythonisse as an attempt on Saül's part to deny or cover up Samuel's murder, but the only reason for reading in this way would be an attempt to make sense of this one point, and the text does not lend itself to such a reading. Furthermore, at no other point in the drama does Saül attempt to hide anything: he is entirely straightforward in his attitude to God and in his murderous intentions towards David and Achimelech; and none of the others dramatis personae seem to know of any part Saül might have played in Samuel's death. Saül's reaction to the appearance of Samuel's ghost is initially surprise, and his admission of guilt seems to be in response to seeing the ghost of Samuel for himself. When he recognizes his guilt he uncovers his

75. *Saül*, ll. 491-92.

chest, inviting Samuel to avenge himself. Is it possible he did not know he
was culpable? An understanding of the problem may be gained by recourse
to authorial intent: in a letter to his friend Virieu, Lamartine writes,

> It is true that Samuel died naturally but I needed his ghost for the effect of
> the scene in the second act. If the scene works, I may be quite pardoned in
> having implied that he was assassinated, although this is an error.[76]

The scene is one of anagnorisis, or recognition, a motif that receives
commendation by Aristotle. Impressively dramatic though the effect may
be, the scene's success must to some extent depend on its integration in the
drama. At times following this scene Saül makes reference to having killed
Samuel, so one is left wondering how it came to be that this guilt revealed
by the Pythonisse was a guilt of which he was previously unaware.

Despite his recognition of guilt, Saül is not prepared to yield to fate. The
revelation of the future has done nothing to ease his distraction, and his
chief concern is for Jonathas, who, together with Micol, is alarmed by his
renewed distraction since they both believed that the return of David and his
amicable reunion with Saül indicated that all would now be well for their
father and for their people. Saül finds it ironic that the God who has been
persecuting him has revealed the truth to him while his son and daughter,
who have professed a trust in the deity, are deceived. Saül's concern for
Jonathas, which prompts David to offer to fight in his place, is naturally
heightened at David's claims of strength and divine favour, to the point
where Saül desires to kill his adversary, but is prevented by Micol and
Jonathas. The king is extremely bitter at this betrayal by his offspring and at
the missed opportunity to avert his fate by removing the man whom he
believes is its agent. The consequent onset of another attack of raving, during which his delirious mind engages in fantasies of killing David, is eventually eased somewhat by his daughter's recitation of David's psalms, and
once more there is a glimmer of hope that the two men might once more be
reconciled. However, as the soldiers return from battle singing of David's
victory, Saül's mood swings violently back to enmity and he marches out of
the tent to seek out Jonathas.

Saül still hopes to alter the destiny of his line, and in Act 4 Scene 2 he
attempts to persuade Jonathas that David is a perfidious enemy and deserves

---

76. Quoted by de Cognets, *Saül*, p. 46, note on l. 616. De Cognets later suggests
that the idea of introducing Samuel's ghost in this manner probably came from a
remark by Petitot in his translation of Alfieri. Petitot refers to a scene involving Saül
and the ghost of Samuel which occurs in a tragic play by an 'almost forgotten' French
author named du Ryer.

to die. Jonathas's loyalty to David and his refusal to adopt Saül's combative approach to his fate is the cause of friction between them. Saül confesses his ambivalence towards David, and attributes it to divine manipulation:

> It feels as if an invisible and bizarre hand
> Always attracts me towards him and always parts me from him.[77]

and the tension is chiefly marked by their differing attitudes towards the deity. Saül's complaints against the heavens are growing increasingly unrestrained since the revelation of the fate that awaits his son, but Jonathas remains pragmatic.

Saül's next line of approach in his quest to ward off the fate of his line is to question David directly concerning his loyalty to Saül's house. However, David's assurance of loyalty does not satisfy him, and David's remark that he is second after Saül and nothing before the heavens does little to calm Saül's fears. The mere hint of David's status in God's eyes drives Saül to distraction, which intensifies when David offers divine injunction as justification for carrying the sword of Goliath. Saül considers this the final proof that David has pretensions to the throne and is ready once again to kill him, but Achimelech's interruption with the information that David is a king stops him in his tracks. Easily persuaded, Saül hears Achimelech's prophecy of David's immortal race with terror; he asks whether David is a God, and as all present except Abner bow before him, Saül feels compelled to join them,

> A God forces me to recognise
> In my happy rival my conqueror and my master,[78]

with devastating results.

Up to this point Saül has frequently swung back and forth between affection and hatred for David, but now he makes his final choice. He is outraged at his abasement before his enemy and he reverses once more his perception of status: 'I have yielded before him, I his king, I his master!'[79] He resolves to have Achimelech put to death and, despite the protests of Micol and Jonathas, Abner dispatches him, but not before the priest has reminded him of his rejection by God, which Saül turns back at him to taunt him, 'May this God, if he can, save therefore his oracle!'[80]

77. *Saül*, ll. 1220-21.
78. *Saül*, ll. 1400-401.
79. *Saül*, l. 1437.
80. *Saül*, l. 1456.

As Achimelech is led away he comments on his expectation that Saül will follow him soon. However, Saül is unperturbed and, now ready to face the Philistines, he leads Abner and Jonathas away to prepare for the battle which, he says, will tempt their fate.

Fate is evidently too tempted to resist, and Saül's part in the battle ends in an encounter with his dying son. He is ready to kill himself in an attempt to regain control of his fate from the deity, who has left him in an impossible position:

> heaven, constant in persecuting me,
> Snatches my empire and condemns me to live![81]

However, the thought that Jonathas might have survived and might need to be rescued stays him, and despite the heavens he hangs onto this hope. The discovery of his injured son, barely alive, wrests that last spark of hope from him. He exclaims, 'This then is how, great God, your hand repays me!'[82] Their last moments are marred by argument regarding David and God, beginning with an outburst from Saül at Jonathas's request that David take his place as Saül's son. Saül fantasizes about killing David and then himself, and Jonathas advises him not to irritate God. However, Saül's attitude towards God is now even more incautious than ever. Now that Saül has lost everything but his life, he feels there is nothing more to fear:

> I have feared this God, my son; you die, I defy him!
> His cruelty cannot increase my torment.
> I fall beneath his blows, but blaspheming him![83]

Jonathas's dismay at his father's blasphemy and his attempts to act as Saül's intercessor meet with the Saül's fury and provoke him to further outrageous ranting at God:

> I do not repent of the crimes of my life.
> It is you who commits them and who justifies them...
> You were of my *forfaits* both cause and accomplice...
> That which was crime in the one, is justice in the other:
> Your virtue is nothing but a name, your law nothing but a caprice,[84]

so that Jonathas's last breath is spent entreating divine clemency for his father.

---

81. *Saül*, l. 1668-69.
82. *Saül*, l. 1703.
83. *Saül*, ll. 1745-47.
84. *Saül*, ll. 1756-57, 1761, 1764-65.

At Jonathas's death Saül curses the false oracles which promised king-ship to his line. However, his fury suddenly evaporates and he wonders what has become of the shadowy persecution that has tormented him for a long time:

> Persecuting spirits, authors of my misery!
> What! you abandon me in my final hour?[85]

He seems to desire a witness to his last moments, the witness of the author of his suffering; and indeed the author of his fate has ordained a final tragic irony for Saül: his suicide at the approach of soldiers who turn out to be his own men. As he looks up with his last glance he sees David weeping over Jonathas, the Philistines defeated, and sees not a man in mourning but one who has defeated him along with the enemies of Israël.

The relationship between Saül and David is inherently unstable. The two most significant causes of this instability are David's piety, of which Saül is suspicious, and David's military success, of which Saül is resent-ful. The two are linked insofar as David paints God as the source of his power and success; when Saül discovers from the Pythonisse that his line is to be extinguished, David's devotion to God is still more threatening.

The characters in Lamartine's drama may be recognizable as those portrayed in 1 Samuel, but they have been allowed motivations and modifications which in some cases throw the case for Saul's status as a tragic hero into a different light. David's character forms a sharp contrast with Saül's. David appears to be a moral and devout human being: reason-able, pious and above all sane. He is loved by Saül's son and daughter and by Achimelech, and he is admired by Saül's soldiers. His words are always courteous, yet he somehow always succeeds in infuriating Saül, and one may begin to wonder whether David is being deliberately provocative. His frequent appeals to God and his boasts of superior military talent (cf. ll. 678-684) are calculated to enrage Saül. Even when Saül dismisses David's claims as presumptuous ('Do you think that Saül cannot conquer without you?'[86]) the remark is somewhat hollow, since Saül is on the verge of defeat against the Philistines and David is the only hope of victory. This scenario is repeated throughout the drama. Regardless of the frame of mind in which Saül starts out, the result of any encounter with David is rage and loss of control whose expression ranges from insults to accusa-tions to attempted murder. David serves as a vehicle through which to

---

85. *Saül*, ll. 1800-801.
86. *Saül*, l. 695

perceive God's rejection of Saül and also the nature of Saül's madness and irrational behaviour.

Saül's relationship with his children is similarly blighted. Whenever Saül is distracted or plunged in despair, Micol and Jonathas attempt to cheer him up. However, nothing they can say to him is what he wants to hear, and their attempts to make him feel better in fact only serve to worsen his distraction. He is incapable of seeing the situation as they see it, though one might wonder at points whether they have grasped the gravity of the situation, considering that they remark on the beauty of the day and their hope and joy at David's return when they are being besieged by a Philistine army against which they can barely hope to win. This separation leads to isolation for Saül: he becomes so distressed that he can no longer engage with Jonathas and Micol.

Saül in Lamartine's drama is unquestionably the victim of his character flaw, his rage, his jealousy, his paranoia, as much as he is of divine manipulation, though at the same time the theme of divine manipulation is much more fully developed than in 1 Samuel. In Lamartine's drama the cause and effect work in the opposite direction: it is Saül's paranoia which leads to his raving. We are able to view the internal struggles and pleasures of the characters without restraint (with the possible exception of Abner who gives little away), and the creation of characters who so manifestly exhibit the traits of those in 1 Samuel while at the same time maintaining their own identities is undoubtedly the work of an author with a consummate understanding of character.

Conclusions

In dramatizing the story of Saul, Lamartine retains its force and its fascination. Since the time of Aristotle, tragedy has been conceived of chiefly as a dramatic form; when Lamartine takes the elements of tragedy from a narrative and composes a tragic drama out of them, essentially he attests the existence of the tragic vision in the Hebrew Bible, a notion remarkable in his time. Lamartine's Saül, for all his hubris, his murderous behaviour and his blind rages, is a man who is exceptional but not as exceptional as his rival. One may admire his audacity in cursing the heavens and one may rue his downfall. Lamartine's Saül is not a pitiful figure, but he can evoke *eleos* and *phobos*, sympathy and a dismay and apprehension of fate.

Analysis of the plot has shown that Lamartine has changed many significant events, and the examples that I have investigated more closely demonstrate this. Aristotelian categories[87] are adequately fulfilled: the events are played out in a matter of hours, there is reversal in David's return from exile, which brings with it the possibility of victory, and there is recognition both of a person (Samuel, with all its implications) and of Saül's destiny. Saül is clearly the tragic hero of this drama: he is characterized as a noble man but having in his jealousy and paranoia a fatal flaw. He also perceives himself to be menaced by the heavens, against which he struggles. He displays hubris in both senses in which the word is understood, in his decision to combat God and in his murder of Achimelech (and Samuel). The type of collision that Hegel identifies is also to be found in *Saül* in the conflict between Saül and David: both positions are morally justifiable. Furthermore, most of the five conflicts that Steiner identifies[88] are to be found in varying degrees in the drama. There is clearly a conflict between old and young in Saül's relationship with Jonathas, as can been seen from Saül's declaration that he can see into people's hearts whereas he implies that Jonathas has not yet learned to do this. Curiously, the conflict between Micol and her father, while a conflict between a male and a female, is never developed into a conflict between positions that are perceived as essentially male or female. This enhances Micol's characterization as closely aligned with her father's pessimism. Saül's attempts on David's life and David's return to exile contain elements of a conflict between Saül as an individual and the society for which he is responsible: he knows that without David there is little hope of victory against the Philistines. The appearance of Samuel's ghost hints at a conflict between the living and the dead, and this theme makes a brief reappearance in Saül's designation of David as 'another Samuel'. The conflict between the human and the divine emerges as Saül attempts to kill (and succeeds in some cases) all those who claim to have some kind of divine authority, and is developed in Saül's combative attitude towards God as the drama progresses. These conflicts are developed in a manner that diverges significantly from their correlatives in 1 Samuel, in particular Saül's conflict with the deity. This, therefore, will be treated in more depth in the following chapter.

---

87. Not only those of Aristotle himself, but also those that have been attributed to Aristotle, such as the necessity of hubris.

88. Steiner, *Antigones*, p. 231.

Chapter 4

ONCE VICTIM, ALWAYS VICTIM:
BLIND INSANITY AND CONFLICT WITH THE DIVINE

Introduction

Lamartine's use of plot and character are central with respect to the relationship of *Saül* to its sources, but the features that define the work as
Lamartine's are its thematic material and stylistic devices, and the matter
of the role of the deity. While Lamartine has based his plot and characterization on the biblical narrative, albeit with several significant differences, his use of theme and style and his treatment of the role of the deity
are fundamentally different from 1 Samuel's account. The plot and characterization of *Saül* are recognizable as being in a source relationship with 1
Samuel, but much of the thematic material of Lamartine's drama depicts a
different world, a world informed by Lamartine's interest in Greek tragedy
and Romantic lyricism. Many of the themes found in *Saül* recur throughout Lamartine's work, such as the connection between natural phenomena
and human emotion and remembrance. The difference in style is almost
inevitable, since *Saül* is drama rather than narrative, and yet Lamartine has
used stylistic devices that recall biblical narrative. However, the divergence
that is the cardinal sign that *Saül* is taking place in a different world from
that of 1 Samuel is the omission of the deity from the dramatis personae.
This, coupled with the absence of the character of Samuel, renders it
impossible for the drama to represent the divine perspective, and Saül's
perceptions are the only indications of divine activity. Therefore, whereas
in the previous chapter the intertextual focus was primarily one of comparison, here the emphasis is chiefly one of contrast. The points of connection between the two primary texts are less numerous and *Saül* asserts
its autonomy, yet the appearance of certain devices and themes creates
borders between Lamartine's drama and 1 Samuel.

Thematic Schemes And Stylistic Devices

The thematic material in Lamartine's drama is of particular interest because its treatment differs substantially from that of 1 Samuel and is also so typically Lamartinienne. Crucial to the tragic vision, particularly in the Greek tradition, are themes such as hiddenness and blindness, recognition and revelation; and these are central themes in Lamartine's drama. Crucial to Lamartine's poetry is the theme of the identification of natural features with human emotion[1] and this proves to have an important role in *Saül: Tragédie*. This theme is featured as a stylistic device, and also relates to the theme of remembrance, which again is central to Lamartine's work.[2] In this drama, vocabulary is used as a marker both of thematic material and of stylistic devices, and so I will examine the manner in which this operates.

Darkness, Blindness and Hiddenness

Central to the tragic vision is the struggle for meaning within the limits of human capacities, and thus the significance of the senses and their inadequacy both literally and metaphorically for providing meaning is one of the most common motifs in tragic literature. Hence *Saül* capitalizes on the theme of blindness, which in occurs in the drama together with motifs of light and darkness, symbolizing knowledge and ignorance, good and evil. From the beginning of the drama Saül is struggling to make sense of his suffering, and as he lists inexplicable forces at work on him he tells Jonathas,

> I have made overabundant efforts to tie them up,
> My son, for a long time God has no longer informed me.[3]

Enquiry of the deity cannot provide any answers. Meaning cannot be achieved through sensory communication with the deity, and the motif of loss of senses is applied to the articles of divine inquiry: heaven has closed its mouth to its oracles and despite Saül's attempts to snatch the truth from heaven, the altars are deaf and the ark is mute. Furthermore, God deliberately orders events without supplying meaning to those who are affected:

---

1. Birkett, *Lamartine,* p. 23.
2. Birkett, *Lamartine,* pp. 32-36.
3. *Saül,* ll. 287-88.

> Inexorable, at the mercy of his supreme order,
> He guides mortals, peoples, even kings,
> Blind instruments of his secret designs.[4]

This thwarted search for meaning causes bafflement. As Saül prepares for his meeting with the Pythonisse he expresses his frustration at his inability to discern meaning:

> It is too much, too long to await, in the night,
> The invisible blows of the arm which persecutes me![5]

David, meanwhile, is associated with light. At his reunion with Saül, the king hopes that David's presence signifies a change of fortune and invites him, 'Come in bright days, to change the dreadful days'[6] and tells him '[I] Add a new lustre to the glow of your life'.[7]

The drama provides an interesting twist by placing the moment of revelation and recognition relatively early in the plot and continuing to develop the theme of blindness following it. Like Oedipus who responded to the Delphi oracle by leaving the arena in which he believed his terrible fate would enact itself, Saül hears the revelation, understands it, and attempts to escape it. He projects his own blindness onto his son and daughter in the hope of convincing them to engage in his struggle and he holds God responsible for their lack of perception,

> The God who persecutes them
> Hides from them the abyss where his arm guides them!
> O unfortunate Race! o miserable father!
> Is it you God deceives? Is it me he enlightens?[8]

His plan to kill David to secure their protection fails with their defence of Saül's enemy, and the king is outraged,

> It is you whom he persecutes, and who preserves him?
> What have you done? O heaven! victims too blind[9]

but Micol and Jonathas remain loyal to David. Saül's subsequent ravings are further demonstration of his blindness. His loss of reason is the ultimate incapacity in the process of making sense of his suffering, for it is

4.   *Saül*, ll. 265-67.
5.   *Saül*, ll. 532-33.
6.   *Saül*, l. 360.
7.   *Saül*, l. 370.
8.   *Saül*, ll. 655-58.
9.   *Saül*, ll. 752-53.

precisely this kind of suffering which demands a search for meaning. Even his memory is unreliable, and in his vague awareness of his condition he exclaims,

> In the chaotic night my soul is confounded;
> Take off this blindfold which covers my sight![10]

The same image is used again when Saül discovers the sword of Goliath in David's possession: David's odious act in taking the sword which only the king may touch has finally caused the blindfold to fall from Saül's eyes.

Once Saül has regained his reason he is determined to continue his fight against fate and irascibly asks Jonathas, who will not be persuaded or convinced, whether he should blindly hand over to his rival the throne, the people, his children and himself. The irony is that it is Saül's blindness which prevents him from delivering up his sovereignty to David, and it is this blind struggle against his fate which ensures its consummation. Jonathas acknowledges his blindness to his fate, but accepts that it cannot be altered and so his fate is not tragic but unfortunate. Micol on the other hand, so like Saül in many other respects, shares his sense of darkness. Her final scenes, in which her preoccupation with death is attenuated, takes place in the darkness of the night-time battle. This moderates the integral tension between her share in the fate of Saül's line and her marriage to David, which in the biblical material is overcome by her separation from David (and in 2 Samuel her childlessness).

The use of specific vocabulary to indicate thematic material is crucial to Lamartine. A component of the theme of darkness is the motif indicated by the use of the word *ombre*. The word means 'shadow' or 'shade', and is used to signify a variety of images, particularly Saül's distracted state of mind, but *ombre* is also used to describe the physical state of Samuel in his appearance during Saül's consultation with the Pythonisse.[11] It refers to that which cannot be understood or controlled, and for Saül at least such forces are threatening. However, the word occurs for the first time on David's lips, in the first scene:

> Invoking the night, the protective shadows,
> I come home as fugitive among my brothers[12]

Although in terms of the drama's internal chronology there is no indication yet of the importance of *ombre*, outwith this constraint one can

---

10. *Saül*, ll. 984-85.
11. The word can be translated 'ghost'.
12. *Saül*, ll. 9-10.

observe that there is a certain irony in the notion of protective shadows
returning David to his comrades; his return necessitates encounter with
Saül, whose dark mental state causes David to depend for his life on protective comrades.

The word *ombre* is the principal word that Saül uses both metaphorically
and symbolically to indicate his confusion. In his first appearance, in Act 1,
Scene 4, he contrasts *l'ombre* and *la lumière* ('light'), yet fears both. However, the word does not have solely negative connotations for Saül at this
point. He speaks thus of his kingdom: 'Israel reposed in the shadow of my
tents'.[13] However, after his consultation with the Pythonisse and his encounter with the *ombre* of Samuel, his use of the word is almost without exception a reference to his state of mind. To begin with it is a metaphor of
suspicion, particularly Saül's suspicion of betrayal by God's agents; for
example his suspicion of the priests:

> David is the instrument of cruel priests...
> In the shadow of the altar their plottings betray me,[14]

and of David,

> It is time again: you are not yet King
> In vain you lift up your shadow against me[15]

His desperation at the end of the battle also falls into this category, since it
takes up once again the motif of his state of mind together with a suspicion
that this is a consequence of his divinely ordained fate:

> Where to flee? or; to find again, in these deadly shadows
> Of my destroyed soldiers, their wretched remains?...
> Alone I saw—and heaven, constant in persecuting me,
> Snatches my empire and condemns me to live![16]

The word is also used to describe the location in which his state of mind is
at its most distracted: Jonathas speaks of Micol's enclosure with Saül in
the *ombre* of his tent (l. 781); and by other characters it is used to describe
Saül's state of mind: Micol remarks on the shadow on Saül's forehead and
the grim fire in his eyes (ll. 1141-42).

Eventually, in Saul's final outcry against God, the *ombre* has become a
symbol of God's persecution: now that all his soldiers have fallen in the

13. *Saül*, l. 241
14. *Saül*, ll. 1227, 1229
15. *Saül*, ll. 1346-47.
16. *Saül*, ll. 1656-57, 1668-69.

'deadly shadows' and he alone is left alive, he discovers his dying son. At Jonathas's death, Saül is ready to succumb to his fate:

> Die then! Come all to enjoy my torture,
> You shadows which sacrificed my bloody injustice[17]

The symbol extends also to his perception of David's persecution, as when David discovers him in his last moments,

> Detestable rival, in the dark mansions
> Your voice pursues me even among the shadows?[18]

The word *ombre* in the mouths of other characters does not tend to take on this dark symbolism, except when they are describing Saül's state of mind. However, Micol's usage is occasionally closer to Saül's, just as her attitudes to fate and the deity are closer to Saül's. Most of the other characters associate the word with positive images: the returning soldiers in Act 3 Scene 5 sing in praise of David who has saved them from the shadows of death (l. 1134) and Jonathas hopes the shadow will hide from the Philistines the small number of soldiers (ll. 1496-97). Micol uses the word in her recitation of David's psalms as a reference to Saül's past victories over Israël's enemies,

> Get up, O Saül! and may the eternal shadow
> Engulf even their name![19]

and the Pythonisse responds to Saül's question concerning his *forfaits*:

> The shadow has covered them, the shadow covers them again,
> Saül, but heaven sees what earth ignores,
> Do not tempt heaven![20]

Micol, however, whose attitude to the fortunes of Israël is closest to Saül's, believes the sombre night during the battle hides the destinies of Israël in the horror of its shadow (l. 1569). Nevertheless, she and the other women and priests are able to hide in the shadows from an unknown approach, so Micol has reason to be grateful for the *ombres*. Thus the motif of *ombre* runs throughout the drama, and its significance is aligned with the development of character, while still underpinning the notion of the unknown and incomprehensible.

---

17. *Saül*, ll. 1796-97.
18. *Saül*, ll. 1816-17.
19. *Saül*, ll. 1035-36.
20. *Saül*, ll. 609-11.

Another component of this thematic strand is that represented by the verbs *cacher* and *dérober*, which indicate what is hidden. The theme of what is hidden and what is revealed has been central to the tragic vision. At the first level it is frequently the dramatis personae themselves who are hidden. The drama opens with David hiding himself on his return to Saul's camp, and through his revealing of himself to Jonathas and Micol we learn that he is hiding from Saül, who has threatened his life. Jonathas hopes 'May this dense foliage hide you from his eyes!'[21] Later, in Saül's confusion which prevents him from taking part in the battle, he asks where David is hiding, to be told that he has driven him away.

At the next level fate is hidden. The overriding concern for Saül, Jonathas and Micol at the beginning of the drama is that they cannot be sure of victory in the coming battle, which they understand as God's hiddenness. God is no longer the helper of Israel, nor of them personally. It is not that God is absent, but that God does not choose to help Israel; God watches Israel's fate without intervening. Thus Micol says,

> You whose word formed humans
> To serve as a spectacle for your divine glances,
> O God! leave this ardent, inaccessible throne,
> Where your terrible majesty is hidden from our eyes...[22]

Or, if God intervenes, it is to harm; so Saül,

> Inexorable, at the mercy of his supreme order,
> He guides mortals, peoples, even kings,
> Blind instruments of his secret designs.[23]

Not only is future outcome of fate hidden, but also the present connection with fate. Saül feels that God is causing him to suffer unreasonably,

> And now, what am I? A shadow of myself,
> A king abandoned at his supreme hour!
> Battling vainly this fate,
> This unknown power which troubles me,
> Persecuted, punished, without knowing my crime,[24]

and the sense of uncertainty which this produces in him leads to a decision:

21. *Saül*, l. 211.
22. *Saül*, ll. 103-106.
23. *Saül*, ll. 265-67.
24. *Saül*, ll. 245-49.

Prudence injures me, doubt bothers me,
And I want hand-to-hand to confront my luck…
And, diving boldly into the funereal shadows,
To snatch my fate from the midst of their gloom![25]

and Abner arranges for him to consult the Pythonisse. After her revelation, Saül believes that David has been hiding more than just his body, and tries to persuade Jonathas,

Know better a perfidious enemy,
Hiding under deeds of virtue wishes for crime,[26]

and he asks whether his son does not perceive the parricidal blade, whether he does not pierce the perfidious mask (or masque). Saül encourages Jonathas to look into human hearts to throw light on their hidden designs, and claims his own age and experience enable him to read in people's hearts more than can be read on their faces,

I know how to divine them, I know how to draw out of them
The mask where their plans seek to hide[27]

But Jonathas is more concerned with the secrets God holds back from humans. His acceptance of God's hand in his fate prompts him to tell his father, 'Let us respect the secrets which God wishes to hide from us.'[28]

Saül is the primary centre of the *cacher* motif. Either people are hiding from him, or he believes people are hiding from him, or his concern is to uncover hidden plans and schemes. Micol to some extent shares this concern. The secondary focus of the motif is the Philistines: Jonathas hopes the silence and shadow will conceal from the Philistines the small number of Israël's soldiers; Micol and her companions hide in the shadows from soldiers they think may be Philistines. The manner in which the motif is used links Saül's enemies (David, God and the Philistines) against Saül. Simultaneously the motif functions within the tragic vision as Saül attempts to uncover and then to combat his fate.

Revelation and Recognition
Revelation is the matrix within which a tragic hero may encounter his fate. Revelation brings together the elements of the hero's suffering with their

25. *Saül*, ll. 485-86, 489-90.
26. *Saül*, ll. 712-13.
27. *Saül*, ll. 1186-87.
28. *Saül*, l. 1247.

causes, and its source is inevitably outwith the hero whose blindness has prevented him from grasping the meaning of the evil that afflicts him. In the effort to make sense of his anguish the hero seeks out revelation in the hope that meaning will provide relief, but the obstacle to the success of this manoeuvre is that enlightenment, or recognition, brings with it greater suffering. The significance of the role played by revelation in *Saül* works on several levels: David returns from hiding in exile and reveals himself in turn to Jonathas, Micol and Saül; the Pythonisse reveals the fate of Saül, Jonathas and David; Abner reveals the threat of David's interest in the throne to Saül, and Saül communicates it to Jonathas. The decisive moment of revelation in *Saül* comes early in the drama, in Saül's encounter with the Pythonisse. The Pythonisse claims to be 'the voice of the supreme God' and so what is revealed to Saül is divinely ordained fate. It is the revelation of his fate that Saül is seeking, and which he would be seeking from God, but is unable: 'everywhere heaven closes its mouth to its oracles'.[29] However, the Pythonisse is an agent of God, and moreover has come looking for Saül to prophesy on his fate and that of David. This gives Saül hope that perhaps the heavens are tired of persecuting him. The fatal book of destiny 'Every day, every moment, alas! reveals a word',[30] but Saül wants to read 'in one deed, my whole destiny'.[31]

He goes to the Pythonisse fearless, and even her opening words of doom do not shake him. He thinks she is trying to unsettle him, and her reluctant timidity exasperates him, so that he wants her to speak up or depart. She would prefer not to speak, but considers herself to be under the divinely furious power of a God who pushes and persecutes. As her vision begins and she calls out the names of the central characters, it is her naming of David and Jonathas that changes Saül's manner. Not only his own fate will be revealed, but also that of his line and of David. As the Pythonisse foresees David's coronation, which Saül has feared since his discussion with Abner, Saül would prefer to hear no more. He is at the same time terrified and furious at the confirmation of his worst suspicions and at the following prediction of Jonathas's death, which is revealed together with the king's culpability.

So far Saül has not been able to read a single page of the book of his own fate, and the Pythonisse persists in revealing the coming power of David and his descendants, seeing in her vision a God. Apparently this is

29. *Saül*, l. 494
30. *Saül*, l. 528
31. *Saül*, l. 534

not what Saül expected to hear, and he clings to God's promise of the throne, unable to accept his rejection. He does not appear to believe there could be any reason for God to reject him, and as the Pythonisse finally addresses Saül's own fate, telling him that his own arm will punish his *forfaits*, he asks for clarification. The Pythonisse tells him that nature of these *forfaits* is not for her to reveal but for Samuel. Saül does not understand and pushes her further, and she accuses him of Samuel's assassination. Now Saül intends her revelation to end with her death, but the revelation continues with the dramatic appearance of Samuel's bloody ghost. Samuel reveals nothing but himself, he does not speak to Saül, but in Samuel's silence Saül recognizes his own guilt. It is only now that the moment of recognition and comprehension arrives, and Saül leaves the encounter understanding the reason for his rejection, the meaning of the torment he has endured and the suffering of his people. He knows the price that must be paid for his guilt: the blood of his son. He must now respond to the revelation: to accept his fate or to combat it.

The function of revelation in the encounter with the Pythonisse differs substantially from that of the biblical material. The involvement of the deity in *Saül* precludes any notion of paganism and legitimizes the Pythonisse's role as agent of revelation, while the appearance of Samuel functions as a dramatic device which provides the interpretation rather than the source of revelation in contrast to 1 Samuel. Revelation is the tool by which Saül comes to understand his fate, without which he has been unable to respond to his suffering. In recognizing the person of Samuel, Saül recognizes his destiny.

Having decided to combat his fate, another moment of revelation for Saül comes at Achimelech's prophecy concerning David and his descendants, which continues the thread of the Pythonisse's revelation. Saül's terror at the veiled references to the One who is to come prompt him to stare at David and exclaim 'Is he a God?'[32] The revelation of David's greatness is thrust upon him and he is compelled by God to respond with adoration. He has temporarily lost the struggle against his fate and acknowledges that David will reign. His only plea is that David not shed the blood of his family. On this occasion, as with the Pythonisse, the source of the revelation is divine. Saül's earlier protests at his lack of communication with the heavens is now shown to be a misapprehension: rather than being ignored he is manipulated by forces that torment him, on this occasion into acceptance of his fate. This attention from the deity increases his struggle, and it is signi-

32. *Saül*, l. 1376

ficant that on neither occasion does he plan to seek out revelation. Revelation functions as one of the torments to which God subjects him, since he cannot escape it and it brings him unwelcome information. Following his meeting with the Pythonisse he is able to choose his own response; at Achimelech's prophecy his response is coerced. However, the effect is temporary and he is able to continue his struggle against the fate revealed to him, winding himself tighter in the web of disaster that surrounds him. Here his recognition of David as quasi-divine is a recognition that his struggle against his destiny cannot be won.

Nature Symbolism and Remembrance
The significance of landscape in the work of Lamartine is well attested, particularly the apparatus of projection of human emotion and memory onto natural features.[33] Although the device is not widely used in *Saül*, the locations in which it appears are of consequence, as they function as a characterization tool.

David's description in the first Act of his life in exile emphasizes his bravery and intrepidity. He searched for deserts, enjoying their horror, he welcomed the vast shadows of dense forests, as he snatched the bloody skins of lions and survived on throbbing flesh. Climbing the mountains at night, the moon lent him its placid light and he saw once more the places inhabited by his people, recognizing the plains where he had engaged in the glories of his youth. He became tired of this shameful existence and seized once more his spear in his idle hands. He went to seek death, but he found glory and victory after victory and an astonished people demanded him as king. He preferred to die rather than to reign far from Micol, so he eventually returned. This account sets the scene for the development of David's background and characterization as a military hero and loving husband. It is interesting that in this long speech, which comes as a response to Micol's question 'What God has protected you? What God has restored you?' (l. 171), David does not once mention God, which is odd in view of his later predilection for speaking of the heavens.

The most significant of the examples of nature symbolism comes in Saül's opening lines, which introduce the king of Israël as a disturbed man. The introduction of Saül at sunrise provides a contrast between the early light and Saül's inner darkness, and places David's return from exile within the context of a new phase in Saül's life. He regards the dawn with a simultaneous memory of a past time when he enjoyed God's favour. Now that he

33. See Birkett, *Lamartine*, ch. 2, and Ireson, *Lamartine*, pp. 44-46.

is out of favour with God each new day announces a new misfortune; furthermore at each nightfall he fears the shadows. As he looks up at the dawning sun he sees it veiled in a bloody cloud, covering nature with a livid light. Every landmark is stained with a horrible colour. He exclaims, 'Sun! I understand you and I shudder with horror!'[34] His shuddering is given perspective by Micol's reply, 'The Dawn has never appeared more serene and more pure',[35] and Jonathas's response, 'Never has a more beautiful day shone in the heavens!'[36] These contrasting views serve to differentiate between the relative states of mind of Saül and his offspring, but the significance extends beyond this. Saül projects his state of mind onto nature; in the bloody cloud, the livid illumination, and the horrible stain Saül sees the destruction of his soldiers, his divinely ordained torment, and the abandonment of God. After an outcry over God's treatment of Israël's people and king, he returns to the theme, exclaiming 'Ah! I read my arrest in the whole of Nature!'[37] What he sees is evidence that soon he and his line will have disappeared because God has broken him. Immediately after this scene, when Saül realizes that he is about to meet David again, his words continue this theme:

> Happy and terrible day!
> For a great and proud heart, oh! God! How distressing it is
> To present oneself, in shame and in adversity,
> To the consideration of a hero whom one has persecuted![38]

Later, in his confusion in Act 3 Scene 5, he sees the sun approaching the horizon and is troubled:

> Where am I? o heaven! Where am I coming from? What dense cloud
> Hides from me the image of the past, the present?[39]

Again, he projects his state of mind, his confusion, onto his view of nature.

The treatment of remembrance is necessary for *Saül* since a work the length of this drama depends on the plot background of the biblical material being incorporated somehow into the drama as there is no room to relate each of the events of many chapters of 1 Samuel. Remembrance provides the background which gives meaning to the plot and characterization.

---

34. *Saül*, l. 224
35. *Saül*, l. 226
36. *Saül*, l. 228
37. *Saül*, l. 274
38. *Saül*, ll. 347-50.
39. *Saül*, ll. 968-69.

However, the device is also used as a motif which serves the drama's own plot development and characterization. The dramatis personae all look back to happier times of acceptance: David remembers his acceptance within society as a hero before his enforced exile, Saül remembers his acceptance within God's favour as rightful sovereign over Israël. Both Saül and David remember times of military glory, which David is able to regain while Saül loses his reason and is confined with only his memories. Again, the device functions as a characterization tool as well as providing background to the plot.

Stylistic Devices

There are several stylistic devices found in *Saül* that Lamartine has used deliberately to recall biblical style because of their prevalence in biblical narrative. There are two such devices in *Saül* that are especially indicative of this trend: synecdoche and the technique of naming. With synecdoche 'there is contiguity between the literal and non-literal meaning, [and] the relation between the two is one between the part and the whole'.[40] This technique is very common in biblical literature, and its occurrences in *Saül* are reminiscent of biblical style. The incidence of synecdoche in the drama is overwhelmingly concerned with body parts and the whole body, and is used with particular reference to the senses. Thus when Saül gives David his weaponry, David asks God to make him conquer under the eye of the king, indicating David's desire that Saül should see David's victory as an act of God, and when Jonathas hopes the dense grove will hide David from Saül's eyes he fears that if Saül sees David there will be trouble. The device is also used metaphorically: the arm that pursues Saül and rains blows upon him is a metaphor for the actions of God, while it is Saül's own arm that will punish his *forfaits*, a metaphor for his suicide. These examples represent a deliberate device that is used for the purpose of recalling biblical style; however, many examples of synecdoche that are used idiomatically in modern languages have their origin in biblical synec-doche and these idioms are also found in *Saül*: for example, Saül tells Jonathas that he reads more in people's hearts than in their faces. Such devices bridge the gap brought about by the vastly differing technique of characterization, which drama necessitates, whereby the characters speak long and often and reveal their innermost feelings and thoughts.

The other device that bridges the characterization gap between 1 Samuel and *Saül* is the technique of naming in a manner that recalls biblical

40. Bar Efrat, *Narrative Art*, p. 208

narrative, whereby a character is named or addressed according to relationship.[41] This technique is used with particular effect in 1 Samuel, where
Michal is variously David's wife or Saul's daughter; or where Saul
addresses David as his son. In the same vein in *Saül* David refers to
himself as the son-in-law of his king (l. 12) and to Jonathas as his brother
(l. 33), while Micol is addressed by Jonathas as David's wife (l. 137).

The significance of this naming technique is that it establishes closeness
of relationships. Thus when Micol is praying in her first scene while
looking after Saül and Jonathas addresses her as David's wife, it emphasizes that although the content of her prayer is mainly concerned with the
situation of the people and of Saül, her chief concern is really her husband,
whom she mentions only at the end of her prayer. In the following scene,
Saül is addressed by Micol as her father (l. 125) and by Jonathas as his
king (l. 127) and this distinction continues throughout Act 1 Scene 4,
distancing Jonathas from Saül until the subject of David is broached, when
Jonathas for the first time addresses Saül as his father in order to make the
connection from which he can ask the question, 'Did you not have two
sons? Did I not have a brother?'[42] Saül recognizes that David was once his
son, but says he isn't any longer, but wishes he were again (ll. 304-305).
When he knows he will be reunited with David he refers to him as his son,
but his first address to David is as 'friend of God' (l. 343). Since Saül has
already stated his view of God's activity with regard to himself, and since
he has also displayed an ambivalence concerning David, this naming
technique heralds adversity.

The absence of a name can also be significant; for example Reinhartz, in
her work on Judges in *JSOT* 55, she forges a connection between Samson's
unnamed mother and the unnamed angel who announces the impending
birth of her son. In *Saül* the most important unnamed character is the
Pythonisse. The woman of Endor is also unnamed in 1 Samuel, but since
Lamartine has excluded significant dramatis personae (e.g. Yhwh) and
included non-biblical dramatis personae (e.g. Esdras), one might assume
that the Pythonisse could have been given a name. That she remains
unnamed is crucial because Saül asks her identity and instead of giving her
name she claims to be 'The voice of the supreme God'.[43] Her identity thus
connects her with God, which will be more important than her name in
view of her revelation.

41. See Alter, *Biblical Narrative*, pp. 126-27.
42. *Saül*, l. 302
43. *Saül*, l. 537

Abner also uses the technique of naming by association when he refers to David as 'the son of Jesse'[44] when attempting to manipulate him to command Saül's army. So far David's relationship as son has been in connection with Saül as father, but Abner's concern has been with the succession of Saül's son Jonathas, to which he believes David is a threat. He therefore emphasizes David's relationship as son to Jesse in order to distance David from the throne. The technique serves a double purpose, because as well as distancing David from the throne it is used in the context of David's past military success to remind David of his duty to his people but at the same time to discourage him from using this duty as an opportunity to usurp the throne.

The technique is used again as an accusation in l. 1316 where Saül refers to David as 'son of Melchizedek' and as 'another Samuel'. Melchizedek was a priest according to Gen. 14.18, but it is the references to the order of Melchizedek that are most appropriate to Saül's accusation. In Psalm 110, which has been interpreted as a Messianic psalm, the subject is a priest forever after the order of Melchizedek (v. 4). This reference is taken up in the New Testament, in Heb. 5.6, 6.20 and throughout Hebrews 7, where it endorses the eternal priesthood of Jesus as Messiah. By addressing David with this title Saül is foreshadowing Achimelech's prophecy of David's messianic connections. Meanwhile the reference to Samuel connects David with the murdered prophet and signals Saül's intention to dispose of him. Both titles connect David with God's favour and connect Saül with his *forfaits*. By these examples it is evident that Lamartine has picked up on the technique of naming in biblical narrative and used it in *Saul* in order to create association, thereby aligning the drama with some of its source material.

The Role of God

The most crucial of all the points of departure from the biblical material is the omission of Yhwh as one of the dramatis personae in *Saül*. In 1 Samuel, Yhwh unambiguously rejects Saül and favours David, but no such claim can be made for this drama. This technique is consonant with most Greek tragedy (though cf. Euripides' *Heracles*) and colours the understanding of the tragic vision, since divine activity is perceived by the characters without the confirmation of a narrator, and thus the deity's role in fate is called into question. Undoubtedly all the characters are depicted

44. *Saül*, l. 803

as believing that the deity controls or orders their destinies, but it is precisely the intertextual reading that opens up the question of whether the Yhwh portrayed in 1 Samuel, who intervenes in human activity, plays the same role in *Saül* without a voice.

Ultimately one cannot be sure what Saül has done to incur the wrath of God. One can only note the effect, which is Saül's perpetual *égarement*. The biblical narrative presents Saul's affliction as a kind of madness which leaves him either depressed or hostile. Lamartine depicts a distraction whose symptoms range from confusion to fury. At some points Saül is incapable of reason; at others he appears wild and barbaric. The evil spirit from Yhwh, which in the biblical narrative is the cause of Saul's madness, has a correlation in *Saül* as a spectre,

> An implacable phantom upsets my sleep
> An implacable phantom besieges my awakening;[45]

as a cloud,

> ...what sinister cloud
> Rests on [Saül's] brow, obscures his face![46]

as an invisible hand,

> It seems that an invisible and bizarre hand
> Always attracts me to [David] and always parts me from him;[47]

and as God,

> A God stronger than me, agitating in my breast,
> Makes me change a hundred times my wishes and designs.[48]

However, though Saül appears to perceive the deity, he is less inclined than the Saul of 1 Samuel to placate the deity, either by religious observance such as sacrifice or by accepting his fate.

Conception of God

The picture of God built up by the characters changes somewhat during the course of the drama as their fates move in different directions. At the beginning of the first act all the characters are suffering misfortune and their understanding of God is accordingly bitter. David is overwhelmed by

---

45. *Saül*, ll. 275-76.
46. *Saül*, ll. 773-74.
47. *Saül*, ll. 1220-21.
48. *Saül*, ll. 1278-79.

God's severity; he feels his past good fortune was short and dearly bought and wonders 'Why do you not leave me in my obscurity?'[49] Jonathas speaks of the scourges with which God overwhelms his people, believing that 'God no longer remembers the people which adores him'.[50] Micol believes when she prays that she invokes in vain a God whose throne is inaccessible and whose majesty is terrible. She prays that God will

> Regard with pity this people overwhelmed by misery,
> Regard with pity this King who pursues you anger . . .
> Restore your power to Saül, and David to my heart![51]

Saül's perception of God is the most bitter of all. He believes he has been punished without knowing his crime. God has put the crown on his head but God has abandoned him. He feels that God intervenes capriciously in human affairs, 'And God, when it pleases him, rejects us and breaks us'.[52] He has no hope in God.

The whole scheme is reversed, still in the first act, by the reconciliation between David and Saül's family, at which all the characters begin to hope in God. Jonathas thinks that perhaps God looks upon Israël with a less severe regard, Micol displays signs of hope, while David asks God,

> Come, come down and do battle, and under the eye of my King,
> Make me conquer today for my people and for you[53]

and even Saül believes that in David's return there may be reason to hope in God, 'Ah! blessed be heaven which sends him back to us!'[54] He addresses David as 'friend of God' and refers to him as 'the work of God'.

God is therefore a severe ruler, but one who works through individuals for the defence of the people who worship him. He is a manipulative God who can choose to break individuals if he chooses without explicitly revealing the meaning of their suffering. Thus if Saül wishes to understand his rejection he must search it out for himself. He hopes when David returns that his suffering is now at an end, but he nevertheless does not comprehend it. It appears that at his reconciliation with David in Act 1 he is prepared to go forward without the understanding he has craved so long as his anguish is over. This amounts to trust in God and God's purposes.

---

49. *Saül*, l. 15.
50. *Saül*, l. 70.
51. *Saül*, ll. 113-14, 116.
52. *Saül*, l. 270.
53. *Saül*, ll. 407-408.
54. *Saül*, l. 333.

Any trust in God that Saül has regained is tied up with his continuing sovereignty and the succession of his son, and so it is not strong enough to withstand the pressure of the seeds of doubt that Abner sows. Abner's words cast doubt on the people's fidelity to Saül, which he models on the infidelity to God practised by the people,

> Which, foolish adorer of foreign gods,
> Has twenty times for Belial betrayed the Lord,[55]

and who equally will betray their king and his line if there is an ambitious youth raising his eyes to the throne. Since Saül has attempted to gain meaning from deaf altars and a mute ark and wishes to know his fate, and since Abner convinces him that the priests are so corrupt that the spirit of God no longer descends upon them, it is necessary to take Abner's advice and consult a pious person who can tell the future as easily as the past. Conveniently, there is just such a person who wishes to reveal Saül's fate to him, who in fact claims to represent God and who has refused to be driven away until she speaks with the king.

The claim of the Pythonisse to be the voice of the supreme God raises the question of the ambivalence of a deity who, one the one hand, refuses to answer Saül's questions by the usual means, and in fact taunts him with symbolic dreams without revealing their meaning, but who on the other hand sends a female necromancer to reveal Saül's future ruin, who insists on speaking to the king even when he screams for silence, but who will not answer the one question that overwhelms him: what reason is there for his rejection and that of his son? What has he done to deserve his fate? Why has God turned away his face from Jonathas and condemned him? Before his meeting with the Pythonisse, Saül believed his question was 'How?'—how should he proceed? how would the people respond in a situation of victory or defeat? how could he manage the threat of an usurper? Whenever he is strong and in possession of his reason, his mind turns to 'How?', but in his weakness under pressure from the deity his only question can be 'Why?', and the sign he receives in response is the bloody ghost of Samuel. For the time being, this answer appears satisfactory to Saül, but despite Saül's recognition of his guilt God's ambivalence continues.

Does Saül believe that the Pythonisse speaks for God? His initial impatience and his surprise at her sex suggest that to begin with he is unsure. When he hears the fate that awaits him and Jonathas his outrage

55. *Saül*, ll. 467-68.

points to lack of belief in her claim to divine inspiration. His certainty that he will retain the throne that God has promised him is only shaken when he sees the ghost of Samuel. As in 1 Samuel, it is the sight of Samuel's ghost (in this case Saül's vision rather than that of the woman of Endor) which is the decisive moment, yet there is no word from God, only a sign which represents Saül's culpability. Now he believes the words of the Pythonisse, that 'God will vindicate all that God inspires in me!'[56]

Only Saül has encountered the designs of God in this manner, and other characters remain hopeful. Micol imagines that God is tired of his harshness and that the end of their misfortunes is at hand. David declares his belief in God's infallible assurance, and believes his arm alone will suffice to save Israël. This apparent confirmation of Saül's fears is compounded by what he has heard in his confrontation with the Pythonisse, and so the conflict is set up with David on the side of God and Saül in combat with God. If God has truly inspired the Pythonisse's words to Saül, then God has implicitly manipulated Saül and David into their present positions. Although Abner's advice may have caused Saül to doubt the wisdom of his reconciliation with David, it was the consultation with the Pythonisse which confirmed his position. David has not been privy to this consultation and so does not appreciate what is at stake for Saül. This removes the possibility of David's deliberately altering his behaviour to accommodate Saül's concerns. That David speaks of God, as he is wont to do, inevitably rouses Saül's jealousy, but until the consultation with the Pythonisse the king was in control of his jealousy. On this reading it may be concluded that God has engineered the tension between Saül and David by seeking out Saül to reveal the future while at the same time keeping David ignorant of these proceedings. However, since we are dealing with a drama in which God is not one of the dramatis personae, such a reading must be carefully considered, as the possibility remains that Abner has set up the entire episode for the same purpose: to engineer conflict between the king and David. On such a reading, the absence of an explicitly stated motive leads to the necessity of taking Abner at face value: Abner genuinely fears for Saül's sovereignty and believes that if Saül knows the future he will be able to take control over his own fate. The question is left open, and therefore the answer remains ambiguous until we can determine whether God is an agent in the drama or whether the activity attributed to God is merely perceived by the human agents. The answer centres around

---

56. *Saül*, l. 602.

the vision of Samuel's ghost: is Saül hallucinating, or does Samuel appear at the behest of the Pythonisse?

Without a doubt, if there is one protagonist who is sceptical of God's power it is Abner. Having witnessed the conflict emerging between Saül and David, his attitude towards David becomes sarcastic:

> What! the son of Jesse, what! the messenger of heaven
> At the moment of battle abandons Israel?[57]

What does it matter if no prophet has spoken to confirm God's will? The only prophet is necessity, according to Abner. David's unease can only be inverted by the priest Achimelech confirming what Abner has suggested: that David command the army in battle against the Philistines, and David comes to believe that God will confound the malice of his enemies. Meanwhile, Saül has lost his reason, and Jonathas describes how the king blasphemes the heavens or invokes them on his knees. The source of his confusion is outwith him:

> What sleep, righteous gods! what sinister cloud
> Rests on his brow, obscures his face![58]

It seems almost paradoxical that it is the words of David's psalms which eventually restore his reason, but in fact they deal with the victories of Israël in which Saül once played a major role. Again there is a tension between Saül's trust in his divinely appointed position, which David in the past supported, and his present situation of limbo, where David is perceived as a perfidious enemy because of his alliance with the God who torments Saül in these times of confusion.

It is exactly this question which Saül tackles in Act 4. Is his ambivalence towards David human confusion or divine vengeance? Act 4 is the nexus in the debate concerning God, since it is this point at which the characters' fate is cemented, the point from which their destinies fulfil themselves. It is the point of no return, because the discussion of God's attitude and will offers them the chance to change their attitudes and prompts them all to make choices that will play themselves out to the conclusion. The discussion centres among Saül, Jonathas and David.

Jonathas is presented with the choice of joining Saül in the struggle against fate or accepting the possibility of losing the throne. Without divulging the mechanism by which he comes to fear for his line, Saül

---

57. *Saül*, ll. 803-804.
58. *Saül*, ll. 773-74.

advances the argument that one must defend the privileges of God's promises. Jonathas chooses to remain loyal to David and accept the fate with which Saül has threatened him. He bases his choice on his understanding of God's will, which he believes Saül is ignoring,

> And do you not hear another voice, yourself,
> You cry: 'It is David whom I have chosen, whom I love;
> It is me who protects him and who guides his steps'?[59]

Jonathas is willing to cede the throne to David on the orders of the heavens, and even if he wished otherwise, humans cannot force God to slacken his vengeance. Jonathas now understands that his fateful demise will pay for his father's guilt, but he also understands

> And, on the battle fronts, the divine anger
> Passes, without breaking them, sweeter and lighter![60]

Unfortunately for Jonathas, bending his head in prayer will not prevent him from being broken in death as punishment for his father's crimes. As Jonathas makes the choice to acquiesce, he challenges Saül to rethink his attitudes. Saül questions whether his constant changes in attitude towards David are human confusion or divine vengeance. Saül does not appear to have the scope for choice that his son enjoys, since his answer is ultimately that his loss of control is attributable to divine manipulation. He believes David is the instrument of cruel priests who hate him and have betrayed him with conspiracies. Since God is stronger, Saül finds himself unable to shake off this influence,

> A God stronger than me agitating in my breast,
> Makes me change a hundred times my wishes and designs[61]

but no sooner has he thus appealed for David's understanding than David speaks about God in a manner that seems to Saül to be calculated to enrage him. Saül returns to the matter that he has discussed with Jonathas: that cruel priests have forbidden the king the altar, which recalls Saül's belief that David is the instrument of these disloyal priests. Saül now gives the answer to his earlier question concerning whether he suffers from human confusion or divine vengeance:

59. *Saül*, ll. 1204-206.
60. *Saül*, ll. 1264-65.
61. *Saül*, ll. 1278-79.

That for him my incense is a profane incense,
That his hand persecutes me, that his voice condemns me,
And that, repenting of having elected me king,
There is nothing in common between heaven and me.[62]

The divine manipulation of Saül removes his capacity for choice in honouring David, but it is precisely because he perceives himself forced to do so that he makes the decision to fight against God. The heavens, which are too strong for Saül's vain courage, and force him to kneel before David, will certainly be too strong for Saül's counter-attack, but Saül refuses to go down without a fight. Jonathas's horror at the crime of Achimelech's murder prompts an outburst from Saül in which the king states exactly what his decision has been:

What is this avenger God of whom you always speak?
He ruins you, and protects the days of a monster!
He guides him to the throne, he makes you his victim,
And if he has favours, it is only for crime.
If he puts this price on them, I want to deserve them;
Being unable to yield, I want to imitate him:
I take, just like him, my hatred for justice,
And of all my forfaits I make him accomplice![63]

As a result of this decision Saül has Achimelech put to death, and from this point he cannot change the course of his destiny, if indeed he ever could. He prepares to meet his fate with the words,

What pleasure! How fine it is for a simple mortal,
To do battle at once both with men and with heaven![64]

Is Saül's decision reasonable? Jonathas considers his father's attitude to be blasphemy, and Micol is horrified at the crime that Saül commits as a result of this decision. Saül feels his punishment far outweighs his errors. There is something here of Job and his companions, where those round about accuse and the afflicted one denies their charges and challenges God. Of course, the similarity cannot be pushed, since Saül is guilty and has acknowledged it. Saül's anger towards God and combative attitude are without parallel in 1 Samuel; indeed in 1 Samuel it is never explicitly stated how Saül feels towards God after the onset of his torment, and it may be that in the touch of Job-like qualities of both Saül and Jonathas we

62. *Saül*, ll. 1296-99.
63. *Saül*, ll. 1474-81.
64. *Saül*, ll. 1510-11.

find another of Lamartine's intertexts. Supporting this is language that recalls the biblical text of Job: at ll. 1451-52. Saül declares his intention

> And first, avenging my fall and my death,
> To struggle against heaven and deserve my fate!

This characterizes Saül as a Job figure who takes the advice of Job's wife: he will curse God and die (Job 2.9). Jonathas's words at l. 1650, on the other hand, recall Job 1.21, 'The Lord wished it, blessed be the Lord!' Jonathas is the innocent man who is prepared to accept that the Lord has given and the Lord has taken away; the difference for Jonathas is that his fate does not allow for a tenfold restitution of all that he once had. By blending these themes with the characterization of 1 Samuel, the contrast to Job is emphasized: Saül is not innocent but believes that his punishment is too harsh for his crime, and Jonathas's innocence is disregarded in the punishment for his father's guilt. The comparison with Job accents their attitudes towards God.

David also must make a decision in Act 4. He intends to return to exile, on Saül's request, but Saül asks him to stay. However, David's penchant for mentioning heaven in almost every speech immediately irritates Saül. The choice facing David is whether to placate his king or to justify his language, and he chooses the latter. It has become clear that if David wishes to wait 'until heaven has changed your heart' then he will be waiting a long time, at least with a view to a permanent change. Saül explains that God continually makes him change his will, and therefore David must decide whether to return to his exile or whether to stay and risk death at Saül's hands. David believes there may still be hope for a reconciliation between Saül and God:

> If your heart, faithful to recognition
> In him, but in him alone, grounds its hope.[65]

The matter becomes more complicated when Achimelech becomes involved by prophesying concerning David: that David is the elect of God and the king of glory, while God condemns Saül. Throughout this David remains passive. As Micol, Jonathas and even Saül fall down before him, claiming that God ordains this action, David neither confirms nor denies their interpretation. After Saül's impassioned acknowledgment of David's superiority and pleas that David not shed the blood of his family (cf. 1 Sam. 24.20-22), David leaves the scene in silence, presumably to resume his exile as Saül

65. *Saül*, ll. 1312-13.

requests. Perhaps he has realized that the relationship between Saül and God is more complex than his earlier assessment accounted for, and that he will never be safe from Saül and the forces that drive him to distraction.

Confusion over God's role and will is not limited to Saül and his daughter. Although Jonathas does not question God's will and David believes he knows it, they are the exceptions. In Act 5, as the women and priests hide from the enemy soldiers, one of the priests asks, 'Avenger God, what have you therefore decided?'[66] In the darkness of the night's battle the position is unknown and there is uncertainty even from the priests as to whether God will save Israël. Micol, typically, expects the worst: in order to ruin Israël, celestial vengeance removes David in the funereal night. David, on the other hand is characteristically optimistic and has retained his trust in God; in fact, he says it was God who has guided his steps back to Micol. However, the principal questions about God arise from Saül and Jonathas. Jonathas believes he has been rejected by God, who loves David. He recognizes God's severity, but imagines that the destinies of humans are written in God's eternal laws. If Jonathas dies it is because God intends Jonathas to die. God has also supplied the meaning: Jonathas dies in divine vengeance for his father's crimes, and Jonathas accepts that whatever evil comes from God is justified, because,

> Man, work of these hands, can he murmur?
> Dare he judge that which he must adore?[67]

Saül's view of God differs in that he does not believe God's activity in persecuting him is justified. Although he has admitted culpability in Samuel's death, although he has even killed Achimelech knowing that he was committing a crime against the heavens, he believes that God's response is unjustified. Saül wants neither blessing nor pardon from God. God is cruel and bloodthirsty, but Saül will infuriate him, and all God's might cannot lessen Saül's courage. God triumphs, but although he batters Saül, Saül will get up again to insult his arm. Saül does not repent of the crimes of his life; God committed them and justifies them. Since this is Saül's disposition, what then did Saül expect? Perhaps he expected to be killed himself in divine vengeance; what he cannot accept is the loss of all his men and the death of his son while he himself survives. Yet, oddly, at his last hour, he feels abandoned by the forces that persecute him. His suicide becomes a way of appeasing the shadows, of reuniting himself with the powers

---

66. *Saül*, l. 1530.
67. *Saül*, ll. 1788-89.

which have left him alive but stripped of all that he once valued. Why does he no longer sense persecution at this supreme moment? Is there reconciliation between Saül and God? Does his decision for suicide satisfy the vengeful countenance with which the heavens have regarded him? Saül makes the decision for himself: he chooses not to live on because he knows he has lost the battle against God. He expected to lose his life but instead he has lost his son and his soldiers, his sovereignty and his significance. He has no more energy to combat the heavens, and so in his acknowledgment that he has lost there is no more need for his persecution. If God has been listening to Saül's outbursts, God has proved him wrong. He cannot make God an accomplice in his death, for in his decision to die he is no longer persecuted. Whatever responsibility God may have had in the crimes of Saül's life, the evil of his death is his own choosing.

Identity of God

So far what has been examined is the characters' perception of God's activity and motivation with respect to their experience. However, unlike in 1 Samuel, God never speaks directly either through a narrator or to any of the characters. If God is not one of the dramatis personae, then the question to be addressed is whether God manifests himself; and if so, whether any of the other characters act in God's place. There are four candidates, all of whom have a claim to a special relationship to God, and it is through them that God is perceived to manifest himself: the Pythonisse, Achimelech, Samuel and David.

The only character to claim directly to speak divinely inspired words is the Pythonisse. Her role is brief but significant. If she is speaking the word of God, then God is a deity who certainly manipulates the work of his hands, as Saül bitterly complains in Act 5. The God who inspires the Pythonisse to insist on speaking to Saül intends the king to know in advance the terrible ruin that will befall him and his line. The question is, what motivates God? Does God expect that after the torment that Saül has been experiencing he will admit that David will be a better king for Israël and simply withdraw from his kingship? Knowing Saül's tendency for confusion and madness, perhaps even responsible for it, does God consider that his protégé David will live to become king once Saül knows what the future holds for Jonathas? This deity must be very secure in his ability to manipulate mortals if he has no qualms about putting the life of his chosen successor at risk. Fortunately for God, it seems he is able to induce an attack of madness in Saül at any time, and it is this, together with the loyalty and protection of the intended victim Jonathas, which keep David from succumbing to Saül's spear.

Achimelech purports to know God's will and by this means convinces David to take up the sword of Goliath, which only the king may touch. Again, if Achimelech really is representing the will of God, it seems that God is not concerned about stepping into human politics for his own ends. What is a king before the king of kings, Achimelech asks, and well he might. In 1 Samuel, Ahimelech gives the sword to David at David's claim to be without weaponry on a mission from Saul. However, in *Saül*, the king has recently presented his own sword to David. Why should God deem it necessary that David carry the giant's sword? Would David fail to conquer without it? Is Saül's sword somehow cursed? Or does God perhaps wish to stir up human politics by setting up a confrontation when the king discovers what has become of his privilege? This is, after all, the consequence of the action. Once again, God's motivation should be subjected to suspicion.

Samuel has no role at all as a living character: his only appearance is in silent ghostly form. Although Saül confesses to his murder, there is no hint given at any point in the drama as to Saül's reason for killing him. Extrapolating from 1 Samuel (for example, Samuel's fear that Saul might kill him if he should anoint a new king) would be merely speculation. Nevertheless, Samuel must be considered because it is by means of the vision of Samuel's ghost that the meaning of Saül's fate is revealed. No word comes from God through this vision, but if God is responsible for it, then one may assume that God wishes to confront Saül with his crime.

Twice in the drama it is asserted that David is somehow holy and has divine connections: by the Pythonisse in Act 2 Scene 3 and by Achimelech in Act 4 Scene 3. These assertions have a messianic flavour which doesn't quite mix with the rest of the material. The messianic nuance is distinctively Christian since it identifies David's descendant as God, and this identification enhances David's piety. That Saül fails on both occasions to understand the nature of these relationships or their content is an indication that these assertions may be understood as Christian apology, and we know from Lamartine's life that at the time he was writing *Saül* he was questioning the devout Catholic principles that his mother had so carefully instilled in him since his childhood, although at that point he had not abandoned them.[68] Saül's rejection is crucial from the perspective of Christian

---

68. See remarks by de Cognets, *Saül*, p. xi, and Fortescue, *Lamartine*, p. 27. Three of Lamartine's later works were put on the Vatican Index.

doctrine since David must succeed in order to be the regal ancestor of the messianic figure of Jesus.

What these characters all have in common is Saül's attempts on their lives. Although in 1 Samuel Saul throws his spear at Jonathan, in *Saül* there is no such attempt on Jonathas's life. Saül succeeds in having Achimelech put to death, and apparently Samuel's assassination was at the hands of Saül. The king also threatens the Pythonisse and David, but without success. It is precisely because they tell Saül what he does not wish to hear concerning God's protection of David and rejection of his line that Saül wishes them dead. We cannot be sure what caused Saül to kill Samuel, but we could extrapolate from the context of his other attempts, especially in the light of l. 1317, where Saül compares David to Samuel: 'This other Samuel which heaven sends back to me!' But David is not like Samuel since he has divine protection from Saül's murderous intentions, and he is certainly not like the Samuel of the biblical material, who tells Saul that Yhwh will not repent of his decision, for he is not a man that he should repent (1 Sam. 15.29). David has just told Saül that he should repent, indeed that if Saül repents God will judge him a second time, the implication being that this time he may not be convicted. That Saül does not appear to believe him is another example of the drama's tragic irony.

Did Lamartine intend any of these conclusions about his representation of God? De Cognets quotes from his correspondence,

> I believe that everything is subject in the physical and moral universe to an all-powerful Providence which I sometimes call fate; it ruins us and it saves us by the least things that we never foresee because they are above our foreseeing.[69]

It is likely that, at this point in Lamartine's life, conceiving the divine as fatality was the furthest extent of his theological challenging of his Catholic upbringing. That God's motivation might be questionable was undoubtedly anathema to him. He must certainly have intended to represent a severe God, but it is likely that he intended that this God, being God, should be allowed the final say in justification of evil. This does not mean that Lamartine's intention (if one can discern it) is the most, or only, appropriate reading. It may certainly be appropriate, following the examples of Linafelt's essay in *Reading Between Texts* and Schüssler Fiorenza's article on ethics in biblical interpretation, to raise the question of God's morality.[70] The task

---

69. Quoted by de Cognets, *Saül*, p. xi
70. See above, pp. 111-13.

is made simpler through Lamartine's characterization of David as loving, loyal and without significant faults. The plot of 1 Samuel has thus been altered in such a way that a suspicious reading of God's motivation becomes an easier option.

Conclusions

Lamartine's use of theme and style has lent elements of Greek tragedy to the biblical myth. The emphasis on the failure of senses, particularly sight, to contribute to understanding and meaning is highly reminiscent of *Oedipus* in particular, while the centrality of revelation and recognition is more widely associated with Greek tragedy. Other themes and stylistic devices are more peculiarly Lamartinienne, though some are consonant with the biblical material. It is impossible to say whether Lamartine's use of devices that recall biblical style is deliberate; however, their existence is a feature of the intertextual relationships between 1 Samuel and *Saül*.

There are a number of tensions in the portrayal of the deity in *Saül*. In the manner of much Greek tragedy, divine activity is perceived rather than experienced in a directly attributable manner. However, Lamartine is working with an ancient Judaic narrative in a Catholic social context, and the deity depicted in the drama has a variety of characteristics and involves three different conceptions of the divine. The God of *Saül* is in a Greek locus (off-stage), but has Judaic manners (concern for the chosen people) and a Christian face (in David's messianic connection).

Unfortunately for Lamartine, *Saül* was not well received outside his immediate circle. It was rejected by the eminent actor François-Joseph Talma, whom Lamartine had approached in the hope of having the play performed at the Comédie Française. This rejection seems to have coloured the attitudes of critics, since the drama has been largely ignored ever since, gaining only a mention from Lamartine's biographers (due no doubt to the events in Lamartine's life at the time of its composition) and virtually no critical commentary, with the exception of de Cognets. In fact, de Cognets devotes the beginning of his introduction to the question of the importance of *Saül* for literary history, yet his conclusions have not, thus far, captured the critical imagination of his successors.

On the basis of Alfieri's work, Lamartine has interpreted the source material from 1 Samuel as tragic and has reworked the material into a tragedy. To what extent has he been successful? Probably on any definition of tragedy, including the Aristotelian, *Saül* is tragedy. The success or failure of the drama is not so much in the definition of tragedy, but in the matter of questions such as why Sophocles' *Oedipus* is still successful after two-and-a-half millennia but Corneille's or Voltaire's *Oedipe* is hardly known after a couple of centuries. The success of the drama stands or falls on audience or reader response. The same issue affects Lamartine and his source: Alfieri's *Saul* has been translated into several languages and attracts critical attention two hundred years on, yet Lamartine's *Saül* gathers dust on library bookshelves.

The reasons for the lack of critical success of Lamartine's Saül are broadly the same as the reasons for the lack of illumination the drama provides in respect of 1 Samuel: it fails to provide adequate opportunity for engagement with social and political texts. Although de Cognets has suggested that the political motives in the drama may be allegorical, the details of such an allegory are difficult to specify, and de Cognets does not elaborate. Perhaps in the context of the French revolution and counter-revolution Saül could be cast as Napoleon, ultimately defeated, or perhaps, in view of Lamartine's monarchist sympathies and the date of writing, David takes over Napoleon's role as one who provides hope of restoring the monarchy. There are no clear parallels, and in any case, such parallels might be difficult for twentieth-century audiences to perceive.

The social texts with which the drama interacts are a second factor, and it is here that significant problems arise. Looking at the theme of the troubled paternal–filial relationship, we find that the tension in 1 Samuel between Saul and his children, and also David, centres around deceit, disloyalty and violence, whereas in *Saül* the tension between Saül and Jonathas and David (and perhaps Micol, where her sympathies lie with David) centres overwhelmingly on theology. To understand why this is problematic we can usefully consider Sigmund Freud's analysis of *Oedipus*. Freud's fascination with the Oedipus myth has been well documented. His view was that the success of the ancient Sophocles drama with modern audiences is due to its focus on a universal human anxiety. The problem with this view at a literary level is that other writers have treated this so-called 'universal' theme with much less success (cf. Voltaire and Corneille, noted above). Similarly, Kaufmann points out that the greatest tragedies focus on relationships that most people experience, for example the parent–child relationship or the relationship of lovers,[71] but, as Kaufmann is aware, this is no substitute for poetics. Hugh Pyper uses Freud's explanation of the power of *Oedipus Rex* to raise questions of biblical narratives:

71. See above, p. 44.

> Freud's work suggests that the impact of any text depends on the under-
> lying anxiety that it activates. If the impact of *Oedipus* relates to the
> audience's repressed desires in relation to their parents what might be the
> implications for accounting for the impact of biblical narratives on their
> readership? What anxiety do they activate in the reader?[72]

These questions are the key to the reason Lamartine's *Saül* does little to
illuminate 1 Samuel. Lamartine's drama does not activate universal anxie-
ties in those who engage with it. Furthermore, a key anxiety raised in 1
Samuel is that of human comprehension of the deity's activity: an anxiety
which is effectively distanced in *Saül* due to the absence of God among
the dramatis personae.

The tragic conflicts in Lamartine's drama, as I have stated above, centre
around theology. The conflict between Saül and Jonathas occurs as a result
of Saül's jealousy and paranoia (apparently caused by the deity), but its
content concerns the nature and activity of the deity. Similarly, Saül's
conflict with all the other characters is worked out at this level. His conflict with David centres primarily around theology, and his concerns for
his power and his line appear at times to be secondary to the gulf between
the way he perceives the deity and the way David perceives the deity.
Often his jealousy of David focuses on the favour David claims to find
with God (which claim is supported at the dramatic level by all the
available evidence) in comparison with his own perceived divine abandonment (again, supported by the evidence). While a collision between the
human and the divine is one of the five tragic collisions identified by
Steiner, the problem with the conflicts represented in Lamartine's drama is
that they are collisions between humans regarding the divine.

Conflict about the nature or identity of God is a prevalent feature of
human existence, but it tends to be played out across cultural boundaries. If
such conflicts occur at a familial level they are usually accompanied by
fears of social upheaval; for example, such threats may be perceived in
cases of 'mixed marriage' or underlined by racial or class tensions. It is
simply not the experience of most people in contemporary Western societies
to be engaged in collision with their parents, employers or monarchs over
the nature and identity of the deity. Because of this, *Saül* is unable to fulfil
its tragic potential, and thus is able to provide little illumination on texts
within its intertextual matrix, whether they be written, social or political

---

72. Hugh S. Pyper, *David as Reader: 2 Samuel 12.1-15 and the Poetics of
Fatherhood* (Biblical Interpretation Series; Leiden: E.J. Brill, 1996), p. 3.

texts. This is also the primary explanation for the ascription of little literary value to the play. Thus it would be accurate to say that the reason Lamartine's drama does little to illuminate 1 Samuel is bound up with questions of construction of literary value. This is not to state that the choice of Lamartine's *Saül* as an object of intertextual study is invalid, since there are clearly intertextual relationships between *Saül* and 1 Samuel, and the question of why a relationship is ineffective is as relevant as the question of why it is effective. While *Saül* is a tragedy in terms of its genre and form, it is not tragic enough in terms of its audience appeal to comment convincingly on the elegant poetics of 1 Samuel.

Face III

HENCHARD IN HARDY'S *THE MAYOR OF CASTERBRIDGE*

Chapter 5

THAT NO MAN REMEMBER ME: THE CHARACTER
OF HARDY'S TRAGIC VISION

Introduction

If 1 Samuel were given a title, it might surely be 'The Life and Death of the King of Israel: A Story of a Man of Character'. Thomas Hardy's monumental study of 'the sorriness underlying the grandest things, and the grandeur underlying the sorriest things'[1] in *The Mayor of Casterbridge* is deeply informed by his pervading interest in biblical narrative. Strangely enough, the obvious clues to the extent to which *The Mayor of Caster-bridge* owes a debt to 1 Samuel, such as physical descriptions of the protagonists, stylistic devices which point to more than a passing rela-tionship, not to mention plot and characterization, have elicited little attention, except for two brief articles: one by Julian Moynahan, who suggests that '*The Mayor of Casterbridge* [is] a much less highly evolved example of the framed novel'[2] (than for instance Joyce's *Ulysses*) and the other by Nehama Aschkenasy, in which *The Mayor* is compared to a Hebrew language novella by S.Y. Agnon. Their perspectives differ in one significant respect: despite his confidence in having 'demonstrated the existence of extensive parallels between Hardy's account of the Henchard–Farfrae rivalry and the biblical account of the Saul–David conflict',[3] Moynahan remains unwilling to commit himself to the notion of 'fully conscious intention of the artist'.[4] Aschkenasy, on the other hand, argues

---

1.   Thomas Hardy, *The Life and Work of Thomas Hardy* (ed. Michael Millgate; London: Macmillan, 1984), p. 178.

2.   Julian Moynahan, '*The Mayor of Casterbridge* and the Old Testament's First Book of Samuel: A Study of some Literary Relationships', *PMLA* 71 (1956), pp. 119-30 (129).

3.   Moynahan, 'Relationships', p. 127.

4.   Moynahan, 'Relationships', p. 127.

that Hardy has deliberately used Saul as a 'prototype' in order to introduce a non-tragic dimension into the novel.

I propose to examine a number of elements in *The Mayor* that point to a reading implying a biblical substructure. The relationship between Henchard and Farfrae may be considered to be structured on that between Saul and David, and this raises the issue of parallels in their relationships to other characters who are drawn from the biblical material, notably Elizabeth-Jane, and the parallel role of paternity in the tragic vision of 1 Samuel and of *The Mayor of Casterbridge*. Moynahan's work has a number of shortcomings, and by means of an intertextual approach to 1 Samuel and *The Mayor* these may be addressed. By means of this intertextual approach the more plausible of Moynahan's arguments may be expanded and clarified. That Hardy consciously used material from 1 Samuel may be argued from the interest he expressed to Leslie Stephen, and Stephen's suggestion that he read Voltaire's drama merits investigation of the drama itself in preparation for the intertextual examination of the relationships between 1 Samuel and *The Mayor of Casterbridge*. This examination may profitably take place from three major perspectives that preoccupy Hardy scholars. Therefore, despite Lascelles Abercrombie's warning that

> Art like Thomas Hardy's fiction is not to be abstracted in analyses of plot and character,[5]

I shall explore intertextually the characterization in *The Mayor* and its relationship to tragedy in this chapter; the following chapter will take account of two other approaches to Hardy's work.

The Present State of Scholarship

Any examination of the state of Hardy scholarship, even of scholarship on this novel, would be beyond the scope of this study. What is of immediate concern is the question of critical approaches to the specific issue of 1 Samuel's relation to *The Mayor of Casterbridge*. On this, despite most critics making a comparison between the description of Farfrae (p. 106) and that of David (1 Sam. 16.12) very little has been written, Moynahan's 1971 article and Aschkenasy's 1983 article being the only approaches, and with this in mind a discussion of their work will therefore be productive.

---

5.   Lascelles Abercrombie, *Thomas Hardy: A Critical Study* (London: Martin Secker, 1912), p. 128.

Moynahan begins by taking as his interpretive centre the idea that 'the major theme' of the novel is not the relationship between character and fate but rather 'the conflict between generations'.[6] He argues that the bitterness of Henchard's failure might be related to the lack of 'a generally accepted religious outlook which could transform Henchard's sufferings into a mitigating ritual and his death into a sacrificial symbol'.[7] This is somewhat curious in view of the development of his article. He points to extended parallels between the Henchard–Farfrae conflict and the Saul–David conflict, which he claims work by a strategy of association. However, he maintains that the 'identification of characters and incidents with their biblical counterparts does not extend beyond the central dramatic situation of the novel' which he takes to be 'the aggressive rivalry of the two men in their careers and in their personal affairs'.[8] Moynahan then outlines some of these parallels: that between the corn trade and the Philistine assaults, the part played by music, the physical descriptions of Farfrae and David, the descriptions of Henchard's and Saul's mental state, the praise by women of Farfrae and of David, and the twice-occurring opportunity to kill which results in the sparing of life. This latter pair of incidents, Moynahan asserts, is not a 'regular' parallel, but 'a sort of transposed or inverted parallelism'.[9]

Moynahan deals with the motif of music in detail, noting parallels between Henchard's reaction to music and Saul's, and also between Farfrae's musical ability and David's. He goes on to compare the enounter between Saul and the witch of Endor with that between Henchard and Fall, the weather prophet. In the penultimate section of his article, Moynahan turns to the question of authorial intent, remarking,

> Whether these parallels result from the fully conscious intention of the artist, or whether we are dealing here with a degree of unconscious influence from the older narrative are extremely difficult questions to answer. We do know that Hardy's mind was saturated in the imagery and episodes of the Bible and that he constantly employed a wide range of biblical allusions in his novels.[10]

6.   Moynahan, 'Relationships', p. 118.
7.   Moynahan, 'Relationships', p. 118. D.A. Dike argues the reverse: that Henchard's sufferings are based on a mitigating ritual in which his death is a sacrificial symbol on the Greek model of the Seasonal King (D.A. Dike, 'A Modern Oedipus: *The Mayor of Casterbridge*', *Essays in Criticism* 2 [1952], pp. 169-79 [169]).
8.   Moynahan, 'Relationships', p. 119.
9.   Moynahan, 'Relationships', p. 123.
10.   Moynahan, 'Relationships', p. 128.

With this question left open, Moynahan then maintains that the parallels are of no relevance to literary criticism if 1 Samuel is merely a source for *The Mayor*, and he goes on to suggest that the Saul–David conflict represents a framing action, on a similar model to that of Joyce's *Ulysses* although 'much less highly evolved'.[11] Thus it is through the identification of Henchard with Saul that the unity of experience is stressed. Moynahan concludes by discussing the theme of history in *The Mayor* and connecting it with the reflection of Saul and David's struggles in those of Henchard and Farfrae.

Moynahan's article has not received a great deal of attention from later critics, and the few remarks on it appear to dismiss it as divergent. Laurence Lerner refers to it in a bibliography as an 'unusual and illuminating approach'[12] but makes no reference to it in the body of his text. J.C. Maxwell accords Moynahan's article 'some plausibility' but objects that the problem with his interpretation is

> not that it is wrong but that it covers too much: that the 'conflict between generations' is 'so archetypal that it is omnitypal'.[13]

Roger Ebbatson also knows of the article, and provides a similar catalogue of analogous themes. But whereas Moynahan sees in these features a series of parallels, Ebbatson stresses their capacity as sources,

> [*The Mayor of Casterbridge*] is, in a real sense, an *intertext* whose meanings are to be identified through the relationship with other texts,[14]

and this position concedes creative imagination on the part of the author.

While Moynahan's approach may be considered unusual in Hardy studies, it is evident that he has struck a chord in pointing out that there are numerous parallels between the two texts. Furthermore, the idea of the conflict between generations may be 'omnitypal', but this does not make it irrelevant: Steiner cites this in his inventory of tragic conflicts. My own view is that in his article Moynahan has not covered enough, and that while his interpretation is doubtless illuminating, some crucial questions

11. Moynahan, 'Relationships', p. 129.

12. Laurence Lerner, *Thomas Hardy's The Mayor of Casterbridge: Tragedy or Social History?* (London: Sussex University Press, 1975), p. 110.

13. J.C. Maxwell, 'The "Sociological" Approach to *The Mayor of Casterbridge*' in R.P. Draper (ed.), *Hardy: The Tragic Novels* (London: Macmillan, 1975), p 150. Maxwell quotes George Douglas Wing, *Hardy* (Edinburgh: Oliver & Boyd, 1963), p. 64.

14. Roger Ebbatson, *Thomas Hardy: The Mayor of Casterbridge* (London: Penguin Books, 1994), p. 7.

have not been addressed. It is precisely the intertextual approach through which some of these questions may be raised.

Moynahan's conclusion that the extended parallels which he notes are of no relevance to literary criticism if 1 Samuel is merely a source for *The Mayor* cannot pass without challenge. The question of source is crucial to literary criticism, and within literary criticism it is the intertextual approach which investigates the relationships between anterior and posterior texts. The identification of a source is a primary step which necessarily raises questions of function and relationship. While the notion of a framing action is interesting, it is limited by Moynahan's view that the identification of characters and incidents in *The Mayor* with their biblical counterparts does not extend beyond the rivalry of the two central characters. Other identifications, for example, are the theme of problematic paternity and the role of supernatural forces in the chief protagonist's destiny.[15] Furthermore, since Hardy was rarely inclined to reveal his sources[16] it might appear that the very concept of framing would be contrary to his preferred techniques.

It is crucial to read the texts carefully when hypothesizing on the relationship between them. Moynahan's comparison of Henchard's gloom with Saul's is one of several examples of a parallel being pushed further than it ought to be: Henchard's gloom may be traceable to the rash act of the wife sale, but Saul's disobedience to Yhwh's commands during his campaign against the Amalekites is hardly a rash act, as Moynahan contends. In fact if Saul acts rashly it is in his sacrificing in 1 Samuel 13, but, leaving that aside, in 1 Samuel 15 Saul believes his actions have been satisfactory, and needs to be persuaded that he has failed. Moynahan goes on to connect the description of Henchard's introspective inflexibility with the image of a brooding Saul troubled by an evil spirit from the Lord. While this aspect of brooding is important, there are much closer parallels to be drawn between Saul's torment by the evil spirit and Henchard's manner. For example, Henchard feels that 'The movements of his mind seemed to tend to the thought that some power was working against him' (p. 263), and asks himself 'Why should I still be subject to these visitations of the devil, when I try so hard to keep him away?' (p. 382). Moynahan comments on Henchard's and Saul's gloom thus: 'we are

15. Moynahan deals with the supernatural, but the parallels are much more extensive than his treatment allows for.

16. 'Hardy was always nervous of admitting what could be taken as his sources, and annoyed when they were pointed out to him.' Martin Seymour-Smith, *Hardy* (London: Bloomsbury, 1994), p. 330.

seldom privileged to see them in any other state of feeling'.[17] In fact it is crucial to the tragic vision that we do see them in more positive moods, as of course we do on numerous occasions, for two reasons. First, moments of relief set the scene for reversal, and second, a perpetually gloomy tragic hero would be difficult to characterize in a sympathetic manner. If, after Aristotle, the hero should not be too bad or too good, she or he also should not be too gloomy, for the same reasons.

Again, a careful reading is necessary simply to determine the exact events being paralleled. Moynahan conflates two accounts when he writes of the parallel between the encounter in the hayloft and the encounter at En-gedi (1 Sam. 24). David does not cut off the edge of Saul's robe while Saul sleeps; rather, Saul goes in to 'cover his feet' and does not see David in the darkness of the cave. The episode in which David comes on Saul asleep is in 1 Sam. 26. With an intertextual approach it is not enough merely to point to a transposed or inverted parallelism that fits the dramatic structure of the novel, as Moynahan does. It is imperative to question here the relationship between the textual world of 1 Samuel and that of *The Mayor*. The world of *The Mayor* is one in which Farfrae makes no subversive political manoeuvres against Henchard because there is a different social power dynamic between the two men. Henchard, after all, is not a king, has no claim on absolute power over Farfrae, has no army of three thousand men with which to hunt him down, and moreover does not have the power to be so threatening to Farfrae as to be able to drive Farfrae into exile. It is not only the dramatic structure of the novel but the whole textual world which is under consideration in the relationship between these paralleled episodes. Furthermore, against Moynahan, it may well be that the dramatic structure of the novel is able to sustain straight-forward parallelisms but may not wish to. However, I am not convinced that it is the parallelism of who wants to kill whom that is transposed. In 1 Samuel it is Saul who wants to kill David. Moynahan does not mention the two incidents in the biblical narrative where Saul attempts to kill David whilst under the influence of the evil divine spirit, and we must remember that on both above-mentioned occasions in 1 Samuel it is Saul who is pursuing David with the intention of killing him, and both times lets him go unharmed for two reasons: firstly he is not by nature a murderous criminal, and secondly David is able to manipulate him. These features are reproduced in *The Mayor*. First David's voice and then David's words

17. Moynahan, 'Relationships', p. 121.

remind Saul of the love he once had[18] (and still has) for the man he is
seeking to destroy. So the parallelism remains, but there has been a shift of
responsibility. This can be demonstrated in the reference to Henchard's
'unmanning': after he lets Farfrae go, Henchard is ashamed,

> So thoroughly subdued was he that he remained on the sacks in a crouching
> attitude, unusual for a man, and for such a man. Its womanliness sat
> tragically on the figure of so stern a piece of virility.[19]

David's cutting off of the skirt of Saul's robe has a similar flavour. This
action has been interpreted as having a certain sexual association[20] which
signifies a symbolic umanning. The crucial difference is that Henchard is
responsible for his own unmanning. The effect is to stress Farfrae's pas-
sivity and to accent Henchard's implication in his own downfall. While
the biblical narrative emphasizes the gulf between the protagonists'
declared intentions and their actual deeds, Hardy's narrative uses these
episodes to stress the connection between character and consequence.

In a similar vein, Moynahan attributes Henchard's bankruptcy to the
weather prophet Fall's inaccuracy of prediction. In fact, like the woman
of Endor, Fall's prediction turns out to be right. What actually ruined
Henchard was his lack of business acumen. He bought so much grain early
in the season that when the weather changed for the better and the price
fell he was forced to sell, making a huge loss. This was compounded by
another change three days into the harvest which caused an unsuccessful
gathering (p. 263). If Henchard had been able to wait another week before

18. Cf. 1 Sam. 16.21. Good thinks that it is David's love for Saul which is being
described here, and he correctly points out that David is the subject of the verbs in 21a
and of 'he became his armour bearer'. Therefore it makes grammatical sense for David
to be the subject of 'he loved him greatly' (see Good, *Irony*, p. 73). However, this
would be in striking contrast to the characterization of David in 1 Sam. as a whole, in
which he is never said to reciprocate the love of Jonathan or Michal. In fact 'love' is
something of a *Leitwort* in 1 Sam., with David as the object of the word, as Brueggeman has pointed out ('Narrative Coherence', pp. 232-33, 240). So it seems more
likely that, in the case of 16.21, Saul too loves David, while David's emotions are
characteristically left unreported.

19. Thomas Hardy, *The Mayor of Casterbridge* (Penguin Classics Edition; ed. with
an introduction and notes by Martin Seymour-Smith; London: Penguin Books, 1985)
(hereafter *The Mayor*), p. 348.

20. See Gunn, *Fate*, p. 94. Gunn argues that there is a strong sexual metaphor in 1
Sam. 24. The Hebrew word for 'cave' recalls the word 'to be naked', the word for
'foot' is a euphemism for 'penis', and the word for the 'skirt' of a robe also means
'extremity'.

selling his mountains of grain he would have received a better price and, though still losing, might have avoided bankruptcy. This inaccuracy undermines Moynahan's argument.

Perhaps the weakest point of Moynahan's article is the suggestion that the parallels he points to may not 'result from the fully conscious intention of the artist'.[21] I would argue that Hardy was indeed fully conscious when he brought to fruition an intention to rework elements of the story of Saul and David. Some ten years prior to his beginning work on *The Mayor of Casterbridge*, he had been discussing the merits of the biblical narrative with Leslie Stephen and his family, as he recalled in 1906:

> Somehow we launched upon the subject of David and Saul… I spoke to the effect that the Bible account would take a deal of beating, and that I wondered why the clergy did not argue the necessity of plenary inspiration from the marvellous artistic cunning with which so many Bible personages, like those of Saul and David, were developed, though in a comparatively unliterary age. Stephen, who had been silent, then said, 'Yes. But they never do the obvious thing'; presently adding in a dry grim tone, 'If you wish to get an idea of Saul and David you should study them as presented by Voltaire in his drama'. Those who know that work will appreciate Stephen's mood.[22]

Presumably having read that moderate man's drama, the seed was sown, I would suggest, in Hardy's mind.

Aschkenasy's treatment of Hardy's novel is extremely brief, and much of what she has written covers points that Moynahan had already made. However, there are a few details that must be discussed. In Aschkenasy's view, the tragic dimension in the novel is reinforced by analogy with *Oedipus Rex*, while the 'introduction of the Biblical pattern takes the novel away from the exclusively tragic domain'.[23] There is a strong influence in her article of Steiner's notion that tragedy is 'alien to the Judaic sense of the world',[24] and Aschkenasy's adherence to this unravels her argument. She claims consistently that the 'Biblical figures who function as the

21. Moynahan, 'Relationships', p. 127.

22. F.W. Maitland, *The Life and Letters of Leslie Stephen* (London: Duckworth & Co., 1908), quoted in Michael Millgate, *Thomas Hardy: A Biography* (Oxford: Oxford University Press, 1982), p. 158.

23. Nehama Aschkenasy, 'Biblical Substructures in the Tragic Form: Hardy, *The Mayor of Casterbridge*, Agnon, *And the Crooked shall be Made Straight*', *Modern Language Studies* 13.1 (1983), pp. 101-110 (104).

24. Steiner, *Tragedy*, p. 4.

archaic prototypes of Henchard are remote from the tragic sphere',[25] and
that Hardy 'used the Biblical prototypes for the non-tragic dimension that
they would introduce in the novel',[26] but that Saul is singled out because
of his tragic potential. However, it seems questionable that a character
with tragic potential would introduce a non-tragic dimension in a novel,
and moreover Aschkenasy offers no evidence in support of her theory that
Hardy intended to introduce a non-tragic dimension. Furthermore, she
attributes the concept in the novel of 'the existence of malevolent forces'[27]
to the influence of *Oedipus*, yet does not consider the possibility that the
existence of such forces could be due, at least to an equal extent, to the
influence of the biblical narrative. Her final remark concerning the novel is
that 'the architectural support that the Biblical frame offers Hardy is
mechanical, imposed by a skilled artisan to perfect his fictional creation'.[28]
It is by means of an intertextual approach that a claim such as this may be
addressed, in which textual relationships between *The Mayor* and 1 Samuel may be explored and found to be more numerous and more significant
than simply the use of one text to improve or 'perfect' another.

Voltaire

The connection between *The Mayor of Casterbridge* and Voltaire's *Saül* is
not at all the kind of structural relationship that may be found between
Lamartine's *Saül* and Alfieri's *Saul*. Furthermore, though Alfieri's work
gave Lamartine his idea, it appears that Hardy had already had his idea
before being directed to Voltaire's drama. Nevertheless, Leslie Stephen's
remark undoubtedly confirmed the idea for Hardy, and although we do not
know for certain whether Hardy followed his suggestion, it will be useful
to make a brief examination of Voltaire's work since by virtue of its
discussion it becomes one of the texts in the network of intertextual
relationships of which *The Mayor* is the focus.

    Voltaire's *Saül* was published in 1763, allegedly in translation from an
original English text, but the 1775 edition of Voltaire's works contained
the following notice following the title,

---

25. Aschkenasy, 'Substructures', pp. 104-105.
26. Aschkenasy, 'Substructures', p. 105.
27. Aschkenasy, 'Substructures', p. 104.
28. Aschkenasy, 'Substructures', p. 109.

Although this translation has been attributed to M. de [Hut], we know that it is not his; however, in order to respond to the eagerness of the public, we believe that we must insert it here as it has been in a great number of editions in the same collection.[29]

The date of writing is also open to speculation, since Voltaire frequently antedated his work. However, suffice to say that it appears unlikely that the drama was written in English, neither does it appear to have been translated since, so if Hardy read it, it is likely that he read it in French. It is written in prose rather than in poetic form and is offered as a drama rather than specifically as a tragedy, though, as Leslie Stephen implied, Hardy may have found it disturbing.

The drama begins with Saül and his servant Baza at Galgala (Gilgal), and Saül is distressed. Since the day he found the kingdom he has known only unhappiness. He comments,

Alas! I was looking for my father's asses, I found a kingdom; since that day I have known nothing but pain. God grant, on the contrary, that I had looked for a kingdom and found some asses! I would have had a better deal.[30]

Saül believes that Samuel is plotting with David in order to elevate David and give him the crown. When Samuel enters it is to bring Saül word of God's repentance and rejection, and Saül exclaims,

God repent! Only those who make mistakes repent; his eternal wisdom cannot be rash. God does not make mistakes.[31]

There is a connection here with Henchard's 'fetichistic' beliefs: to Henchard the deity seems to operate by means of symbols, hence the importance for him of swearing his oath of abstinence on a Bible. To Voltaire's Saül the deity is a symbol: Samuel's God is more real than Saül's.

Samuel complains that Saül has spared Agag, and Saül protests that he thought kindness was the primary attribute of the supreme Being, but Samuel tells him he has deceived himself. This theological perspective is echoed throughout *The Mayor*, which depicts a deity either absent or uncaring in relation to Henchard, and who could certainly not be described as principally kind. Henchard also deceives himself over the deity's

29. Voltaire, Saül, in *Oeuvres complètes de Voltaire: Tome quatrième* (Paris: Garnier Frères, 1877), p. 571.

30. Voltaire, *Saül*, p. 576.

31. Voltaire, *Saül*, p. 578.

attitude: when the sight of the effigy at Ten Hatches Hole prevents his committing suicide, he believes he is 'in Somebody's hand'. In fact, by remaining alive he must endure even greater misery when Elizabeth-Jane rejects him at the appearance of Newson.[32] As Agag pleads for his life, Samuel tells him he will die, but would he like to be a Jew? Would he like to be circumcised? Agag thinks this may be an escape from death, but Samuel informs him that he will die anyway, though he could have the satisfaction of dying a Jew. After killing him, Samuel plans to make a burnt offering of him so that his flesh might nourish the servants. Saül appears to be the only character who is horrified by all of this. The indication of Saül's superior moral awareness, notwithstanding his mental health, has a parallel in Henchard: for example, we learn that Henchard had paid his employees better than Farfrae and that he had supported Abel Whittle's mother.

The first act ends with the approach of David's armies against Saül and the second begins with Michol's attempt to persuade David to spare her father's life. This is the reverse of the episode in 1 Samuel where Michal rescues David from Saul's attempts on his life (19.11-17), and indeed Elizabeth-Jane's attempt to persuade Farfrae that her father wishes him harm.[33] In typically gruesome Voltairian manner, David reminds Michol of the marriage present Saül demanded, remarking that 'Two hundred foreskins are not so easily found',[34] and reassuring his wife that he only wants to succeed Saül, not to kill him. In this drama it is Akis, the king of the Philistines, with whom David is in a son-type relationship (p. 583). David boasts of slaughtering Israel's enemies and telling Akis he has slaughtered Jews, but Michol interprets this as betrayal of Israel and believes David will also betray her, which he denies, promising unending fidelity. Immediately Abigail arrives on the scene, having already married David. Michol demands to know how many other wives he has, and he admits to 18, of which he declares, 'it's not too many for a nice guy'.[35] Michol finds this more satisfactory than having only one rival. David must now decide with whom to fight, since Saül is marching from one direction and Akis from the other. David decides that there is more to be gained from fighting with Akis. After his departure a messenger brings news that Jonathas had been condemned to die due to his breaking Saül's oath, but

32. See below, pp. 246-47.
33. See below, p. 214.
34. Voltaire, *Saül*, p. 582.
35. Voltaire, *Saül*, p. 585.

the army saved him and then began to eat and drink, causing Samuel to die of apoplexy.

Michol and Abigail join Saül and Baza, and Saül complains that Jonathas and David are rebels. Abigail fears Saül: she remarks on his rolling eyes and grinding teeth, and Michol explains calmly that he is sometimes possessed by the devil (p. 588). Similarly, Lucetta fears Henchard's wrath and his threats terrify her, while Elizabeth-Jane, despite finding Henchard's moods incomprehensible, accepts his anger and tries to please him. Saül then leers at Abigail and intends to take her for himself after the battle, so Michol and Abigail determine to hide from his madness. This has a parallel in Henchard's attempt to take Lucetta forcibly away from Farfrae, first by trying to prevent their marriage and then by attempting to destroy it when he reads Lucetta's love letters aloud in Farfrae's presence. Lucetta runs away from him and marries Farfrae in secret, and Elizabeth-Jane runs away from him to live with Lucetta as her companion.

Saül turns to Baza for advice: he wishes to know in advance the outcome of the battle. Baza asks whether he isn't a prophet like any other, but Saül complains that God doesn't reply to him any longer. He is certain that the pythonisse will be useful, however, since she has a spirit of a Python. He doesn't know what kind of spirit this is, but she is skilful and he will be able to consult the ghost of Samuel. A similar incomprehension of the mechanics of the occult, but a belief in it nevertheless, is exhibited in Henchard's visit to the weather prophet Fall.[36] Baza advises Saül not to waste his time with foolish women but to lead his troops in battle. When the pythonisse arrives she demands payment: money is an important theme in the drama, and this is reflected in *The Mayor* in Henchard's massive losses when he sells the grain he has bought because of his doubt in Fall's accuracy. The scene's comedic note continues as the pythonisse commands the sun to appear in broad daylight. An *ombre* appears[37], with a white beard identifying him as Samuel, and the woman tells Saül the vision is making terrible eyes at him. Saul knows he is lost, but the woman exits the scene pleased that she has the money of the foolish captain. She has not recognized him as Saül.

The third act begins with David discussing the death of Saül and Jonathas. Far from lamenting them, he is concerned with whether he is now legitimately king, and whether Saül has left riches. Likewise, Farfrae

---

36. See below, p. 249.

37. There is word-play here with the use of *ombre*, which means both 'shadow' and 'ghost'. Cf. Lamartine.

does not lament Henchard's death, and indeed while he and Elizabeth-Jane are searching for Henchard he is unwilling to invest the money required to carry out a thorough search.[38] Although it transpires that there is no money, David intends to rule the world. The action continues with 2 Samuel's Bathsheba material. David continues to be characterized as a villain: when Bethsabée tells him of her condition and Urie's refusal to sleep with her because of his loyalty to David, David comments, 'nothing is so odious as eager people, who always want to render service without being asked',[39] and he writes the letter commanding the death of Urie, which he sends by Urie's hand. Urie's farewell to his wife, 'always be as attached as I am to our master',[40] is ironic, but though one might expect tragic irony in these circumstances, the tone of the entire drama, together with the double entendre, colours the nuance of the remark, so that it becomes comedic, verging on farce.[41]

The fourth and fifth acts cover very briefly the rebellion of Absalon, Nathan's rebuke of David, the census of the people, the discussions over the succession, and David's death. Although the drama has been entitled *Saül*, the first king of Israel meets his end in the second act. The drama is not tragedy: the only elements of tragic vision are Saül's conflict with David and his death, which in the context are not treated as tragic, since Saul has every reason to be in conflict with David and since his death is not suicide. Neither is Henchard's death suicide, but it is nevertheless tragic. There is no sense of fate and no character flaw in Saül: David is without a doubt a perfidious enemy who explicitly states that he wishes to succeed Saül, and Saül's madness (rolling eyes, gnashing teeth) are brought on by demonic possession. In *The Mayor* Henchard attributes his own behaviour to 'visitations of the devil' (p. 382). Saül's desire to know the future is not the desperate act of a man pursuing his fate, since he neither requests nor receives meaning from the revelation. The python-isse's exiting words suggest she has invented the vision she has described. Thus the significance of this drama for Hardy is not the characterization of Saül as inept (though there are certain parallels, such as Henchard's

38. See below, p. 211.
39. Voltaire, *Saül*, p. 595.
40. Voltaire, *Saül*, p. 596.
41. In *The Life*, Hardy writes, 'If you look beneath the surface of any farce you see a tragedy; and, on the contrary, if you blind yourself to the deeper issues of a tragedy you see a farce' (p. 224).

dependence on and misplaced trust in Jopp) but rather the characterization of David as a womanizing, perfidious entrepreneur.

Saül indeed hardly appears in the work: he is in all four scenes in the first act and three of eight scenes in the second, but even his death is off-stage. It is David who shines through this drama as a ribald villain, and his characteristics are evident in the biblical material. His numerous wives and concubines, compared with a mention of one wife of Saül's (1 Sam. 14.50), taken together with the Bathsheba episode, depict him as a man who uses women to acquire power. The aspect of political gain can be seen in his marriage to Abigail (1 Sam. 25), by which he allies himself with the northern peoples in addition to his alliance with Saül's family. His pleasure in killing is demonstrated in his activities against the Geshurites, Girzites and Amalekites (1 Sam. 27), and his interest in accumulating material goods is illustrated in his repeated questioning concerning the reward for killing Goliath (1 Sam. 17) and in his running a protection racket while in exile (1 Sam. 25). Some of these characteristics may be found in Farfrae in *The Mayor of Casterbridge*, for example Farfrae's glee as he tells Lucetta of the profits he has made (p. 231) and the fickleness of his attentions to Elizabeth-Jane, whose attractions are quickly replaced in his heart by Lucetta's (p. 235). However, the fascination with violence is, in this case, peculiar to Voltaire.

Voltaire's drama is grimly comedic and grisly. If it may be termed tragic, it must be a tentative appraisal: David appears to have no redeeming quali-ties, and many of the complexities of the biblical narrative have been lost in Voltaire's portrayal of Saul's fate, not least in the manner of his death, which Voltaire has not dramatized, but which is not reported as suicide. Both Saul and David have been caricatured; David is obsessed by women, money and killing people, while Saul's ingenuousness has been accentuated to the point where he appears foolish and his madness manifests itself in a sexual advance on Abigail. The plot is a fast-moving series of scenes which serve to reinforce this characterization but which resist any notion of development. Perhaps this is too harsh; the first note on the text reads:

> I have not observed, in this kind of tragi-comedy, unity of action, place or time. I believed, with the illustrious Lamotte, I had to escape from these rules. Everything happens in the space of two or three generations, in order to render the action more tragic by the number of deaths according to the Jewish mind; whereas with us the unity of time can only stretch to twenty-four hours and the unity of place in the enclosure of a palace.[42]

---

42. Voltaire, *Saül*, p. 575 n. 1.

However, the fact remains that this has never been considered one of Voltaire's more exceptional works, as testified by the lack of critical interest.

Nevertheless, the effect of such an approach is to emphasize a comedic tone, and it is very funny: for example the report of Samuel's death of apoplexy. Importantly for Hardy, Voltaire's comedic framing of the material provides a forum in which the kinds of questions are raised which Hardy seemed to find absent in the clergy's arguments on the subject. The irony that Yhwh considers David to be a man after his own heart, in view of David's character, is crucial to Voltaire's portrayal of David, as may be inferred from the closing lines of the play, where the comment that David is the man after God's own heart follows David's instruction to kill Semeï, and his blessing on Solomon, with the petition that God give him a thousand women. Voltaire characteristically exaggerates the portrayal of David's interest in wealth and women; in 1 Samuel David's financial aspirations are less pressing but nevertheless apparent in the narrative. Similarly, Saül's remark that he would have been better off had he searched for a kingdom and found asses reveals Voltaire's recognition of the undeserved measure of Saul's suffering. Continuous with the idea of *The Mayor* as an intertext is the probability that Hardy has drawn on Voltaire's interpretation of the biblical material.

Character

We can see very clearly in the characterization of *The Mayor of Casterbridge* evidence of that endeavour of which Hardy writes in *The Life*,

> Art consists in so depicting the common events of life as to bring out the features which illustrate the author's idiosyncratic mode of regard; making old incidents and things seem as new.[43]

Since the relationship between Henchard and Farfrae is structured on the relationship between Saul and David, we might reasonably expect to find common aspects of characterization. Yet these aspects, and incidents of parallel plot, do indeed seem as new, since Henchard and Farfrae are not Saul and David. Just as Sophocles, Euripides and Aeschylus might remodel character and plot within the framework of narratives concerning pre-existing legends,[44] literary interpreters of 1 Samuel such as Voltaire,

---

43. *The Life*, p. 235.
44. For example, Vellacott writes in his introduction to Euripides' *Medea*, 'The

Gide, Alfieri and Lamartine remodel their characters within a limited scope in the sense that attempts to represent the biblical world persist, along with constraints of 1 Samuel's characterization. Hardy is doing something quite different in *The Mayor*, where neither the characterization nor the plot trajectory, nor for that matter the narrative world are subject to such constraints. Hence where we find parallels of characterization they are old things which have been made to seem as new, and of course part of the reason for this is that 1 Samuel is not the only source for *The Mayor*. Although the primary parallels between *The Mayor* and 1 Samuel are in the structure of Henchard's relationship with Farfrae, Hardy has adapted additional aspects of 1 Samuel's thematic material and incorporated it into his framework. Hardy has not composed a work based on the biblical narrative, but has taken core elements from the story and created a work of such complexity around them that an intertextual approach rather than a source-oriented approach is the necessary context for examination.

The two most straightforward parallels of character are in Henchard with Saul and Farfrae with David. Elizabeth-Jane takes on the role of Michal to some extent and the other characters are without direct parallel, though some aspects of the biblical characterization appear to be reflected in Hardy's. Susan has no direct parallel in 1 Samuel, and Jonathan has no direct parallel in *The Mayor*. Nevertheless, in their relationships with one another, all the primary characters in 1 Samuel may be shown to have connections with the biblical material.

Henchard

The priority that Hardy scholars have given to the significance of character is taken from the association of the novel's subtitle, 'A Story of a Man of Character', with the quote purported to be from Novalis, 'Character is Fate.'[45] While to a great extent this is discussed in connection with Henchard, Farfrae also is connected with both the title and the quotation, since Farfrae also becomes the mayor of Casterbridge and since the context of the quotation is the description of Farfrae's character as 'just

---

king of Athens and his friendly offer to Medea were part of the unalterable legend, and would be accepted as such by the Athenian audience; but the treatment of the episode in this play is not only curiously arbitrary and unrelated to the rest of the action, but more than a little satirical; and the figure of Aegeus provides the one flicker of relief in the otherwise uniform sombreness of the drama' (Euripides, *Medea and Other Plays* [trans. with an introduction by Philip Vellacott; London: Penguin Books, 1963], p. 8.).

45. *The Mayor*, p. 185.

the reverse of Henchard's'.[46] Jeanette King, who gives a literal translation of Novalis's words, curiously does not raise the problem of the source of Hardy's quotation,[47] but makes the very important point that

> Hardy highlights the disjunction between these two concepts of character—
> 'character' as individuality and 'character' in the sense of reputation—and
> their inevitable interaction; in the process I believe he also questions the very
> existence of 'character', of self, independent of these social constructs.[48]

It seems to me that highlighting this disjunction is a feature of the tragic vision rather than simply a technique of Hardy's. A similar process may be found in Sophocles' *Antigone*, for example, or in Miller's *Death of a Salesman*. The same disjunction is evident in the characterization of Saul in 1 Samuel, where Saul's reputation is crucial to his successes and failures with his subjects. The parallel episodes concerning the praise of women in *The Mayor* and in 1 Samuel demonstrate this point: Henchard learns that the women have a higher esteem for Farfrae than for him when a child tells him the women have said,

> '[Farfrae's] a diment—he's a chap o' wax—he's the best—he's the horse
> for my money… He's the most understanding man o' them two by long
> chalks. I wish he was the master instead of Henchard'.[49]

The parallel in 1 Samuel is the victory songs of the women after David's military successes (1 Sam. 18.7-9), that Saul has slain his thousands and David his ten thousands. The disjunction of individuality and reputation is evident from Saul's and Henchard's responses. In 1 Samuel it is Saul who imagines that the logical conclusion is the loss of his kingdom to David; in *The Mayor* the women themselves voice this usurping of authority explicitly, and Henchard murmurs it in echo of the child's words. Henchard is aware that his reputation has been harmed, and when he discovers that Elizabeth-Jane has served in the Three Mariners he believes that this is the cause (p. 203). However, the narrator attributes Henchard's decline in popularity over the previous two years thus,

46. *The Mayor*, p. 185.

47. Seymour-Smith comments in his note on the quotation that in all probability Hardy got it from George Eliot's *The Mill on the Floss* rather than from Novalis, and in Novalis's context it does not mean what we normally understand by it (*The Mayor*, p. 428 n. 188).

48. Jeanette King, ' "The Mayor of Casterbridge": Talking about Character', *The Thomas Hardy Journal* 8:3 (1992), pp. 42-46 (42).

49. *The Mayor*, p. 171.

His friends of the Corporation... had voted him to the chief magistracy on account of his amazing energy. While they had collectively profited by this quality of the corn-factor's they had been made to wince individually on more than one occasion.[50]

Similarly, Saul's reputation is crucial in relation to his character. At the public announcement of his kingship there are a few men who oppose him, but he takes no action against them (1 Sam. 10.27). After his first military success his supporters intend to put to death those who had opposed him but he refuses to allow it (1 Sam. 11.12-13). However, in 1 Samuel 13 he is deserted by much of his army and rejected by the deity, and after this point his reputation is fundamentally important. When Jonathan breaks Saul's oath that the army should not eat, Jonathan's error is pointed out by one of the soldiers, but Jonathan criticizes the making of such an oath. Therefore when Saul receives no answer to his enquiry of God and asks how this sin has arisen not one person will answer him, though they all know that it was Jonathan who broke the oath. Saul determines that his son must die but the people will not permit it. Then in 1 Samuel. 15, after Samuel tells Saul that Yhwh has torn the kingdom from him for his error, Saul asks Samuel to return with him and honour him before the elders and before Israel (1 Sam. 15.30). Saul's reputation is here dependent on Samuel's authenticating his position, and Saul appears to fear that if he loses Samuel's support he will no longer be regarded as worthy of honour, and in Jonathan's criticism he has experienced the decline in authority that a blow to the reputation entails.

The role of rumour, scandal and gossip in *The Mayor*, which King emphasizes, is also a feature of 1 Samuel in episodes such as Michal's reported interest in David and the role of Saul's messengers in the process of setting David up as the king's son-in-law. The scandal of Merab's being given to another man and David's remarks on social status all contribute to a similar notion of character as a social construct, which King terms 'a surprisingly modern conception'.[51] Her assertion of doubt thrown in *The Mayor* on the existence of an inner self points to the similarity between characterization in this novel and in biblical narrative style in which there is rarely any narratorial information on a protagonist's feelings. An example of the same kind of process by which it is left to a reader to infer emotion and its meaning may be found in Elizabeth-Jane's departure from

50. *The Mayor*, p. 184.
51. King, 'Character', p. 46.

Henchard's house to be a companion, and Henchard's request that she remain, which she declines. This is how Henchard learns that she is to live with the woman with whom he has been incautiously intimate, whom he rejected for Elizabeth-Jane's mother, and who has come to Casterbridge with the intention of marrying him:

> He nodded ever so slightly, as a receipt of her decision and no more. 'You are not going far, you say. What will be your address, in case I wish to write to you? Or am I not to know?'
> 'Oh yes—certainly. It is in the town—High-Place Hall'.
> 'Where?' said Henchard, his face stilling.
> She repeated the words. He neither moved nor spoke, and waving her hand to him in utmost friendliness she signified to the flyman to drive up the street.[52]

On occasion the narrator describes in more detail Henchard's motivations and designs, but often any inner self he may have can only be inferred from outward interaction.[53] Thus the self is a social construct.

Certainly the interaction between the self and society in *The Mayor* has elicited much comment, largely because it is within this construct that the tragic vision is expressed. R.P. Draper points to the distinction between the divinely predetermined tragedy of Sophocles' Oedipus and Henchard's tragedy as the product of his character. While this distinction highlights many contrasts between 1 Samuel and *The Mayor*, it also accents the correspondences of character between Saul and Henchard, since both protagonists are caught in the balance on the one hand of character and on the other hand of forces that are beyond their control. Draper discusses the manner in which the 'life of the individual is set against the life of the whole community', a perspective that is crucial to the story of Saul, who is both responsible for his people and dependent on them.[54] At the renewal of the kingdom in Gilgal, Samuel tells the assembled people that if they and their king fear and serve Yhwh all will be well (1 Sam. 12.14) but if they do wickedly they will be swept away together with their king (1 Sam. 12.25). Such an understanding of character is one that engenders incongruity: Draper remarks that Hardy 'is prepared to allow contradictions to lie

---

52. *The Mayor*, p. 217.

53. Crucially, the narrator's report is sometimes contradictory, as when Henchard wonders whether someone might be 'roasting a waxen image' but claims not to believe in such powers, when this not only it implies that he does, but also the narrator persistently describes him as a superstitious man.

54. For discussion of social and sociological concerns, see below, pp. 223-35.

side by side; he feels no compulsion to integrate them into a unified imaginative world'.[55] Draper is writing about the inconsistency of comments in *The Mayor* on the effect of history on the town's inhabitants. This is strikingly reminiscent of the inconsistencies of the narrative of 1 Samuel; inconsistencies which have been labelled by many biblical scholars as source conflations. Draper contends that these inconsistencies 'point to ambivalence rather than ambiguity' and this is precisely why the inconsistencies are so reminiscent of 1 Samuel.

The question of ambivalence is also raised by Robert Schweik, who remarks,

> The fact is that *The Mayor of Casterbridge* is capable of supporting a variety of... conflicting assessments both of Henchard's character and of the world he inhabits, and further discussion of the novel must proceed, I think, by giving this fact more serious attention.[56]

Precisely the same sentiment might be applicable to 1 Samuel, where inconsistencies of narrative are attributed by many scholars to processes of redaction and motivations of redactors, as if the text of 1 Samuel as it stands were incapable of supporting such conflicting assessments. One of these is of course character, and Schweik notes the emphasis on Henchard's good qualities: he is not the 'thoroughly bad man' depicted by Martin Seymour-Smith. The

> disjunction between Henchard's moral stature and the circumstance which has blindly nullified his repentance[57]

is crucial to the intertextual relationship between *The Mayor* and 1 Samuel since precisely the same disjunction occurs between Saul's moral decision to sacrifice to Yhwh (both in ch. 13 and in ch. 15) and the divine forces that inexplicably nullify his repentance (ch. 15, 24 and 26). This disjunction and that with which the novel closes are elements of the tragic vision strongly emphasized in both *The Mayor* and 1 Samuel: 'the distinction between what men deserve and what men receive'[58] is central to the final meaning of both Henchard's tragedy and Saul's.

---

55. R.P. Draper, 'The Mayor of Casterbridge', *Critical Quarterly* 25:1 (1983), pp. 57-70 (69).

56. Robert C. Schweik, 'Character and Fate in *The Mayor of Casterbridge*', in R.P. Draper (ed.), *Hardy: The Tragic Novels* (London: Macmillan, 1975), pp. 133-47 (133).

57. Schweik, 'Character and Fate', p. 144.

58. Schweik, 'Character and Fate', p. 145.

If inconsistencies of narrative and character are associated with the tragic vision, so are inconsistencies of the reader's response. Seymour-Smith comments on Hardy's transformation of Henchard,

> who is by any reasonable standards a thoroughly bad man, into a tragic hero. Simultaneously for the majority of readers he somehow justly robs Farfrae of his apparent virtue.[59]

Interpreting the tragic vision seems inevitably to return to the 'somehow'. 'Somehow' the man is not thoroughly bad, and his elusive good qualities are 'somehow' more appealing than the more abundant good qualities of those with whom he is in collision. It is the 'somehow' robbing Farfrae of his virtue which points overwhelmingly to an intertextual relationship with 1 Samuel. Tragic collision does not inevitably transform character thus; in fact very frequently the tragic lies in both parties in the collision retaining their full complement of virtue. Creon is as virtuous as Antigone in his ethical judgments, and they are both right. This is not to say that 1 Samuel is the only possible connection, but rather to assert that 1 Samuel is a very important connection, since this is precisely what happens to David: he is robbed of his apparent virtue. When Seymour-Smith raises the question of 'somehow' he eventually concludes that

> The more we *think* about [Henchard], the more repelled we may fairly be. Yet the more we *feel* about him, the more we can sympathize with his anguish. That anguish, and his attitude to his fate, is something deeper that anything Farfrae could ever feel.[60]

Woolf makes a similar point when she writes that 'the true tragic emotion is ours'.[61] Seymour-Smith associates Henchard's depth of character with self-destructiveness and Schopenhauer's influence in crystallizing Hardy's thought, specifically the influence on Schopenhauer of the idea of nirvana, which is the

> dissolution and extinction of the individual will in order to bring peace and release from the eternal cycle of human suffering.[62]

This chimes with Henchard's final action, and inevitably with Saul's suicide as well. Self-destructiveness characterizes Saul: his actions against

---

59. Seymour-Smith, *Hardy*, p. 325.

60. Seymour-Smith, *Hardy*, p. 334.

61. Virginia Woolf, 'The Novels of Thomas Hardy', in Draper (ed.), *Hardy: The Tragic Novels*, pp. 73-79 (78).

62. Seymour-Smith, *Hardy*, p. 331.

David bring isolation from Jonathan and Michal and drive him to further excesses, to the point of threatening Jonathan's life and the absurd excess of leading three thousand men against the exiled former object of his love. Saul's suicide is the culmination of a long process of self-destructiveness.

The parallels between Henchard in *The Mayor* and Saul in 1 Samuel may be classified by three categories: general parallels, parallels of self-destructiveness, and parallels of destruction by external forces, which are more concerned with fate than with character. Moynahan has pointed to several parallels, but there are problems with many of them which he has not addressed. For the parallels to be allowed to stand, these problems must be accounted for. The first parallel that Moynahan mentions is that between the context of Henchard and Farfrae's rivalry in *The Mayor* and Saul and David's rivalry in 1 Samuel. Moynahan writes,

> In *The Mayor of Casterbridge* the hazards of grain speculation seem roughly to correspond with the constant threat of Philistine invasion which haunts the reign of King Saul. When Farfrae arrives in Casterbridge, Henchard is at the height of his power as leading merchant and civil magistrate. But for the moment he is seriously embarrassed from having been forced to sell spoiled corn to the townspeople. Farfrae, appearing from out of the blue, saves Henchard from embarrassment and financial loss by showing him a method for restoring the corn.[63]

Moynahan does not make explicit exactly where the parallel lies, but it is in 1 Samuel 17 in the Goliath episode. However, the parallel goes much further than this. Saul sends David out against the Philistines in the hope of having him killed (1 Sam. 18.25); Henchard's price war with Farfrae is described as 'mortal commercial combat' (p. 186) and when Henchard hires Jopp in Chapter 26 his instructions are to ensure that Farfrae is cut out. Moreover, Moynahan's argument is misleading because of the erroneous statement that 'Henchard does not actually dismiss Farfrae from his employment'.[64] He dismisses him in Chapter 16.

Although Moynahan notes the similarity between the physical description of Farfrae and that of David, he makes no mention of a similar parallel between Henchard and Saul. As Henchard remarks on a physical similarity between his dead brother and Farfrae he says, 'You must be, what—five foot nine, I reckon? I am six foot one and a half out of my shoes' (p. 117). This remark is striking because it has no referent in the novel. Henchard makes no further comparison with his brother here, only

63. Moynahan, 'Relationships', pp. 119-20.
64. Moynahan, 'Relationships', p. 122.

with himself, and immediately goes on to talk about business. The remark finds its referent in 1 Sam. 9.2: 'from his shoulders upward [Saul] was taller than any of the people' (RSV). Henchard is tall, about a head taller than Farfrae, and David, while handsome, is not described as being especially tall—in fact the depiction of him as a youth unable to bear Saul's armour (1 Sam. 17) suggests the reverse. Other general parallels are missed by Moynahan. Elizabeth-Jane's eventual marriage to Farfrae and Michal's eventual marriage to David is a case in point. In *The Mayor* Henchard interferes in the process by which Farfrae might become his son-in-law (in name at least) by forbidding the courtship of Elizabeth-Jane, and then later allowing it. In 1 Samuel Saul interferes in the process by which David might become his son-in-law by giving his elder daughter to another man and then later allowing David to marry Michal.

The question of inheritance is another parallel neglected by Moynahan, which is curious considering his emphasis on the conflict between generations. Henchard's heir should be Elizabeth-Jane, but this is problematic. He expresses the sense of possession of an heir when he complains that he shouldn't have let Susan take the child:

> She'd no business to take the maid—'tis my maid; and if it were the doing again she shouldn't have her![65]

Naming is another function of this sense of having an heir, since naming indicates possession. Henchard is keen that the girl should take his surname after his reunion with Susan, and when he later tells Elizabeth-Jane she is actually his own daughter he impresses on her the information that he named her and repeats the request that she take his surname. Yet his relationship with her becomes as marred by his response to circumstance as is Saul's relationship with Jonathan. In 1 Samuel 14, Saul clashes with Jonathan over the oath that none of the soldiers should eat, which leads to Saul's pronouncing Jonathan's guilt and attempting to levy the death penalty. Later, in 1 Samuel 20 Saul throws his spear at Jonathan, enraged that he has jeopardized his own succession by his friendship with David. Although Henchard never makes any attempt on Elizabeth-Jane's life (again, the narratives operate in different worlds), his response when he discovers her true paternity is to reject her. She is not his legitimate heir and he is bitterly disappointed. His chiding of her use of dialect and his criticism of her handwriting as inappropriate to his heir recalls Saul's fury at Jonathan's behaviour which Saul feels is inappropriate to his heir

65. *The Mayor,* p. 80.

(1 Sam. 20). It is interesting to note that these reactions of Henchard and Saul appear to involve an issue of gender propriety: Elizabeth-Jane's handwriting is not feminine (p. 201) and Jonathan's affection for David is not masculine (1 Sam. 20.30-31). Like Saul, Henchard dies with no suitable heir and his line becomes extinguished.

The parallels that relate to self-destructiveness are the closest parallels between *The Mayor* and 1 Samuel. Both Henchard and Saul display hubris with reference to their respective declarations of war on their rivals, and this hubris is self-destructive since its consequence is reversal. Saul and his three thousand soldiers stalk David but cannot hope to succeed because Yhwh has rejected him from being king and Yhwh is now with David. In the framework of the narrative Saul cannot prevail against Yhwh. Saul's assaults against David are self-destructive, resulting in betrayal by his son and daughter and by the priests at Nob, and in David's accumulation of power while in exile, when he secures the alliance of the discontented in the cave of Adullam (1 Sam. 22), and that of Abigail. David's alliance with Abiathar, the one priest who escapes Saul's attack on Nob, leaves Saul without access to the ephod. Similarly, with Jopp's help Henchard intends to cut Farfrae out of the corn market, but it is the weather which is outside his control. Henchard's attempts to banish Farfrae are unwisely enacted, and it is Henchard who makes a great loss, which will shortly result in bankruptcy. As with Saul's struggle against David, uncontrollable forces do not act in isolation, but rather it is a rash decision which leads to self-destruction. Saul furiously orders the priests of Nob to be slaughtered, cutting himself off from the ephod; Henchard is uncertain of Fall's advice and makes poor business decisions, ruining his economic advantage. Just as David will succeed to Saul's throne, Farfrae will take over Henchard's corn enterprise and mayor's chair. But, like Saul, Henchard is not abandoned completely after his fall. Saul retains followers and remains king; Henchard is set up in a small seed and root business by some of the Town Council. In both cases the effect is to postpone the final outcome, which then takes on a heightened tragic aspect. Both Saul and Henchard struggle against their fates, but every moment of relief precedes a greater reversal.

Self destructiveness is evident for both Saul and Henchard in lack of self esteem and isolation. Saul is described as being little in his own eyes (1 Sam. 15.17) and similarly Henchard arrives at the point where he values himself or his good name so little that he will not speak in his own defence. In Chapter 43 the narrator suggests that Henchard might not have made any extenuation for his deceit in telling Newson that Elizabeth-Jane was dead, and in Chapter 44 he is about to plead his case at Elizabeth-

Jane's wedding but stops himself because he does not value himself. This lack of self-value is connected to isolation. Saul's isolation from those closest to him is the same kind of isolation felt by Henchard after he lies to Newson about Elizabeth-Jane's death:

> There would remain nobody for him to be proud of, nobody to fortify him; for Elizabeth-Jane would soon be a stranger, and worse. Susan, Farfrae, Lucetta, Elizabeth—all had gone from him, one after one, either by his fault or by his misfortune.[66]

Both by fault and misfortune Henchard, like Saul, attempts to destroy those he once cared for. His repeated threats to Lucetta, culminating in his reading of her letters to Farfrae, and his rejection of Elizabeth-Jane on finding she is not his daughter correlate to Saul's attempt on Jonathan's life and his treatment of Michal, who allows David to escape and who is given in marriage to Palti. The sense of misfortune is particularly apparent in the loss of David and Farfrae since, despite the element of fault, circumstance too plays a role. Saul casts his spear at David under the influence of the evil divine spirit, while Henchard dismisses Farfrae after poor weather has thrust them into competition at the entertainment. The central misfortune for both Saul and Henchard is that they are not suited to their positions, whereas both David and Farfrae are. It is perhaps because of his loss of Farfrae that Henchard wishes for music at the thought of his isolation, and sacred music at that:

> If he could have summoned music to his aid his existence might have been borne; for with Henchard music was of regal power. The merest trumpet or organ tone was enough to move him, and high harmonies transubstantiated him. But hard fate had ordained that he should be unable to call up this Divine Spirit in his need.[67]

The idea of 'regal power' points to David and recalls Henchard's singing of Psalm 109 in the Three Mariners. Like Saul, Henchard finds in music a cure for his ills, but has no influence with any 'divine spirit'. Thus Henchard's existence cannot be borne because, like Saul's actions against David, Henchard's actions against Farfrae lead to isolation from those who must choose between the two men.

Farfrae
The Novalis quotation about character and fate has been discussed with reference to Henchard, but its application to Farfrae is rarely considered,

---

66. *The Mayor*, p. 371.
67. *The Mayor*, p. 371.

yet the context is precisely the contrasting of Henchard's character with that of Farfrae. As the narrator expresses it, 'Farfrae's character was just the reverse of Henchard's'.[68] In context, the quotation comments on Farfrae's business success, likened to Jacob's herd-breeding success at Padan-Aram. In the notes to his critical edition of *The Mayor*, Seymour-Smith remarks upon this comparison,

> It is significant that Jacob, cheater of Esau, used sorcery as well as superior breeding techniques to achieve this result—though the Lord remained with him when he fled from Laban, who was also a cheat. In the time of Hardy's keen interest in the scriptures Jacob was not regarded by theologians as noble: he was seen as passive and acquiescent (cf. Farfrae). But his fear of the Lord and trust in Providence (cf. Farfrae again) were seen as his saving qualities.[69]

Seymour-Smith elaborates on the sense in which Farfrae's character is the reverse of Henchard's: 'it is the latter's archetypal weight that he lacks... He has principles, he has charm, but nothing in him is deep... Farfrae does not possess the capacity to alienate himself from himself'.[70] It is by reason of Farfrae's lack of depth that his losses have no tragic dimension. He is always able to transform setbacks into opportunities to improve his position. When he is dismissed by Henchard he sets up his own business, and when Henchard wrestles with him in the corn stores he is able to turn the situation to his advantage, conquering Henchard verbally. Even the miscarriage and death of his wife are not as personally disastrous as they might have been, owing to her guilt, and he takes the opportunity to marry a woman more morally suitable, as Dike comments,

> Donald Farfrae is not aware when he marries her that Lucetta is damaged goods; informed of the fact, he reconciles himself to her death and casts about for a more acceptable substitute,[71]

that is Elizabeth-Jane. David's character is similarly shallow in comparison to Saul's,[72] and he has exactly the same quality of adaptability: he spends his time in exile building up a power base, when Nabal refuses to

---

68. *The Mayor*, p. 185.
69. *The Mayor*, p. 428 n. 187.
70. Seymour-Smith, *Hardy*, p. 335.
71. Dike, 'Modern Oedipus', p. 176.
72. This shallow quality is in evidence within the parameters of the Saul narrative; however, a more complex characterization of David emerges outwith these parameters, e.g. in 2 Sam. 18.

give in to his protection racket he prepares for battle and comes away with Nabal's rich widow, and when Saul pursues him he is able to persuade Saul verbally to desist. He allies himself with the Philistines, Israel's enemies, and takes the opportunity to massacre other enemies of Israel, thus building on his power. Soggin describes David as 'a most able and somewhat unscrupulous politician' who 'appears to the redactor as a person who is capable of overcoming the many negative elements in his personality'.[73] This description would be quite apt for Farfrae, whose unscrupulous quality is remarked upon by Seymour-Smith in the introduction to his critical edition of *The Mayor*.

Moynahan compares Henchard's personal qualities with those of Saul, but makes no such comparison between Farfrae and David, except to point out their corresponding musical abilities. In this his work is insightful and thorough. He remarks upon the function of Farfrae's singing in relation to his popularity and its effect on Henchard: when Farfrae approaches the corn stores where Henchard intends to wrestle with him, humming Auld Lang Syne, Henchard is momentarily transported, but like David's music, the effect is only temporary and Henchard, like Saul, continues in his attempt to injure the younger man. Moynahan also details the series of ironies in the scene in which Henchard forces the church choir to sing the verses from Psalm 109, culminating in Henchard's declaration that David knew what he was about when he wrote it. As Moynahan observes, 'It is Henchard's tragedy that he does not know, either in this scene or in the novel as a whole, what he is about'.

This emphasis on music is as far as Moynahan goes in linking the characterization of Farfrae and David, which is curious since there are many other correlations. Besides Farfrae's and David's ability to overcome both fate and flaw, there is the issue of wealth. Dike draws attention to the importance of money in the novel, and Farfrae's interest in money is crucial to the comparison with David: Farfrae accepts the job the third time Henchard offers it to him, when Henchard invites him to name his own terms; David determines to fight Goliath when he has been told three times of the king's reward to the Israelite who kills the enemy. When Farfrae hints that he might ask Elizabeth-Jane to marry him, he frames his remarks in a wish that he were richer; David comments on his inferior economic status when Saul's servants suggest he might marry Michal. There is not a parallel for each and every aspect of this theme, but the

---

73. J. Alberto Soggin, *Introduction to the Old Testament* (trans. John Bowden; London: SCM Press, 2nd edn, 1980), p. 195.

motif is consistent: Farfrae becomes inappropriately excited when telling Lucetta at their first encounter of his manner of making profit. When she suggests he hire a youth and his father, in order to keep the young man and his lover together, Farfrae grudgingly remarks of the old man (in his Scottish accent), 'he'll not be very expensive, and doubtless he will answer to my pairrpose somehow').[74] Having forgotten Elizabeth-Jane, Farfrae marries the richer Lucetta, although Elizabeth-Jane is the more physically attractive of the two women (p. 205). In fact, his reason for intending to call on Elizabeth-Jane on this occasion is the notion that he could marry if he chooses, owing to 'an exceptionally fortunate business transaction' which 'put him on good terms with everybody', and he concludes 'who so pleasing, thrifty, and satisfactory in every way as Elizabeth-Jane?'[75] However, his encounter with the wealthy Lucetta and its result points to his fickle and acquisitive nature. (David's marriage to the wealthy widow Abigail gives him a similar advantage.) When he takes over Henchard's business after the latter's bankruptcy, Whittle tells Elizabeth-Jane he pays the workers less than Henchard had.[76] He won't go so far while searching for Henchard as would necessitate overnight accommodation because 'that will make a hole in the sovereign'.[77] Elizabeth-Jane, though generally careful with money, perceives this attribute of her new husband's, and as Seymour-Smith remarks,

> in keeping with the spirit of Henchard's final self denial, will not allow her husband to gain *credit* (the word is used advisedly) for a large-heartedness that he does not possess. The hint of Farfrae's lack is faint, but, in the context, unmistakable.[78]

Draper points to Farfrae's implicit 'emotional superficiality' which is

> given sardonic treatment when he is represented at his second wedding as singing 'a song of his dear native country that he loved so well as never to have revisited it',[79]

---

74. *The Mayor*, p. 233.

75. *The Mayor*, p. 230.

76. There is another implicit contrast between Farfrae and Henchard with what Whittle later tells Elizabeth-Jane and Farfrae: 'He was kind-like to mother when she wer here below, sending her the best ship-coal, and hardly any ashes from it at all; and taties, and such-like that were very needful to her' (p. 408).

77. *The Mayor*, p. 407.

78. Seymour-Smith, *Hardy*, p. 329.

79. Draper, 'Mayor', p. 59.

and it is this same quality which causes him to forget after his first encounter with Lucetta that he had called to see Elizabeth-Jane. Because of this emotional superficiality, 'Henchard's hell is beyond Farfrae's scope', as Seymour-Smith expresses it.[80] David similarly cannot appreciate Saul's torment. At his encounter with Saul in the hill of Hachilah in 1 Samuel 26 he suggests that if it is Yhwh who has stirred Saul up against him then Saul should make an offering, which David hopes Yhwh will accept. David does not appear to understand the impossible position Saul is in with respect to Yhwh, and of course it is Saul's sacrificing which has incurred Yhwh's rejection in the first place. It is therefore evident that Farfrae is not only characterized as Henchard's rival but also on the model of David's characterization in 1 Samuel. The manner in which Farfrae is characterized on the model of David brings us again to the probability that Hardy drew on Voltaire's interpretation of the biblical material.

Elizabeth-Jane
Moynahan has brought only the two central characters into his argument, since he claims that the parallels are only to be found in the personal and professional rivalry between the two men. However, one might expect that relationships of other characters to the two primary protagonists would be worthy of investigation. There are clear parallels between Elizabeth-Jane and Michal. The significance of Michal's love for David, as it is 'the only instance in all biblical narrative in which we are explicitly told that a woman loves a man',[81] is carried into *The Mayor*. As soon as Farfrae's appearance has been described and he has written the note to Henchard, Elizabeth-Jane's reaction is related:

> Elizabeth-Jane had seen his movements and heard the words, which attracted her both by their subject and by their accent—a strange one for those parts. It was quaint and northerly.[82]

When it comes to be time for Elizabeth-Jane and her mother to find lodging, she suggests going to the same hotel as Farfrae, and when it appears to be too expensive for them she offers to help serve and takes Farfrae's supper to him, and her sexual attraction to him is described in terms which suggest a desire to touch him,

---

80. Seymour-Smith, *Hardy*, p. 333.
81. Alter, *Biblical Narrative*, p. 118. The expression of the love of a woman for a man also occurs in Song of Songs, but of course this is poetry rather than narrative.
82. *The Mayor*, p. 106.

He was now idly reading a copy of the local paper, and was hardly conscious of her entry, so that she looked at him quite coolly, and saw how his forehead shone where the light caught it, and how nicely his hair was cut, and the sort of velvet-pile or down that was on the skin at the back of his neck, and how his cheek was so truly curved as to be part of a globe, and how clearly drawn were the lids and lashes which hid his bent eyes.[83]

Farfrae does not notice her; neither when she takes him his supper, nor when she removes his tray, nor when she goes downstairs to serve. After his singing, she admires what she perceives as his serious attitude to serious things. She believes he is 'refined in his mind' (p. 125). Farfrae eventually notices her and seems to find her appearance 'interesting in some way' (p. 124), and the suggestion is that it is her sober aspect which is interesting, as she comes out of his room from having turned down his bed and they meet on the staircase. Elizabeth-Jane, who has been watching him all the time, feels awkward and keeps her gaze on the candle flame, but notices him smile. However, when Farfrae departs, intending to leave Casterbridge, he glances at her and then glances away without smiling or nodding, and then, when she goes to Henchard's place of business and finds him there, he merely says to her, 'Yes, what is it?' (p. 132).

Throughout the novel Elizabeth-Jane's attraction to Farfrae appears to be stronger than his interest in her, and she is reported to view her interest as 'one-sided, unmaidenly and unwise'.[84] Eventually Elizabeth-Jane marries Farfrae, just as eventually Michal marries David, despite the obstacles. Like Michal, her father places obstacles in the way of her wished-for marriage to her father's rival. Saul's demand of a bride price of one hundred Philistine foreskins has no direct parallel in the different world of *The Mayor*, but the obstacles that Henchard places in the way of the courtship certainly give the impression of finality. After his failure in the face of Farfrae's entertainment, Henchard elicits from Elizabeth-Jane the information that she has made no promise to Farfrae, and then writes to his rival asking him to discontinue the courtship. The narrator comments,

One would almost have supposed Henchard to have had policy to see that no better *modus vivendi* could be arrived at with Farfrae than by encouraging him to become his son-in-law.[85]

83. *The Mayor*, p. 113.
84. *The Mayor*, p. 204.
85. *The Mayor*, p. 185.

However, Henchard is characterized in such a way as to throw doubt on this assertion. One would almost suppose that even marriage to Henchard's step-daughter would not overcome the difficulties of Henchard's jealous nature in his attitude towards Farfrae, as indeed in Saul's case where his plan to have David killed in the mission to acquire the bride price fails and he resorts to a further attempt on David's life from which Michal has to save David. The parallel with Michal's choice of David over her father and her relating to him Saul's intention to kill him is found in *The Mayor* in Chapters 33 and 34. Elizabeth-Jane has heard her father threaten Farfrae in moments of drunkenness, and is so concerned that she goes to work with him to wimble for him, now that Henchard is in Farfrae's employ. While she is there she sees Henchard in the corn stores raise his arm towards Farfrae's back, as if the thought occurred to him to push Farfrae over the parapet. Elizabeth-Jane gets up very early in the morning and warns Farfrae that Henchard might make some attempt to injure him. The world of *The Mayor* is not the world of 1 Samuel and Farfrae has no need to escape from Henchard's anger, but when Elizabeth-Jane's fears are confirmed by the town-clerk, Farfrae abandons a scheme he had been planning to benefit Henchard, and Henchard hears of it, and his enmity towards Farfrae increases. Thus in *The Mayor*, as in 1 Samuel, the daughter is caught between the two rivals and forced to choose between them. Her choice increases the enmity between the rivals and leads eventually to isolation from her father: Elizabeth-Jane marries Farfrae and rejects Henchard, and Michal is given to another man during David's exile.

Use of language is an important signal of analogous characterization, and Hardy's use of naming points to such an analogy. He makes use of the biblical technique of referring to the relationship between two characters in such a way as to point to the tension between, for example, Michal as 'the daughter of Saul' and Michal as 'the wife of David'. This technique highlights the character's feelings concerning the position in which he or she is placed in relation to another, and in the case of Michal accents the conflict between her relationship to Saul and her relationship to David. Thus, when Elizabeth-Jane encounters Henchard in front of the seed drill, 'She looked up, and there was her stepfather',[86] but when he appears at her wedding, 'Oh—it is—Mr Henchard!'[87] Similarly, a little later, 'Mrs Donald Farfrae had discovered in a screened corner a new bird cage.'[88] The contexts of

86. *The Mayor*, p. 239.
87. *The Mayor*, p. 402.
88. *The Mayor*, p. 405.

these three examples are respectively the conflicting views of Henchard and Farfrae on the technological advances in agriculture, the struggle between the two men for Elizabeth-Jane's affection, and Henchard's isolation once Farfrae has succeeded in this struggle.

There are also some remote parallels between Elizabeth-Jane and Jonathan, which are concerned with inheritance. Just as Jonathan should succeed Saul but is prevented by circumstances, Elizabeth-Jane should be Henchard's heir, but is prevented by circumstances. The problem in both cases is a succession outside the model of paternity. Jonathan obviates his succession by recognizing in David the one who should succeed, and Elizabeth-Jane is not Henchard's daughter. Lawton's article, 'Saul, Jonathan and the "Son of Jesse" ', points to Saul's recognition of David as his rightful heir, and similarly in the corn trade Farfrae should be Henchard's heir. The problem is accentuated by Henchard's criticism of Elizabeth-Jane's behaviour which is inappropriate to Henchard's daughter: her use of 'dialect' terms, her 'unfeminine' handwriting, and her having served in the Three Mariners, on which Henchard blames his decreasing popularity. Similarly, Saul criticizes Jonathan's behaviour as inappropriate to Saul's son: his affection for David and his revoking of his right to the throne.

Lucetta

If there is a Jonathan figure then Lucetta as well as Elizabeth-Jane is a candidate. Lucetta 'belongs' to Henchard, although there has been conflict between them centring around Henchard's treatment of her. He has wronged her in terms of the moral stance of the narrative world just as Saul wrongs Jonathan in terms of the moral stance of the narrative world in 1 Samuel 14. Henchard competes with Farfrae for her love just as Saul competes with David for Jonathan's loyalty. For both Lucetta and Jonathan a meeting with the younger man leads to an abdication of responsibility and a change of loyalty. After Lucetta's first meeting with Farfrae she reconsiders her debt to society and the consequent requirement of marrying Henchard. After Jonathan first meets David he performs a symbolic act by which he abdicates his status in his narrative world as next king of Israel, and consequently compromises his loyalty to Saul.

An important role of Lucetta's character within the network of relationships between 1 Samuel and *The Mayor* is centred around her sex, thus making her part of a theme which contrasts Henchard's attitude to women with that of Farfrae. Though the similarities between the two texts are significant, it is also intriguing to find occasions where Hardy has used an episode as a pattern but made significant changes. For example, the introduction of a woman for whose attentions Henchard and Farfrae both compete is a significant alteration to the dramatic structure in comparison with 1 Samuel. It might be argued that this personalizes the competition for the regard of womankind apparent in both texts. For this reading of *The Mayor* it serves to emphasize aspects of sexuality that are present in the biblical narrative, such as Saul's understated virility[89] and David's fascination with glamour. Thus Lucetta also functions as an Abigail figure in her relationship with Farfrae. She is the second woman in the novel to whom Farfrae becomes attracted, the first having been Elizabeth-Jane. In his attraction to her, Farfrae forgets his previous interest in Elizabeth-Jane, and Elizabeth-Jane loses him to Lucetta. When Abigail marries David, Michal loses him: in 1 Sam. 25.42-44 it is reported that David has married Abigail and then that Michal has been given to Palti. We see in this episode another parallel with Voltaire's drama: Abigail's pride in being David's wife is reflected in Lucetta's pride in being Farfrae's wife: for example, she relishes her prominent social position when Farfrae greets the royal personage. Michol's willingness to share David with Abigail finds its counterpart in Elizabeth-Jane's ultimate passive acceptance of Farfrae's rejection of her for Lucetta. Elizabeth-Jane is jealous but quiescent, a characterization that bears no resemblance to Michal, even in 2 Samuel. But what of Henchard's interest in Lucetta? There is no parallel in 1 Samuel. However, if Hardy read Voltaire's drama he may have picked up from it the idea of Saul's sexual attraction towards Abigail and his intention to take her from David, together with the initial rivalry between Michol and Abigail for David's affection. The oppressive character of Henchard's sexuality is influenced by Voltaire's *Saül* rather than by 1 Samuel: Henchard's threatening behaviour towards Lucetta expands Saül's leering at Abigail in Voltaire's drama. Lucetta and Abigail are primarily drawn as objects of sexual attraction for the central male characters. Certainly the relationships between Saül, Abigail, David and Michol in elements of Voltaire's work connect strongly with the relationships between Henchard, Lucetta, Farfrae and Elizabeth-Jane.

89. That Hardy perceived Saul's sexual appeal may be inferred from the emotions Eustacia Vye expresses in *The Return of the Native*: she plans to leave Clym for Wildeve, but feels 'He's not *great* enough for me to give myself to—he does not suffice for my desire!... If he had been a Saul or a Bonaparte—ah! But to break my marriage vow for him—it is too poor a luxury!' (Book Fifth, Chapter 7).

Susan

While Susan has no direct parallel in 1 Samuel, her role in emphasizing the distinction between Henchard and Farfrae's sexual impulses reflects the distinction between Saul's and David's sexual impulses. Saul's wife is mentioned once, briefly, in 1 Sam. 14.50 and never again, while David has four possibilities of marriage in 1 Samuel, the first of which, Merab, is denied him, though he goes on to marry Michal, and he takes Abigail as his wife in 1 Samuel 25 and also Ahinoam of Jezreel. He acquires numerous wives and concubines in 2 Samuel, though he is never reported as loving a single one of them. One might form the impression that David acquires women out of a desire to increase or display power.[90] For Saul, on the other hand, women do not appear to have any significance on a sexual level, though he does manipulate his daughters into marriages. The depiction of Henchard as a self-confessed woman-hater who keeps mostly at a distance from the sex (p. 148) chimes with the picture of Saul's having little involvement with women. Although Henchard says he is 'by nature something of a woman-hater'[91] and thinks 'there's not an inch of straight grain in 'em'[92] he nevertheless cares what they think of him, particularly in comparison to Farfrae:

> A reel or fling of some sort was in progress; and the usually sedate Farfrae was in the midst of the other dancers in the costume of a wild Highlander, flinging himself about and spinning to the tune. For a moment Henchard could not help laughing. Then he perceived the immense admiration for the Scotchman that revealed itself in the women's faces,[93]

though he does not allow such as Abel Whittle that privilege.[94]

90. John Levenson argues on the basis of 2 Sam. 12.8 that the Ahinoam David marries is Saul's wife. His focus is historical, and he contends that David thus laid claim to Saul's throne while Saul was still alive. He also suggests that David may have become king of Judah while Saul remained king of Israel. There is a difficulty with his argument which he does not address: the prohibition involving sexual relations with a woman and her daughter (Lev. 18.17). Although we cannot be certain that Ahinoam is Michal's mother, no other wives of Saul are mentioned. A concubine, Rizpah, is mentioned in 1 Samuel, but she is identified as the mother of sons, not daughters. Levenson contends that Saul's giving of Michal to Palti is a *quid pro quo*. See John D. Levenson, 'I Samuel 25 as Literature and as History', *CBQ* 40 (1978), pp. 11-28 (27).

91. *The Mayor*, p. 148.
92. *The Mayor*, p. 221.
93. *The Mayor*, p. 177.
94. *The Mayor*, p. 170.

When Henchard marries Susan the gossip centres around seeing a man wait so long to take so little, and there is a marked contrast when Farfrae marries Lucetta. Even in the early chapters detailing the wife sale, Susan functions as a tool for characterizing Henchard's antipathy towards women. This antipathy persists despite the impulse of which Seymour-Smith writes, with reference to the wife-selling,

> Impulse, we may be sure—and hot irresistible sexual impulse at that—got him into marriage, and just as hot irresistible impulse has got him out of it.[95]

There is an ambivalence in Henchard's virility on the one hand and his lack of concern for women on the other, and Susan functions to emphasize this ambivalence. Susan is the Ahinoam to Lucetta's Abigail, a woman about whom there is no mystery despite, or perhaps because of, the absence of description of her life.

The Paternal Relationship

The parallelism of characterization is not simply a matter of individual characterization, but also the characterization that arises in relationship between the protagonists, and this is crucial to the network of relationships between 1 Samuel and *The Mayor*, since it shapes the development of Hardy's conception of the biblical material. One crucial example is the paternal relationship in 1 Samuel and in *The Mayor*. The tragic collision between parent and offspring in 1 Samuel has been explored in Chapter 1 of this study, where we found that the anomaly of succession was crucial to the tragic vision. Coming to *The Mayor of Casterbridge* we may note that in a similar manner Henchard's conflicting actions with respect to Elizabeth-Jane are at the apex of the unfolding of the tragic.

The question of the paternity of Elizabeth-Jane is pivotal for the novel's dramatic development. Apart from the suspense it provides, it serves to illustrate the stranglehold by which fate clutches Henchard, and moreover it functions as a means of insight into Henchard's self-questioning concerning the terrible event of his youth. Like many of the emotions that consume Henchard, the passion of his response to the discovery that Elizabeth-Jane is after all Newson's daughter is intemperate; one may comprehend the sense of his courage and his shame, yet the extreme force of his bitterness is at once compelling and repugnant. The fact that Henchard keeps his wife's secret has the result that in the eyes of Elizabeth-Jane herself, she remains

---

95. Seymour-Smith, *Hardy*, p. 327.

Henchard's daughter. Henchard keeps his discovery to himself, but not his resentment.

The key to Hardy's treatment of the material relating to paternity in 1 Samuel is that, like Saul's relationship with his children, Henchard's relationship with Elizabeth-Jane is characterized by increasing isolation. Unlike the examples of Greek tragic drama mentioned above, which tend to handle in a very immediate manner themes such as murder and dishonour in connection with issues of paternity, 1 Samuel draws the tragic through a breakdown of mutual love as a direct result of paternal character flaw. The murder of offspring by parents, and vice versa, in Greek tragic drama tends to be sudden and shocking, and yet off-stage, creating a very immediate dramatic force. Furthermore, the murdered children (or parents) often have little or no capacity as protagonists; their function is basically to exist, as for example in *Medea* and *Heracles*. Though the concept of 'filicide' (for want of a better word) is not absent from 1 Samuel, Saul's failure to have Jonathan put to death following the breaking of the vow[96], and later the lack of success of his attempted murder of Jonathan[97] prolongs the dramatic tension and delays the climax, thus allowing the painful relationship between him and his offspring to contribute further to his suffering. Later dramatists, such as Shakespeare and Middleton, deal with themes such as illegitimacy and isolation in a manner that is more consonant with 1 Samuel than is Greek drama, at least in this respect, and in *The Mayor of Casterbridge* we find that Henchard, like Saul, consciously acts in a manner that causes his 'offspring' to reject him.

The parent–offspring relationship takes on a more subtle dimension when one considers the father–son typology between Saul and David, which is correspondingly built up in *The Mayor of Casterbridge* between Henchard and Farfrae. There are a number of indications of father–son typology between Henchard and Farfrae. Henchard's observation, at their first meeting, of a resemblance between his brother and Farfrae establishes a notion of kinship between them, and provides a reminder of Saul and David's physical characteristics. This remark brings together a number of parallels with the biblical narrative. A we have seen, the conflicts between Henchard and Farfrae have figured in the framework of comparisons between *The Mayor* and *Oedipus Rex*,[98] while Ebbatson remarks,

96. 1 Sam. 14.
97. 1 Sam. 20.
98. Dike, 'Modern Oedipus'.

Henchard is identified as a father, enters into a false relation with his 'daughter', and seeks to overmaster Farfrae, who has become a surrogate son or younger brother.[99]

Lawton, in his article dealing with the complex relationship between Saul, Jonathan and David[100], argues that Saul feels little affection for his son Jonathan and in his heart feels that David, the 'son of Jesse' is his proper son. The passages he cites[101] have their parallels in *The Mayor*, not only as episodes in the plot, but also as characterization, as mentioned above. Thus we can conceive that just as David *really is* in some complex manner Saul's son, Elizabeth-Jane and even Farfrae *really are* Henchard's children. And just as Saul attempts to destroy those who could have succeeded him, so Henchard endeavours to drive away those who would have remembered him.

Conclusions

The examination of relationships in characterization has demonstrated that not only are Henchard and Farfrae modelled on Saul and David, but also that in their relationships with other characters the biblical material has been reworked. Although an intertextual approach will not normally set much store by authorial intention, I have nevertheless addressed what is a valid question from the one scholar who has noted a sustained relationship between the biblical text and the novel, and I have concluded that Hardy did indeed consciously use the characterization of 1 Samuel's Saul and David in *The Mayor*. This has been possible by noting Hardy's stated interest in the biblical story of Saul and the 'bridge' of Voltaire's drama, of which glimpses of influence may be discerned in Hardy's novel, especially in regard to the characterization of Farfrae. The 'obvious thing' to which Stephen alludes in Hardy's description of the events is the characterization of David as violent, over-sexed and acquisitive, and this element is the primary influence of Voltaire's drama on *The Mayor*. I have dealt exclusively with characterization in this chapter, since this is a fundamental perspective in Hardy studies on *The Mayor*, but it is by no means the only perspective. By investigating other perspectives by means of an intertextual approach, many more points of contact may be found between these two texts and other texts in their matrix, and this will be the aim of my final chapter.

99. Ebbatson, *Hardy*, p. 75.
100. Lawton, 'Son of Jesse'.
101. E.g. 1 Sam. 24.9-22 and 1 Sam. 26.17-25.

Chapter 6

THE SOLID, INEXORABLE HAND OF INDIFFERENCE: AMBIVALENCE AND ABSENCE

Introduction

The focus of the previous chapter was an intertextual study of characterization in *The Mayor of Casterbridge* in relationship to 1 Samuel. In this chapter I shall begin with an investigation of the sociological approach and its relevance to the intertextual relationships between the biblical material and the novel. I shall also consider feminist approaches to Hardy in view of these relationships. These categories are determined by movements in Hardy studies, which I shall allow to some extent to dictate the agenda, since to impose an agenda that focuses on the biblical material might be to preconceive the results of the intertextual study.

This chapter will go on to contend that the role of the natural/supernatural is central to Hardy's conceptions in his handling of plot and characterization with respect to the biblical narrative, which gives rise to the question of the role, if there is one, of the deity. Does *The Mayor* convey a sense of what has been termed Hardy's religious pessimism, or can we understand from the text that Hardy is dealing with humanity's inability to find coherence in the nature of God?[1]

By discussing social and cultural approaches and by investigating the role of fate or chance in relationship to supernatural powers and divine ambivalence, the full picture should emerge. This approach will result in a thorough assessment of the intertextual dimensions at work between 1 Samuel and *The Mayor of Casterbridge*.

---

1. See, e.g., a remark in Hardy's personal notebook *Memoranda I*: '1899 later. Pessimism. Was there ever any great poetry which was not pessimistic?' Hardy goes on to cite Rom. 8.22; Job 14.1, 10; Ps. 109.22. Quoted in R.H. Taylor (ed.), *The Personal Note Books of Thomas Hardy: With an Appendix Including the Unpublished Passages in the Original Typescripts of 'The Life of Thomas Hardy'* (ed. with introductions and notes; London: Macmillan, 1978), pp. 27-28.

Social History

Some Hardy scholars have been concerned with *The Mayor* as social
history, or with sociological impulses in the novel. This often remains
within the parameters of discourse analysis rather than source analysis, by
which I mean that discussion takes place within a framework that involves
reading the novel as literature rather than as a historical source (although
the latter aspect of the social approach may also be found). In this respect
the intertextual relationship with 1 Samuel is worth examining, since the
biblical narrative charts its own social history, and despite having been
read for centuries as a historical source, its social comment when read as
literature is in some ways analogous to that of *The Mayor*. Thus it is
primarily with reference to *The Mayor* that I shall consider 1 Samuel as
social history within the intertextual relationship.

One of the most influential exponents of the sociological approach,
Douglas Brown, argues that the novels that represent Hardy's strengths (in
the midst of much 'unserviceable' and 'shoddy' prose) are those which
employ an agricultural theme recording

> Hardy's dismay at the predicament of the agricultural community in the
> south of England during the last part of the nineteenth century and at the
> precarious hold of the agricultural way of life.[2]

Brown assigns to Farfrae the role of the 'invader' figure who 'menaces a
stable, sheltered, but impotent community, and portends disaster' (though
he later revises this view), a figure which Brown contends is recurrent in
Hardy's work, while Henchard expresses 'the harsher aspect of agricultural life' and corresponds to Egdon Heath in *The Return of the Native*.
Thus the story is of the conflict between the native and the invader, of

> the defeat of dull courage and traditional attitudes by insight, craft and the
> vicissitudes of nature; and of the persistence through that defeat of some
> deep layer of vitality in the country protagonist.[3]

Hence the descriptions of the common people of Casterbridge, their daily
lives and their modes of speech. There is little in 1 Samuel to correspond
to this view of *The Mayor*. The daily life of the common people in 1
Samuel is barely described, though significantly the only discussion of

---

2.   Douglas Brown, *Thomas Hardy* (Westport, CT: Greenwood Press, 1980; reprint
of the 1954 edn published London and New York: Longmans, Green & Co.), p. 30.

3.   Brown, *Hardy*, pp. 65-66.

lifestyle occurs in Samuel's warning to the people that they will be worse off if they insist on having a king. Brown's assessment of the conflict between rural and urban in *The Mayor* also has no parallel in the biblical material: there is no distinction between urban and rural apparent in 1 Samuel. However, if we continue with the analogy between the corn trade and the Philistine war, we can perhaps discern a similar conflict. A few remarks in 1 Samuel suggest the situation of the people of Israel relative to that of the Philistines, for example 'there was no smith to be found in all the land of Israel' (1 Sam. 13.19): the Philistines feared the people of Israel might make weapons and so the Israelites had to go to a Philistine smith for any ironmongery they required. If the market in *The Mayor* corresponds to the Philistine war in 1 Samuel, the role of agriculture might be said to correspond to the making of weapons, but the point should not be forced. To read intertextually in respect of Brown's model would require the identification of David with the figure of the invader and of Saul with some kind of harsh aspect of Israelite life that is defeated by David's genius. This reading might be possible if Saul had turned out to be the sort of king about which Samuel warns the people, but there is nothing in the narrative to suggest that Saul ever acts according to this model. In fact, Saul's downfall stems in part from listening to the people and from his concern for his reputation. Furthermore, David's role and characterization do not fit Brown's description of the invader figure. He does not menace the community of Israel and he does not portend disaster, except for Saul. But there we may discern a flaw in Brown's argument, since Farfrae hardly fits this description either.

Maxwell critiques Brown's approach and its focus on the predicament of the agricultural community in late nineteenth-century England. He notes that Brown 'shows a tendency to play down the individuality of the protagonist' and comments that 'it is hard to see his fate as epitomizing that of English agriculture'.[4] The problem is that the action in the novel is set several decades before the date of writing: Hardy's preface points to a concern with the agricultural climate which led up to the repeal of the Corn Laws in 1846, whereas Brown points to a concern with the agricultural climate of the latter decades of the nineteenth century. Also problematic for Maxwell is Brown's treatment of Henchard in comparison to Farfrae in his later work (1962). Brown modifies his portrait of Farfrae, whom he comes to see no longer as the 'invader', but there is no correspondent modification of Henchard's role. Maxwell's solution to the

---

4.   Maxwell, 'Sociological Approach', p. 150.

problems of Brown's work lies in discerning a 'broad contrast between old and new' in Henchard and Farfrae, and ultimately Maxwell occupies an 'author as father' stance, contending that

> At least [the lucid and explicit comments such as Hardy makes in, for example, the preface] are likely to be a safer guide than the critic's judgement of what the historical situation might or ought to have promoted the novelist to offer his readers.[5]

While this stance is open to argument, Maxwell certainly smoothes some of the rough edges of Brown's argument, and the conception of a conflict between 'old' and 'new' is especially pertinent, if somewhat vague. However, I believe that the chief problem with Brown's work is not the disjunction between Hardy's preface and Hardy's contemporary economic environment, but the tendency, which Maxwell mentions, to play down Henchard's individuality. Just as Henchard has a relationship to 1 Samuel's Saul without being Saul recast, Henchard is more than simply 'agricultural man'. Brown's assessment of *The Mayor* appears to reduce Henchard to an almost allegorical figure, whereas, I would argue, Henchard is in relationship to, but not identified with, the agricultural theme. The forces of agricultural economics play their part in Henchard's tragedy, but Henchard functions outside of these forces and there are other sociological forces that contribute to his decline. Furthermore, Farfrae is subject to the same forces and succeeds. The relationship that Henchard has to the agricultural theme is on the same terms as that of Farfrae, who is by no means the urbanizing figure that Brown's analysis suggests.

Peter Widdowson outlines a different perspective on the social approach with his focus on presenting Thomas Hardy as 'a cultural figure in the late twentieth century, as well as of the late nineteenth century'.[6] He critiques the manner in which Hardy 'has been formed and canonized as the supreme literary celebrant of "rural England" '.[7] One of the techniques he employs is to read *The Life* as Hardy's last novel, and argues that in this way

> *The Life* 'reveals' the informing ideology by which its author is so deeply alienated, just as the novels produced by this author can expose in their own discourse the alienating and destructive processes of a class society. For them to do this, however, requires the removal of those accretions of critical

5.   Maxwell, 'Sociological Approach', p. 156.
6.   Peter Widdowson, *Hardy in History: A Study in Literary Sociology* (London: Routledge, 1989), p. 6.
7.   Widdowson, *Hardy*, p. 7.

and educational practice which have sought…to obviate the marks of those processes and to constitute 'Thomas Hardy' as a body of work which colludes with the dominant social and cultural ideology.[8]

Widdowson's work aims to effect 'a radical adjustment of perspective' on Hardy's work. He points out that Hardy is 'historically specific, not a rural idyllist, and very precise in his sociological detail'.[9] However, his work contrasts with Maxwell's author-centric stance, since it embraces a 'trust the tale' perspective. It also contrasts with Brown's work by dismissing the centrality of the agricultural community as one of Hardy's themes and proposing instead that what concerned Hardy was rapid change in class society. Therefore, for example, the narrator in *The Mayor* narrator insists on the distinction of Henchard's original hay-trusser work as that of the skilled countryman rather than general labour.

In fact, Widdowson has little room for *The Mayor*, concerned as he is with rescuing the so-called lesser novels from canonical exclusion, but by extending the implications of his work to *The Mayor* we might observe that Henchard's life and death and Farfrae's rise are indicative of this process of rapid change. Henchard's ruin is centred in his attachment to his determining social environment. Rather than 'agricultural man', he is perhaps 'upwardly mobile man', and he struggles against a harsh but plastic sociological system which, while it offers opportunities, provides no protection. A point of contact with 1 Samuel may be discerned here: neither the choice of Saul by Yhwh, nor his anointing, nor his election by lot can guarantee him protection against threats to his sovereignty, whether the threats be divine or human. Saul, too, is attached to his environment, and therefore inflexible. Although class in the sense in which it is apparent in nineteenth-century England is not at issue in 1 Samuel, there are points at which the biblical narrative engages the question of status. One example is the rumour of the promise of riches and the king's daughter to the slayer of Goliath, which has been likened to a fairytale and which places Saul in a class above David at this point. Saul has risen to this status by virtue of his kingship, but entered the story describing himself as 'from the least of the tribes of Israel' and from 'the humblest of all the families of the tribe of Benjamin' (1 Sam. 9.21). David responds to the two suggestions that he become the king's son-in-law firstly by declaring low social status and secondly by declaring low economic status. However, Saul cannot retain

---

8.　Widdowson, *Hardy*, p. 154.
9.　Widdowson, *Hardy*, p. 204.

his class status because he cannot retain his kingship, while David continues to enhance his status, by rising from Saul's armour-bearer to become
the king's son-in-law and then by acquiring power and influence while in
exile, and ultimately by taking the kingship after Saul's death. It seems,
therefore, that in 1 Samuel, as in *The Mayor*, there is a sociological structure which hinges on fluidity of status, allowing for the same kind of rapid
change that Widdowson expounds.

Lerner explains that, although there are many interpretations, sociological criticism is centred around two factors: first, relating of Hardy to the
social reality of nineteenth-century England (in part this is Widdowson's
focus), and second, viewing Hardy as being concerned with social change
(cf. Brown, Maxwell). There is a corresponding evasion of the notion of
tragedy; Marxist criticism in particular determines 'to show the social
basis of what are presented as universal or cosmic questions'.[10] Lerner,
however, argues that what concerns Hardy is not economics but lifestyle,

> Hardy believed that tremendous cultural upheaval was taking place in rural
> England. There had been an old way of life, characterised by the slow
> rhythms of agricultural work, fixed social relationships, the colourful speech
> of dialect, manual skills passed on through the generations, legends and folk
> tales and superstitions. It was going out before a new way that involved
> rationalised work processes, calculation instead of impulse, lower toleration
> of eccentricity, and influence from the towns penetrating the countryside.[11]

The sense of transition, the progression from the old to the new, is central
to most sociological approaches to *The Mayor*, and it is precisely this
which connects intertextually with 1 Samuel. The story of Saul is set in a
period of transition. Samuel is the last judge and his sons are unsuitable as
his successors. The people have seen that the nations around them have
kings to lead them in battle and request an identical manner of government. Saul, their first king (chosen by Yhwh), belongs to the era of the
judges and is instructed by Samuel until the point at which Yhwh rejects
him. David, who is to become their second king (also chosen by Yhwh) is
anointed by Samuel and protected by Samuel, but receives no instruction
on how to govern and does not belong to the era of the judges. David is the
first king of Israel who has full sovereign authority. Saul, caught between
the era of the judges and the era of the kings, is unable to change with the
times and therefore unable to hold onto his power. He makes a series of

---

10. Lerner, *Tragedy*, p. 75.
11. Lerner, *Tragedy*, pp. 88-89.

disastrous mistakes which lead to his ruin, mistakes which David, despite his faults, will never make.

The movement of the changing times in *The Mayor* which D.H. Fussell outlines also pertains to 1 Samuel, with the supreme 'maladroit delay' for Saul coming in Samuel's arrival in 1 Samuel 13. That which is changing is the political world. Israel's war against the Philistines provides the impulse for Saul's rise, the setting for Saul's fall and the occasion for Saul's death. Social politics play an important role in both 1 Samuel and *The Mayor*. Seymour-Smith argues against Brown that 'the novel is not about agricultural economics—that is only the background'[12] but surely background is not irrelevant. If Brown explains Farfrae's superiority to Henchard in terms of agricultural economics, it is because Farfrae *is* superior in terms of agricultural economics, and this superiority is an important factor in Henchard's downfall, just as David's superior military strategy is a factor in Saul's downfall. A narrative's 'background' provides the impetus for its protagonists' action. However, Brown's sociological approach to the novel which sets Farfrae as representative of the new order against his contemporaries (including Henchard) as representatives of the old order is an approach that raises problems. Farfrae stands against Henchard but not against his contemporaries; the problem for Henchard is that he is among the last of the representatives of the old order and his contemporaries are moving forward without him. It is Henchard's inability to adapt which sets him apart. This can also be seen in 1 Samuel: it is the people of Israel who ask for a king, and Saul's position between the era of the judges and the era of the kings is an isolated position, one in which he cannot progress. It does not matter that the old and new orders which Henchard and Farfrae (or Saul and David) represent extend beyond the narrative scope of the work, since the background of each is not a static phenomenon. The repeal of the Corn Laws, of which so much is made by some (e.g. Brown) and which is disputed by others (e.g. Maxwell) in understanding *The Mayor*, was part of an economic development that extended back before 1815 (when the Corn Laws were introduced) and forward for several decades after the repeal. The corn trade was central to the English economy throughout the nineteenth century. Likewise, combat with the Philistines remained a feature of ancient Hebrew historiography from the beginning of the era of the judges until the end of the era of the kings.

Since agricultural economics forms the background of *The Mayor* and the Philistine war forms the background of 1 Samuel, it is not only the

---

12. Seymour-Smith, *Hardy*, p. 326.

chief protagonists upon whom these forces act. It is evident, then, that consideration must also be given to the intertextual relationship between the people of Israel in 1 Samuel and the inhabitants of Casterbridge in *The Mayor* with respect to their sociological position. Samuel, the last judge, rebukes the people for their request. When Yhwh accedes to the request, Samuel is instructed to warn the people of the disadvantages of having a king. The people want an individual who will lead them in battle, and they want to be like the nations. They demonstrate their desire to progress, to move forward into a new order. The alternative is corruption in the form of Samuel's sons. Similarly, the inhabitants of Casterbridge value the new order. Henchard loses his reputation and Farfrae is invited to become mayor. Old ways and old-fashioned things are in decay, such as the fair at Weydon-Priors and the furmity woman herself with her antiquated wares. Farfrae's new-fangled entertainment with its ballroom made of a 'gigantic tent' that had been 'ingeniously constructed without poles or ropes' (p. 176) is chosen in preference to Henchard's more traditional pig on a pole.

Following Widdowson's example, I shall move at this point from perceptions of social relations to sexual politics. Feminist criticism is an aspect of Hardy studies that merits much discussion but which for the purposes of this work I am able to treat only briefly. Widdowson argues for a reading of Hardy's fiction that takes account of 'the relations of a group profoundly displaced and unstable in their class location, but where the most dynamically unstable group is female'.[13] He points out that most of the women, especially the 'rising' ones, are destroyed or constrained at the end of Hardy's novels, which is the consequence of the trajectory of narrative discourse and not of 'life'. He maintains that there is no necessary logic to these resolutions, 'Lucetta does not have to be so upset by the skimmity-ride that she miscarries and dies'.[14] Elaine Showalter, however, contends that there was a contemporary belief in the delicacy of pregnant women, which, together with the high maternal death rate, undermines this kind of argument. Elizabeth-Jane, whom Widdowson does not discuss, is one of the 'rising' women. Throughout *The Mayor* she shrinks from seeking social status, in fear of the notice and subsequent wrath of Providence, yet she is determined to rise in respect of her education, and her end is one of serenity if not joy.

13. Widdowson, *Hardy*, p. 215.
14. Widdowson, *Hardy*, p. 217.

Penny Boumelha provides an extensive analysis of late nineteenth-century sexual ideology. She asserts that female sexuality was a matter of great discussion, speculation and research, particularly concerning the 'Nature' of women, and writes of C.G. Harper's work expounding the fear that Nature would be revenged on educated women and their children,

> This kind of sociobiology, with its direct and unmediated connection between zoology and politics dominated the sexual ideology of the last two decades of the nineteenth century.[15]

Boumelha goes on to discuss characteristics of Hardy's women and remarks that there is a 'predisposition towards intense physical response to mental anguish',[16] such as Lucetta's death after the skimmity-ride. She also points to the significant 'oddity' common to many of Hardy's bourgeois women in their lack of a father, and comments that in some the absence is not remarked, while 'in others [the father] disappears…at the point where the women [*sic*] accedes to marriageability'.[17] Elizabeth-Jane is not placed in either category, yet she belongs in both, despite Boumelha's notion of embodied patriarchal law in the shape of her step-father. From Elizabeth-Jane's perspective there is a constant vacillation. At first she has no father as Newson is presumed dead, then Henchard lays claim to the paternal relationship but separates himself from her at the time of Farfrae's first courtship. On the first occasion of Newson's return Henchard sends him away (of which Elizabeth-Jane only learns later) but by this time Henchard is once again in a paternal relationship to Elizabeth-Jane. However, shortly before her marriage to Farfrae, Newson returns a second time and Henchard leaves Casterbridge. The final separation from Henchard comes on Elizabeth-Jane's wedding day, and the narrator reports that not long afterwards Newson also leaves Casterbridge. Elizabeth-Jane is flung back and forth between having a father and losing a father throughout the novel, which spans a period throughout which she is marriageable. Also crucial for Elizabeth-Jane is Boumelha's comment on

---

15. Penny Boumelha, *Thomas Hardy and Women: Sexual Ideology and Narrative Form* (Brighton: The Harvester Press, 1982), p. 22.

16. Boumelha, *Women*, p. 38. A further example, which Boumelha has not mentioned, is the death of Lady Constantine in *Two on a Tower*: 'Sudden joy after despair had touched an over-strained heart too smartly' (Thomas Hardy, *Two on a Tower* [Penguin Classics Edition; London: Penguin Books, 1995], p. 314).

17. Boumelha, *Women*, p. 40. Missing from Boumelha's list are Elfride and her father from *A Pair of Blue Eyes*.

the entanglement of women characters in an ideology of romantic love that calls upon them to experience their sexuality rather in being desired than in desiring, and this is obviously related to their confusion of sexual passion and aggression[18]

which has its consequence in Elizabeth-Jane's conflict between her desire for the passionless Farfrae and her feeling that this desire is 'unmaidenly and unwise'. Boumelha also points to an androgyny in narrative voice, which involves 'an attempt to make the central female characters the subjects of their own experience, rather than the instruments of a man's'.[19] This becomes evident in the description of Elizabeth-Jane's appraisal of Farfrae's physical appearance when she brings him his supper in Chapter 6, in which her experience of sexual attraction is related.

Showalter contends that in Hardy's work there is 'a sense of an irreconcilable split between female values and possibilities', but that Hardy 'also investigated the Victorian codes of manliness, the man's experience of marriage, the problem of paternity'.[20] She therefore discusses Henchard's 'unmanning', which is 'a movement towards both self-discovery and tragic vulnerability'.[21] Showalter argues that by means of a process of unmanning, Henchard learns through his vulnerability to cast off his previous 'male' concerns, such as money, paternity, honour and legal contract, so that he is enabled to become sensitive, dependent and attentive; qualities that are associated with femininity in general and Elizabeth-Jane in particular. This ultimately becomes evident in the 'centripetal influence' of the circle he traverses around Elizabeth-Jane's locus, carrying mementoes of his step-daughter. Showalter concludes that 'the moral as well as the temporal victory in the novel is Elizabeth-Jane's'.[22] Hardy may not have been a feminist, but in The *Mayor* one is aware that he rejected misogyny. Two problems with Showalter's work have been identified by Ebbatson: she 'neglects the social and cultural context of Casterbridge' and she 'over-simplifies the ambivalent characterization of Donald Farfrae'.[23]

---

18. Boumelha, *Women*, p. 44.

19. Boumelha, *Women*, p. 32.

20. Elaine Showalter, 'The Unmanning of the Mayor of Casterbridge', in D. Kramer (ed.), *Critical Approaches to the Fiction of Thomas Hardy* (London: Macmillan, 1979), pp. 100-101.

21. Showalter, 'Unmanning', p. 102.

22. Showalter, 'Unmanning', p. 113.

23. Ebbatson, *Hardy*, p. 102.

Ingham criticizes Showalter's essentialism[24], and yet there is a sense in which, within the framework of the text, Henchard shares his 'masculine' concerns with other males, and Elizabeth-Jane shares her 'feminine' characteristics with other females, and that the 'human value' (as Ingham expresses it) of the qualities Showalter identifies is subsumed by their gendering. If there is an essentialism in Showalter's work, it is reflected by the novel. Rosemarie Morgan suggests that 'these so-called innate feminine characteristics are not so much gender-determined as determined by preconceptions of gender'.[25] On this reading, the essentialism is neither Hardy's nor Showalter's, but a historical and cultural construct which is closely aligned with Boumelha's examination of contemporary ideology.

Patricia Ingham's criticism of Showalter's identification of Hardy and narrator is evidence of Ingham's poststructuralist agenda, yet within Showalter's own internal argument the problem is less pressing. Nevertheless, Ingham's concern with relating Hardy's novels to the historical context that produced them, rather than to authorial intention,[26] raises the issue of metatexts and intertexts in a way that is neglected by many other feminist readings.

Morgan, like Boumelha, stresses the importance of a diversity of narrative voice, and, like Showalter, identifies the primary narrator with Hardy. Therefore, for Morgan, Hardy's portrayal of women expresses a 'less-than-typical Victorian view of female sexuality'. Victorian women, she contends, 'were rarely offered fresh active fictions bearing imaginative possibilities of challenge, renewal and change'.[27] In Hardy's novels, however, women's work may be conventional or unconventional and may be outside the home; women travel, initiate relationships and

> struggle to shape their own lives with a vigour and energy and resilience that is, to the reader, the more remarkable for the fact that theirs is a struggle against all odds, a struggle in a world that, as Hardy says in *The Return of the Native*, is *not* friendly to women.[28]

Therefore, women have 'real' bodies and 'real' signs of physical exertion, 'real' emotions which are described and recognized and detailed as closely as those of male characters. They also experience sexual passion and self-

24. Patricia Ingham, *Thomas Hardy* (London: Harvester Wheatsheaf, 1989), p. 5.
25. Rosemarie Morgan, *Women and Sexuality in the Novels of Thomas Hardy* (London: Routledge, 1988) p. 155.
26. Ingham, *Hardy*, pp. 7-8.
27. Morgan, *Women* p. x.
28. Morgan, *Women*, p. x.

awareness of their bodies. However, Morgan is careful to emphasize
Hardy's avoidance of contemporary liberal feminism, and his opposition
to liberal feminists' idealization of marriage, which brought him criticism
and misinterpretation.

Importantly for Morgan, Hardy's women are imperfect. Hardy saw 'the
necessity of freeing women from the tyranny of the doll/madonna imago
in all its incorporeal flawlessness' and 'sought to restore to woman, or to
her fictional counterpart, not only a flesh and blood reality but also a
human nature lovable in all its imperfections'.[29] We can discern evidence
of this in Elizabeth-Jane's 'unmaidenly' sexual interest in Farfrae, in
Lucetta's sexual weaknesses and in Susan's sexual naïvety.

Is there an intertextual dimension relating 1 Samuel to the sexual politics of *The Mayor*? Perhaps the first point to be made is that we cannot
discuss so freely any authorial intention of the writer(s) of 1 Samuel. To
attempt to identify the narrator with the writer(s) would be virtually
meaningless in the case of 1 Samuel. The role of female characters in 1
Samuel 8–31 is minimal, and indeed most females mentioned are entirely
passive, being described in relation to men, or being the objects of verbs
that have men as subjects. Every woman mentioned in 1 Samuel 8–31 is
described in relation to her recent or impending marriage, with the sole
exception of the woman of Endor. In 14.50 Ahinoam is named as Saul's
wife and Merab and Michal are named as his daughters. In 25.43 David
marries Ahinoam of Jezreel, having just married Abigail. Merab is to be
given in marriage to David in 18.17, but is eventually given to Adriel
instead. There are only three women who are active in the narrative, and
they all play a role in empowering David, with imputed consequence to
Saul's decline. Michal loves David and the marriage present which David
must pay for her leads Saul to further enmity towards him. Furthermore,
Michal helps David to escape from Saul's attempt on his life. Abigail's
marriage to David brings him greater political power and wealth and
improves the position from which he can make his claim on Saul's
kingdom. The woman of Endor reveals to Saul that the following day he
will die in battle and that David will gain control of the kingdom. All three
of these women are used by men with the intention of consolidating the
men's positions.

There is little in the way of points of contact with *The Mayor* in terms of
sexual politics. This is not to say that there is no intertextual relationship,
but that the relationship is one of difference. The objectified status of the

29. Morgan, *Women*, p. 157.

women in 1 Samuel 8–31 has cultural parallels with the objectified status of women in nineteenth-century England, where there was a prevailing cultural imperative on women to marry and to provide offspring. Feminist scholars of Hardy have argued that in his novels there is a critique of this cultural imperative, while feminist biblical scholars have argued, for example, against 'romantic' readings of the Abigail narrative. Linafelt comments,

> There is no cause…to read into [Abigail's] offer [of her hand in marriage] any great love for David on Abigail's part. Her shrewd address to David indicates that she knows how power works in an androcentric world. Like it or not, she will be taken, and she might as well prepare as best she can for survival.[30]

There is little female subversion of male constraint in 1 Samuel 8–31, since even Michal's help with David's escape is the choice of one man over another rather than a choice for herself, and the price she pays is to lose David, whom she loves, and to be given to Paltiel by her father. For the most part women in the narrative play no role at all, or a wifely role, and the sexual politics is one simply of straightforward patriarchy.

An interesting break with this pattern is Saul's visit to the woman of Endor in 1 Samuel 28. Saul tells his servants to find for him a woman who is a necromancer (28.7). The question of her sex is largely ignored by biblical scholars, with the focus being on her profession. However, there is no indication that necromancy was restricted to women, and yet it appears that in many cultures the practitioners of 'pagan' religious techniques are predominantly female. It is striking, then, that in *The Mayor* the weather prophet Fall is a man. In 1 Samuel 28, the woman's marital status is not related, as if it were unnecessary in view of her purely professional relationship with Saul. However, there is no sense of androgyny in her depiction: her speech to Saul after the appearance of Samuel, in which she coaxes him to eat, characterizes her in feminine terms. Similarly the offer of a morsel of bread which on acceptance is accompanied by a fatted calf depicts the woman's feminine, even motherly, characteristics.

On balance, then, the portrayal of sexual politics in *The Mayor* differs significantly from that of the Saul narrative. The similarities are cultural in origin and arise from discrete patriarchies. In both texts women have a role determined by preconceptions of gender in which they are subject to the power and authority of men, which they may on occasion subvert, but with disagreeable consequences, such as Michal's remarriage, or Lucetta's fear of Henchard's reprisals and her eventual death.

---

30. Linafelt, 'Taking Women', p. 100.

Fate and Chance

Chance and circumstance play a significant role in Henchard's downfall,[31] and moreover there is often a suggestion of supernatural interference, though where this occurs it is usually framed in reference to a protagonist's suspicion, perception or imagination. Chance, furthermore (or perhaps mischance), may be understood as a force that holds Henchard in its thrall. During his confession to Farfrae he remarks,

> In the nature of things, Farfrae, it is almost impossible that a man of my sorts should have the good fortune to tide through twenty years o' life without making more blunders than one.[32]

The relationship between 1 Samuel and *The Mayor* does not extend to a direct portrayal of divine ambivalence, since Yhwh has no correlative in the novel as one of the dramatis personae. Nevertheless, there is a recurrent suggestion that if there are supernatural forces at work within the context of the narrative, their disposition with respect to Michael Henchard is one of ambivalence. The elements of chance lend themselves to the tragic vision in the novel and, because the theme of chance is closely bound up with plot development, they extend to marked parallels between the plot of 1 Samuel and that of *The Mayor*. It will therefore be profitable to examine these parallels and their relationship to the theme of chance within *The Mayor*, and to investigate the means by which components of the tragic vision, such as reversal and recognition, are framed in relation to 1 Samuel. Furthermore, it will be necessary to explore the role of the supernatural from an intertextual perspective and to ascertain whether the notion of divine ambivalence is carried from 1 Samuel into *The Mayor*. However, we will turn first to the problematic question of fate.

While the emphasis that the subtitle places on the tragic vision in *The Mayor of Casterbridge* is that of character, the reader may remark that Henchard's character does not alone cause his ruin. The narrator comments on the

> ingenious machinery contrived by the Gods for reducing human possibilities of amelioration to a minimum—which arranges that wisdom to do shall come *pari passu* with the departure of zest for doing,[33]

---

31. The connection between character and fate which is made in *The Mayor* has been discussed in Chapter 5. See above, pp. 199-200.

32. *The Mayor*, p. 148.

33. *The Mayor*, p. 395.

and this links the novel's tragic vision with its plot. King in fact asserts that

> For [Hardy], as for Aristotle, the plot was the most important element. His are tragedies of situation, rather than of character... The conflict of ideas or feelings is made tragic by the situation.[34]

She argues that Hardy's vision of life has a deterministic basis expressed as fatalism and that therefore his vision seems to be 'dependent more on concepts of Fate and Nature than on those social elements which are equally, if not more, important to him'.[35] We would, then, expect that such a fatalistic vision of life would be expressed in terms of plot development even if Hardy's principal interest is in development of character.

Fussell, however, emphasizes the significance of timing within the novel and the pattern of change which focuses the tragic vision, which Fussell terms 'the maladroit delay':

> The anguish of the novel derives, to a large extent, from the interaction between...various areas of change, each moving with its own particular timing.[36]

Fussell presents this as a challenge to the idea that the anguish of the novel is the product of destiny or fate, perhaps the sort of idea that Daniel Schwarz advances in arguing that in *The Mayor* the narrator 'increasingly protests against the nature of the cosmos which arouses man's expectations only to blunt them'.[37] D.A. Dike, on the other hand, compares *The Mayor* with Greek dramatic form and thus argues in favour of reading a conception of fate in the novel:

> Hardy, aware not only of Greek drama but also of a theory of Greek drama and of what we have been led to believe was the official Greek position, seems to take Fate and the Wheel more literally [than Sophocles]. Or perhaps 'literally' is too strong, for they stand in relation to the action of his novel as myth stands to ritual, symbolic explanation to imitation.[38]

---

34. Jeanette King, *Tragedy in the Victorian Novel: Theory and Practice in the Novels of George Eliot, Thomas Hardy and Henry James* (Cambridge: Cambridge University Press, 1978), p. 99.

35. King, *Tragedy*, pp. 24-25.

36. D.H. Fussell, 'The Maladroit Delay: The Changing Times in Hardy's "The Mayor of Casterbridge"', *Critical Quarterly* 21:3 (1979), pp. 17-30 (26).

37. Daniel R. Schwarz, 'Beginnings and Endings in Hardy's Major Fiction', in Kramer (ed.) *Critical Approaches*, pp. 17-35 (26).

38. Dike, 'Modern Oedipus', p. 170.

While Fussell's argument is plausible, it cannot preclude the idea of fate because it does not take account of the ambiguities and contradictions that persist in the novel. Dike is more convincing in his assessment of the symbolic function of fate. Schweik, however, discusses a structural cycle in which events move from hope to catastrophe and through which the perception of Henchard's character shifts. Thus it is in the fourth and final episode that

> Hardy emphasizes most strongly the disjunction between Henchard's moral stature and the circumstance which has blindly nullified his repentance, his recantation of ambition, and his new capacity for a higher kind of achievement; and in doing so Hardy seems intent on reversing the fable-like correspondence between character and fate which figures so conspicuously in the first half of the novel.[39]

This structural cycle is the means by which the plot is developed, and within it the concept of fate. The connection between fate and the nature of the cosmos that Schwarz advances is a very important one, and it is the same sort of connection that King is making when she discusses determinism. There is a general agreement, despite Fussell, that the tragic vision in the novel is connected to a conception of fate. The model of the 'maladroit delay' is interesting, but it is difficult to see how time and coincidence must necessarily be outside the scope of a deterministic cosmos. Dike's argument is probably the most effective rebuttal of Fussell, since he points to the novel's debt to Greek tragic form and the significance of fate within it.

Fate and Parallels of Plot

There are analogous plot developments in *The Mayor* and 1 Samuel that frame the working out of fate of Henchard and Saul. Within the parallel between the corn market and the Philistine conflict there are three significant incidents that display this analogy. The first is where Farfrae, having been dismissed by Henchard, sets up his own business on a smaller scale than Henchard's, and Henchard is determined to 'have a tussle with him' at 'fair buying and selling' (p. 184). Farfrae, however, turns away his first customer, who has had recent dealings with Henchard, because he does not want to do anything which would harm Henchard. In a similar manner, David, driven into exile by Saul, accumulates allies at the cave of Adullam, though on a small scale—four hundred men—and Saul is determined to hunt him down and destroy him. David, however, will not harm Saul

---

39. Schweik, 'Character and Fate', p. 144.

because he is Yhwh's anointed. Virginia Woolf makes the point in respect of Henchard:

> Henchard is pitted, not against another man, but against something outside himself which is opposed to men of his ambition and power. No human being wishes him ill. Even Farfrae and Newson and Elizabeth-Jane whom he has wronged all come to pity him, and even to admire his strength of character. He is standing up to fate, and in backing the old Mayor whose ruin has been largely his own fault, Hardy makes us feel that we are backing human nature in an unequal contest.[40]

It is not Farfrae who wishes to harm Henchard, nor David who wishes to harm Saul. Both men are engaged in a struggle with fate and while Farfrae and David may appear to be used as accomplices by forces outside themselves, they will not act in their own right against their former benefactors.

The second incident is in Chapter 32 after Henchard's bankruptcy, when Farfrae offers Henchard the furniture that he has bought from Henchard's former house. Henchard feels he has wronged Farfrae and there is a reconciliation, and Henchard finds himself in Farfrae's employ. However, it is only a partial reconciliation: Henchard's hatred of Farfrae returns and he begins to threaten Farfrae again. The counterpart in 1 Samuel is the episode in which Saul falls into David's hands at En-gedi (1 Sam. 24) when David spares Saul's life and Saul confesses he has wronged David. Again, this is only a partial reconciliation, since Saul returns to his house while David returns to his stronghold, and in 1 Samuel 26 Saul once again seeks David's life. There can be no true reconciliation between Henchard and Farfrae or between Saul and David if fate is to assert itself and thus the inadequacy of this reconciliation leaves the way open for reversal.

The third and most conspicuous parallel is the fight in the corn stores (Chapter 38). Henchard ambushes Farfrae and overpowers him, and Farfrae challenges him to take his life, commenting that Henchard has wished to for some time. His words check Henchard, who bitterly denies it and declares his erstwhile love for the younger man. Farfrae is thus able to escape and Henchard intends him no more harm. In the analogue, in 1 Samuel 26 Saul encamps near to the place where David is hiding, though here it is David who ambushes Saul. David protests his innocence and Saul admits that he has erred and been foolish. David thus enables his escape and Saul pledges that he will do David no more harm and asks him to return. Just as David does not return to Saul after the repeated threats to his life, Farfrae will not come back later that evening when Henchard begs

---

40. Woolf, 'Novels', p. 77.

him to return to his ailing wife. Both Saul and Henchard have lost their credibility through their recurrent assaults. This loss of credibility secures their fate. Saul's loss of David is permanent and nothing can now reconcile them. His fate is to lose everything, while David's destiny is to succeed him, and now that his separation from David is complete his fate is inevitable. In similar manner, Henchard's fate is to lose everything, and having lost Farfrae an inevitable chain of consequences is set up. Farfrae loses Lucetta and so courts Elizabeth-Jane; Henchard will lose her too. King's idea that the illusion of freedom diminishes in the course of Hardy's novels is appropriate to 1 Samuel as well:

> All the main characters of [Hardy's] tragic novels seem, as he suggested of Tess and Angel, under *any* circumstances doomed to unhappiness. Even the most improbable coincidences are merely accelerating factors. Given the principle of heredity, the character and environment of the protagonists, the outcome is inevitable. Heredity and environment, character and society, are each conceived as modern Fates. Primitive superstition and scientific theory reinforce each other. Whether we call this vision 'fatalistic' or 'deterministic' is of relatively minor importance.[41]

Heredity, writes King, is for Hardy 'a rendering of the Greek principle of collective or inherited guilt' (p. 60). So Saul's heredity, the kind of person he is by reason of his birth in the era of the judges and his involvement in the people's request for a king, renders him unsuitable to the kingship, while his environment, particularly his cultic environment, undermines him. Like Henchard, his character and his world provide the motives for his rejection. Whether his end is the product of a jealous deity or the consequence of a series of errors, his fate is a struggle against the inevitable.

Fate and Tragic Themes
Since 1 Samuel is not the only text with which *The Mayor* has an intertextual relationship, it is evident that the intertextual relationships between *The Mayor* and Greek drama are important in understanding the intertextual relationship between *The Mayor* and 1 Samuel. Therefore Dike's work on the novel as 'A Modern Oedipus' is of great value for the examination of the tragic devices used in the novel and their parallels in the biblical narrative. Dike's explanation of the antagonism between Henchard and Farfrae as recalling that between Oedipus and Creon is of particular note with respect to the construction of the latter relationship around the primitive rite of the Seasonal King: 'As conclusion to that

41. King, *Tragedy*, p. 26.

ceremonial combat, the rejected king was torn asunder and spread over the land'.[42] Dike stresses Henchard's profession as corn merchant as a reminder of the religious antecedent. This idea, of course, recalls Saul and his rejection and dismemberment, and the *agon* of his conflict with David. The biblical material that has been used in *The Mayor* has been remodelled in a framework of Greek tragic form, and central to the relationship between the biblical narrative and the novel are the tragic motifs of reversal and recognition.

There are analogies between *The Mayor* and 1 Samuel in the application of the motif of reversal in the novel. Henchard experiences reversal with respect to Elizabeth-Jane's paternity: he intends to claim her as his own but on each occasion where he might possess her he loses her through the workings of chance and circumstance. The intention begins with his second marriage to Susan for Elizabeth-Jane's sake, since Henchard regrets the sale of his daughter more than the sale of his wife, and it continues with his request that she be known by the name of Henchard rather than Newson, a request which is considered undesirable by her mother, who influences Elizabeth-Jane to refuse. After Susan's death, when Henchard makes another attempt to claim Elizabeth-Jane as his own, his declaration prompts him to look for proof and he discovers the reverse. Once he knows she is not his own daughter he rejects her for a considerable period of time, but just as he accepts her again his claim on her is threatened by the arrival of Newson. His desperate attempt to keep her results in his lie and it causes Elizabeth-Jane to deplore his deceit, so once more he loses her. This reversal of paternal intention finds its biblical parallel with Saul's intention to claim Jonathan's loyalty, which results in his losing it (1 Sam. 20) and with Saul's manipulation of his paternal relationship with Michal, so that his plan to have David killed by the Philistines on the quest for the bride price results in the reverse and David becomes his son-in-law. Just as Henchard's conscious purpose 'to atone for his crimes…reverses his fortune and prepares his downfall'[43] so Saul's conscious purpose to alleviate his torment (caused by the evil divine spirit, a consequence of his crimes) reverses his fortune and prepares his downfall.

According to Dike, reversal stems from a sense of duty distorted by hubris, and Dike likens Oedipus to Henchard with reference to this aspect of reversal. One may also argue that this 'profound irresponsibility' is

42. Dike, 'Modern Oedipus', p. 169.
43. Dike, 'Modern Oedipus', p. 169.

evident in Saul as analogue to Henchard: Saul's sense of duty in sacrificing before battle (1 Sam. 13) and in his intention to sacrifice the Amalekite livestock (1 Sam. 15) is similarly distorted by hubris (in the sense of 'man overreaching himself' rather than 'wanton violence'). The reversal stemming from hubris is related to tragic collision as it is hubris that gives rise to such collisions and reversal which destabilizes them: even the collision between the civilized and the barbaric, the 'dangerous incongruity between Nature and Civilization',[44] which in *The Mayor* finds its arena in the marketplace, has its counterpart in 1 Samuel: in the collision between the people of Yhwh and the uncircumcised Philistines. While this collision is not of primary importance in *Oedipus Rex*, it is striking in the comparison between *The Mayor* and 1 Samuel. Saul is king of the people of Israel, and David is one of his subjects. David begins his career in Saul's house and shows his capabilities to be superior to Saul's. Saul comes to realize that David is the threat to his kingship of whom Samuel has informed him, and in Saul's attempts to remove David he exhibits hubris (in both senses). After the initial conflict between Saul and David (Saul's attempts on David's life), Saul drives David into exile and David goes over to the Philistines, the enemies of Saul and his people. From this position David is able to accumulate power and to wage war on other enemies of Israel. Eventually, Saul's hubris leads to reversal and he is ruined, destabilizing the collision. David will eventually take his place as king of Israel. Similarly, Henchard is the owner of a large corn business and leads the marketplace. Farfrae begins his career in Henchard's employment and shows his capabilities to be superior to Henchard's. Henchard comes to realize that Farfrae is a threat to his position of which some of the townsmen warn him,[45] and in Henchard's attempts to remove Farfrae he exhibits hubris. After the initial conflict between Henchard and Farfrae (over Whittle), Henchard dismisses Farfrae and Farfrae goes into business in competition with Henchard and his employees. From this position Farfrae is able to accumulate power and to make profit at the expense of other businesses in the market. Eventually Henchard's hubris leads to reversal and he is ruined, destabilizing the collision. Farfrae then takes Henchard's place in the business Henchard has built up, keeping his employees (but paying them less).

Dike does not examine the collision between the civilized and the barbaric in terms of Henchard and Farfrae, but such an examination would be

---

44. Dike, 'Modern Oedipus', p. 172.
45. *The Mayor*, p. 178.

useful, since the novel's world is the polis of Casterbridge and its environs, and Farfrae is a foreigner.[46] His status in relation to the polis is assessed by the other characters on the evening of his arrival at the Three Mariners. Although none of them seem over fond of their own native territory, they imagine Farfrae's country to be a 'land of perpetual snow, as we may say, where wolves and wild boars and other dangerous animalcules be as common as blackbirds hereabout' (p. 123). But Farfrae's fate is to be assimilated to the polis and Henchard's fate is to be rejected by it. This assimilation and rejection is precisely analogous to David and Saul. Although Moynahan (p. 120) stresses David's position as a foreigner as a member of the tribe of Judah at the court of a Benjaminite king, in fact as a member of one of the Yahwist tribes David is not so foreign. However, in his decision to seek refuge with the Philistine king he aligns himself with Israel's enemies and thereby makes himself a foreigner. Reversal therefore destabilizes the tragic collision and effects the working out of fate.

The other tragic motif that may be profitably examined is that of recognition. Recognition is the process by which the tragic hero 'is brought face to face with the past he tried to escape'.[47] King relates this to reversal and to the 'superimposition of a cyclical pattern on the hero's forward progress', a pattern which 'reflects the interaction of past and present'.[48] She argues that life for Hardy's tragic heroes is their hamartia. However, there are indeed incidents of hamartia in Henchard's past, and the principle of recognition relates to these specific events. A significant moment of recognition for Henchard comes at Ten Hatches Hole, where in his intention to drown himself he sees the effigy of himself, discarded after the Skimmity Ride. He imagines it is himself, and thus is confronted with his past: his dalliance with Lucetta, which arose as a consequence of the wife-selling. This recognition is accompanied by the sense that he is in Somebody's hands. Furthermore, Henchard has previously experienced recognition while presiding at the court at the hearing concerning the furmity woman. This occasion has a direct relationship to Saul's experience of recognition during his encounter with the woman of Endor. The furmity woman reveals Henchard's past and he is confronted with the crime of the sale of his wife

---

46. Although Maxwell, Seymour-Smith and others point out that none of the central characters are native to Casterbridge, Farfrae's foreign status is stressed more emphatically in the novel than Henchard's, Susan's, Elizabeth-Jane's or Lucetta's.

47. King, *Tragedy*, p. 97.

48. King, *Tragedy*, p. 97.

and daughter, the event which is much more closely connected with hamartia than his indiscretion with Lucetta. This revelation results in a blow to his reputation and precipitates his bankruptcy.[49] Similarly, the woman of Endor brings up the ghost of Samuel, a part of Saul's past, who confronts Saul with his past rejection for his crimes. The repetition of his rejection precipitates Saul's failure in battle against the Philistines and his death by his own hand. Central to both episodes is not only recognition by the protagonist but also recognition of the protagonist: the furmity woman who reveals Henchard's past and forces him to confront it must necessarily first recognize Henchard. The woman of Endor at the moment of revealing the ghost of Samuel and Saul's past recognizes Saul, thus drawing in the thread of Samuel's denunciation of necromancy (1 Sam. 15) and Saul's action against its practitioners, and forcing Saul to confront his past crimes and rejection (1 Sam. 15). Recognition for both Saul and Henchard is related to the supernatural, in the shape of a witch figure, and it is to the supernatural that we shall now turn.

The Divine and the Supernatural

It is interesting to note that although Hardy has reworked material from 1 Samuel in *The Mayor*, he has omitted the role of Yhwh, which is central to the story of Saul. A central feature of the tragic vision in 1 Samuel is the collision that takes place between the deity who chooses a king unable to achieve his regal potential and the man who is presented with a divine injunction whose implications are beyond his grasp. However, the God who makes it his business to determine the fate of his creatures and to pronounce judgment on them according to their deeds is excluded from or omitted by Hardy's narrative. Those devastating forces to which Saul is subject, which shape his destiny and which drive him continually towards his destruction, take on a new shape in the narrative structure of *The Mayor of Casterbridge*: the shape of individual character, or of heredity, or of industrialization and technological change. The fact that God is not one of the dramatis personae is unremarkable given the framework of the novel; nevertheless, the fact that Henchard's ruin is not attributable in some way to divine operation is a significant transformation. The absence of a Samuel figure is continuous with this reading, since for Henchard there is no medium between him and the source of his fortunes.

---

49. It is also the furmity woman who directs Susan and Elizabeth-Jane to Casterbridge, so her role has also in this sense been to confront Henchard with his past.

While Saul's rejection and ruin come about because of Yhwh's manipulation of human affairs, Henchard's life is never reported to be directly controlled in this manner. If the forces that subjugate Henchard are not divine forces, it is necessary to consider alternative possibilities as to their origin and nature. Henchard's superstition is frequently stressed, and it comes as no surprise that forces of Nature, such as the weather, serve as the occasion of much of Henchard's misfortune. It seems as though Henchard is unluckier than he deserves with respect to the weather. Indeed, it is bad weather at the corn harvest which results in the problem of the 'growed' wheat, a problem which he cannot overcome without Farfrae and which marks the beginning of his struggles. It is bad weather which spoils the entertainment that Henchard organizes in celebration of 'a national event'. Furthermore, the weather is the catalyst by means of which Henchard bankrupts himself in competition with Farfrae. Yet ultimately it is not the weather which is responsible for Henchard's downfall. Although his superstitious nature provokes him to paranoia, the liability lies not in the circumstances, but rather in his response to them, in 'the momentum of his character'.[50]

It is therefore of consequence that early in the novel the narrator describes Henchard thus: 'there was something fetichistic in this man's beliefs'.[51] Henchard's perceptions and those of other characters concerning supernatural powers take on more than passing significance, though Henchard is also susceptible to conventional religious conviction: he makes his oath by swearing on the Bible that is on the communion table in the church he enters, and when the period of his vow of abstinence is over he joins the churchgoers in the Three Mariners and forces the choir to sing verses from Psalm 109, which he chooses from the Psalter. The theme of the supernatural in *The Mayor* is related to the concepts of chance and fate, since the characters' perception of the supernatural is expressed in terms of the possible existence of deterministic powers. Providence in particular is linked with the concept of fate. Elizabeth-Jane doesn't want to tempt Providence by being too cheerful or extravagant because she fears 'the coulter of destiny, despite fair promise' and thus fears that Providence might punish her and afflict her and her mother, 'as He used to do' (p. 158). Farfrae also speaks of Providence and higher Powers, though in a more positive manner and both times when he is considering leaving Casterbridge. When Henchard offers him the managerial post on his own terms, he believes 'It's Providence! Should any one go against it?' (p. 133),

50. Cf. the quote attributed to Novalis, *The Mayor*, p. 185.
51. *The Mayor*, p. 84.

and when he is offered the mayor's chair he says, 'See now how it's ourselves that are ruled by the Powers above us![52] We plan this, but we do that. If they want to make me Mayor I will stay, and Henchard must rave as he will' (p. 316). The suggestion within the narrative world is that Providence ordains that Farfrae should first bring his superior capabilities into Henchard's path and then once Henchard has given way to uncontrollable jealousy, provokes Henchard further by ordaining that Farfrae should be set up in Henchard's old position.

This is, of course, Farfrae's perception of Providence rather than the narrator's, yet this does not preclude the possibility of such a conception of Providence within the narrative world. That Henchard considers the mayor's chair his rightful position is evident from the episode concerning the royal visitor, when he unsuccessfully attempts to greet the personage himself in Farfrae's place. The Providence that nurtures Farfrae is ambivalent towards Henchard. While this ascription of ambivalence to Providence is never overtly stated in the novel, nevertheless, if there is a force that may be called Providence it manifests itself as chance, and chance is certainly ambivalent towards Henchard. At Ten Hatches Hole, when Henchard sees what he imagines is himself face down in the water, he is profoundly moved:

> The sense of the supernatural was strong in this unhappy man, and he turned away as one might have done in the actual presence of an appalling miracle.[53]

It turns out that he has discovered the effigy. Nevertheless,

> Despite this natural solution to the mystery Henchard no less regarded it as an intervention that the figure should have been floating there. Elizabeth-Jane heard him say, 'Who is such a reprobate as I! And yet it seems that even I be in Somebody's hand!'[54]

There is a strong irony here, since if Henchard is in anyone's hand it is certainly an ambivalent hand.

The parallel between Saul and Henchard with respect to the divine, or as Moynahan terms it, the supernatural (in any case, the two terms are closely

52. This superstitious sentiment recalls Kent's declaration in *King Lear*:

> It is the stars,
> The stars above us, govern our conditions...

(Act IV, iii). Kent and Gloucester are both inclined to superstition.

53. *The Mayor*, p. 372.

54. *The Mayor*, p. 374.

related in the framework of 1 Samuel and of *The Mayor*), is in part informed by Hardy's well-documented interest in pagan religion.[55] Henchard, like Saul, is not a pious man, and does not readily seek out contact with the divine of his own volition, though 'he was superstitious— as such headstrong natures often are'.[56] In Chapter 2 he finds a church in order to make his vow of abstention because 'there was something fetichistic in this man's beliefs'.[57] Once there he does not actually address God, though he kisses the book on the communion table. He places his trust in signs rather than faith.[58]

The theme of the supernatural works to a great extent through Henchard's superstitious nature,[59] which is more commonly displayed in his suspicion that evil forces are at work in his life than in the idea of divine protection. Early in his acquaintance with Farfrae he speaks of his dark moods, which he describes as 'gloomy fits…when the world seems to have the blackness of hell, and, like Job, I curse the day that gave me birth' (p. 149). This sense of the infernal persists throughout the novel. When Henchard discovers that Elizabeth-Jane is not in fact his daughter, he feels a deep misery. He looks out on the night 'as at a fiend'. Because of his superstitious nature he 'could not help thinking that the concatenation of events this evening had produced was the scheme of some sinister intelligence bent on punishing him'. He is aware of the irony of cause and effect and it angers him 'like an impish trick', and he feels that '[l]ike Prester John's, his table had been spread, and infernal harpies had snatched up the food' (p. 197). In Chapter 27, having made an immense loss after a rash gamble with the weather, he asks himself,

> I wonder if it can be that somebody has been roasting a waxen image of me, or stirring an unholy brew to confound me! I don't believe in such power; and yet—what if they should ha' been doing it![60]

55. A particularly macabre example of this interest may be found in Hardy's short story 'The Withered Arm', in which Rhoda Brook is visited by an incubus, an evil spirit in the guise of her former lover's new wife. As she wakes she seizes the apparition by the arm and shortly afterwards Mrs Lodge's arm begins to wither. The two women consult Conjuror Trendle, who explains the affliction as the result of 'being ''over-looked''. He later advises Mrs Lodge of a possible cure: to press her arm against the neck of a hanged man. When the opportunity arises, the dead man turns out to be the illegitimate son of her husband and Rhoda.

56. *The Mayor*, p. 257.
57. *The Mayor*, p. 84.
58. Cf. 1 Sam. 14.41; 28.6.
59. Cf. *King Lear* with respect to Gloucester.
60. *The Mayor*, p. 264. In the prelude to Eustacia Vye's death in *The Return of the*

In fact, it appears that he does believe in such power.[61] Furthermore, some time later, when Farfrae is courting Elizabeth-Jane after Lucetta's death, he considers telling Farfrae that Elizabeth-Jane is not his daughter, so that Farfrae might give her up and she might belong to Henchard once again. The thought appals him and as he shudders he exclaims, 'God forbid such a thing! Why should I still be subject to these visitations of the devil, when I try so hard to keep him away?' (p. 382.) The theme of belief in the supernatural develops in such a way that Henchard begins with dark moods and progresses through language of infernal creatures and suspicions of witchcraft to the notion of satanic visitation. This has a distinct analogue in Saul's torment caused by an evil spirit from Yhwh.

Moynahan makes a comparison between Henchard's moods and those of Saul, but clearly the parallel goes further than mere moods. There is a sense in which Fate or Chance is linked to supernatural interference. King remarks,

> The concept of Fate seems to be contradicted by the idea of Chance, so recurrent a motif in Hardy's fiction. But his novels show Chance conforming to a pattern, taking on the 'air of design' which Aristotle felt made the best kind of tragic plot (*Poetics*, IX).[62]

This 'air of design' in the motif of chance is linked to the sense of a rigid law which King connects with Hardy's frequent allusions to the Old Testament and to Greek tragedy; 'a law which must be adhered to not for the sake of happiness, but because it is the law, inexorable and inflexible'.[63] The importance of the story of Saul for *The Mayor* demonstrates precisely this: the divine commands which Saul fails to fulfil are as inexorable and inflexible as the laws which govern Henchard. If, as King suggests, Hardy constantly asserts the 'moral superiority of the individual over the workings of Necessity or society',[64] does this mean that in reworking the biblical material in *The Mayor* Hardy implicitly asserts the moral superiority of Saul over God? King draws attention to the influence

---

Native, Susan Nunsuch, believing Eustacia to be responsible for the illness of her son, makes a waxen image, complete with touches that would have identified the image as Eustacia to 'anybody acquainted with the inhabitants of Egdon Heath'. She then thrusts pins into the wax and completes the procedure by holding the effigy in the fire with tongs while reciting the Lord's Prayer backwards. See Book the Fifth, Chapter 7.

    61. See above, p. 202 n. 53.
    62. King, *Tragedy*, p. 25.
    63. King, *Tragedy*, p. 35.
    64. King, *Tragedy*, p. 35.

of Sophocles on Hardy's fascination with the notion of the human as a plaything of malevolent gods,[65] so perhaps any inference of Hardy's attitude to the God of 1 Samuel should be considered in this context. Furthermore, Seymour-Smith asserts that

> the narrator's remark that 'character is fate' does not imply that Hardy himself is affirming that men are not, after all, mere playthings of the gods. The statement cannot be taken to imply either pessimism or optimism about the human situation, unless it is to be understood as meaning that 'a strong will, what is called 'character', can turn adversity into good fortune, so we are not mere playthings of the gods'.[66]

Schwarz prefers to speak in terms of an unjust cosmos, which manifests itself through the symmetry of beginnings and endings, making 'a statement about man's inability to progress'.[67] Schweik's perspective coheres with King's in the idea that 'Nature and Chance are repeatedly made to serve what seems to be a larger moral order in the world.'[68] In this sense, then, despite the omission of Yhwh among the dramatis personae, there does appear to be an ambivalent force which appears to the characters as chance or even fate, but which they suspect may be identified as a supernatural or divine force. In the world of *The Mayor* this force plays a very similar role to that played by Yhwh in the world of 1 Samuel. Although, as Draper points out,

> [Oedipus's] tragedy is predetermined by the will of the gods. Henchard's tragedy, however, is more evidently the product of his character.[69]

In fact it often looks as if Henchard's tragedy is predetermined by some malevolent force, aided and abetted by the flaw in his character.

There are in fact two characters in the novel whose function is connected to the supernatural: the weather prophet Fall and the furmity woman Mrs Goodenough. To some extent both of these characters have a parallel in 1 Samuel with the woman of Endor: Fall and Mrs Goodenough fulfil a similar function but from differing perspectives. Moynahan has

---

65. King, *Tragedy*, p. 42. Cf. also Gloucester's remark in *King Lear*:

> As flies to wanton boys are we to the gods;
> They kill us for their sport.

(Act IV, i). Hardy quotes these lines in his introduction to *Tess of the D'Urbervilles*.
  66. Seymour-Smith, *Hardy*, pp. 334-35.
  67. Schwarz, 'Beginnings', p. 34.
  68. Schweik, 'Character and Fate', p. 137.
  69. Draper, 'Mayor', p. 57.

pointed to the similarity between Henchard's encounter with Fall and 1 Samuel 28, but his analysis misses a few key points. Although the text does indeed draw attention to the biblical narrative, it is not only to the incident Moynahan cites.[70] What is significant is that the effect of the statement that Henchard 'felt like Saul at his reception by Samuel'[71] is also to recall Saul's final 'reception' by Samuel, namely the encounter with Samuel's ghost. Like Saul in 1 Samuel 28, Henchard feels that his circumstances are critical. Reduced to desperation by his lack of success in the market (in Saul's case in the warfare with the Philistines), Henchard is keenly aware that his conflict with Farfrae has reached a point of no return, which notion he remarks upon to Jopp:

> 'Now', said Henchard, digging his strong eyes into Jopp's face, 'one thing is necessary to me, as the biggest corn-and-hay-dealer in these parts. The Scotchman, who's taking the town trade so bold into his hands, must be cut out. D'ye hear? We two can't live side by side—that's clear and certain'.[72]

Thus the two men plot to bankrupt Farfrae by means of competition. Crucial to the failure of their scheme is the weather, which, it must be remembered, is a constant source of misfortune to Henchard. The unfavourable weather in June prompts Henchard to consider consulting Fall, though he keeps his intention secret even from Jopp. This secrecy is contiguous with the parallel with 1 Samuel, as it not only highlights pagan superstition but also emphasizes the moment of recognition. A sense of eeriness, already initiated in the description of the path to Fall's house, heightens the drama: Fall not only recognizes Henchard, he appears to have anticipated his arrival and his business. Moynahan observes that the manner of recognition is different, and dismisses the parallel of the offer of food as 'a contrasting touch of homely realism'[73] without recognizing that the offer of food once the matter is concluded, together with its refusal, makes a further connection between the earlier remark referring to Saul's reception by Samuel and the episode between Saul and the woman of Endor.

Crucially, Moynahan states erroneously that 'Fall's prediction does turn out to be wrong'.[74] It is critical to the irony of the novel that the forecaster's advice does indeed turn out to be correct; the rain comes, admittedly not as

70. Moynahan (p. 127) believes the reader is directed to 1 Sam. 9.14-24.
71. *The Mayor*, p. 259.
72. *The Mayor* p. 256.
73. Moynahan, 'Relationships' p. 127.
74. Moynahan, 'Relationships' p. 126.

dramatically as Fall had predicted, but too late for Henchard. Moreover, the events that result from the encounter are very significant in the resemblance between the two narratives, a significance to which Moynahan does not give enough consideration. The fact that 'Henchard, unlike Saul, does not die immediately after his visit to the seer'[75] is not the point. Saul's death in battle the following day is suicide; Henchard's hasty and self-destructive commercial frenzy is in effect financial suicide, by his own hand and characterized by his own idiosyncrasy:

> If Henchard had only waited long enough he might at least have avoided loss though he had not made a profit. But the momentum of his character knew no patience,[76]

as has already been noted.[77]

Fall is connected with tragic reversal. Henchard goes to consult Fall concerning the weather for the harvest, prompted by his superstitious nature. His reluctance to disclose his action even to Jopp is based on the fear that accompanies a course of action frowned upon by religious authorities. The disparity between institutionalized religion and pagan practice is remarked upon by the narrator, who reports Fall to be 'astonished that men could profess so little and believe so much, when at church they professed so much and believed so little'.[78] Similarly, when Saul consults the woman of Endor he goes in disguise because the practice of necromancy has been outlawed (by him) as contrary to the practice of Yahwism (as indicated by Samuel, 1 Sam. 15.23). Fall recognizes Henchard and offers him food, which he declines (cf. Saul). The prediction that Fall gives Henchard is accurate and the outcome ruins him (cf. Saul). The chief contrast between *The Mayor* and 1 Samuel is that the reason for Henchard's ruin is that he does not act wisely on the prediction, which only concerns the weather and not his fate. While Saul is condemned to death the following day, Henchard only receives information. His rash actions in response to that information are, nevertheless, economic suicide, and his reaction to the outcome is to imagine that someone is performing black magic against him.

The furmity woman, Mrs Goodenough, performs the function of tragic recognition, and has been discussed above. What connects her with the woman of Endor (who is usually described as a witch) is not only her function but also her appearance. She appears three times in the novel: the

75. Moynahan, 'Relationships' p. 126.
76. *The Mayor*, p. 263.
77. See above, p. 244.
78. *The Mayor*, p. 258.

first time, at the fair at Weydon-Priors, she is described as 'a haggish creature of about fifty', scraping a large spoon in a large three-legged crock (p. 73). When Susan returns to the spot many years later with Elizabeth-Jane the woman is described as 'haggard, wrinkled, and almost in rags', she croaks 'in a broken voice', she is 'tentless, dirty' and sells 'poor slop', and she is variously described by the narrator as 'the old woman' and 'the hag' (pp. 88-89). When she later appears before the court, charged with committing a nuisance, she is 'an old woman of mottled countenance, attired in a shawl of that nameless tertiary hue which comes, but cannot be made' and 'an apron that had been white in times so comparatively recent as still to contrast visibly with the rest of her clothes' (p. 272). Although the woman of Endor is never described in such terms, which after all are the stereotypical marks of a witch in the world of *The Mayor* rather than that of 1 Samuel, the connection between this depiction and the profession of the woman of Endor serves to enhance the connection between their respective functions. While Fall reveals the future, Mrs Goodenough reveals the past. She has come on bad times during Henchard's rise to power; similarly we may infer that the woman of Endor has lost her means of living, which is more directly due to Saul owing to his prohibition of necromancy. Both Mrs Goodenough and the woman of Endor function as agents of recognition within the scheme of the tragic vision. It may or may not be by chance that Mrs Goodenough is in Casterbridge, but it is certainly by chance that Henchard is acting as magistrate on the day of her hearing and thus suffers a heavy blow to his reputation which precipitates his ruin,

> Small as the police-court incident had been in itself, it formed the edge or turn in the incline of Henchard's fortunes. On that day—almost at that minute—he passed the ridge of prosperity and honour, and began to descend rapidly on the other side.[79]

The imagery of the wheel of fate confirms that the characters most closely related to the supernatural are the agents of fate and function within the scheme of the tragic vision in the novel. Until this point, despite his bankruptcy, he still has Lucetta's promise of marriage, but in despair at learning the fate of Henchard's first wife she marries Farfrae in secret. It is also significant that it is not after the oracle that resulted in his bankruptcy but rather after the revelation of his past misdeed that he begins to consider the approach of the time when he will be released from his oath

---

79. *The Mayor*, p. 291.

of sobriety. In some ways the furmity woman is a better candidate than Fall for a 'witch' of Endor figure because she brings up the ghost of the past into the present, with terrible consequences. Her disclosure is the point of Henchard's ultimate breakdown.

The Significance for an Intertextual Reading

It appears, then, that Hardy's use of tragic form and motif is intricately related to his use of the biblical material as a source for *The Mayor*. The relationship between the two texts is informed by Hardy's concern with the Greek tragic tradition. The absence of Yhwh in *The Mayor* in its intertextual relationship with 1 Samuel is central to the understanding of the tragic vision. The comparisons and contrasts between the two texts are informed by the actions of Yhwh in 1 Samuel and the workings of chance and fate in *The Mayor*. While Fussell's examination of the workings of time and delay is plausible, a reading of the novel's overall stance seems to indicate that there is a concrete sense of Greek tragic form, which may incorporate the 'maladroit delay' but which is not undermined by it. The 'maladroit delay', chance, fate—all these concepts operate as powers which control human destiny in a manner not unlike the manner in which Yhwh controls human destiny in 1 Samuel. In both texts human destiny is controlled in an ambivalent manner, wherein lies a crucial aspect of the tragic vision.

This raises the question of the effects of such a transposition in Hardy's treatment of the biblical material. It is of profound significance for the reading of Henchard as a tragic hero. If there is no deity ordering the sequence of events, or afflicting his creatures with evil spirits, then the tragic is internalized. True to the textbook definitions of tragedy, Henchard is well endowed with hubris, and the actions which arise from his flaw draw out their consequences towards his downfall. Yet unlike, for example, *Antigone*, or more theatrically *Electra*, the divine has no part to play in determining the tragic hero's destiny. Henchard is at no point given any account of or explanation for what happens to him. Electra is commanded by Castor to leave Argos and her long lost brother; Oedipus perceives that Apollo has ordained his agonies; Saul has Samuel to tell him that Yhwh has rejected him from being King and that he will die in battle against the Philistines. Henchard must question alone the circumstances of his plight. Good tragedy demands a degree of self questioning on the part of the hero, for if the hero does not repent or regret or at the very least recognize the past error then the circumstances of fate would be perceived merely as disaster and not as tragedy. That there is nothing that might be interpreted as forgiveness in response to this repentance or regret or recognition; in other words, that fate presses the hero towards destruction regardless of that self questioning is also of the essence of tragedy. For Henchard, not only is there no forgiveness, there is no source of forgiveness to which he might apply. The effect of this is to preclude a resolution, to remove any semblance of catharsis from *The Mayor*'s tragic vision. Yet the novel ends with order restored, with Farfrae governing the political and commercial affairs of Casterbridge, and his wife, Elizabeth-Jane, in a 'latitude of calm weather' and 'equable serenity'.[80]

Conclusions

The exploration of the sociological approach has pointed out areas in which there are parallels between interpretations of *The Mayor* and 1 Samuel, while the examination of feminist approaches to Hardy has drawn attention to the differences between the texts. The investigation into the role of fate and chance in *The Mayor* has shown that there are points of contact with 1 Samuel, particularly with reference to the conception of ambivalent forces which operate in the field of human destiny.

We have seen how a careful intertextual reading results in a more profound understanding of 1 Samuel as a source for *The Mayor* than does Moynahan's sensitive but flawed article. By no means is there any intention here to assert that 1 Samuel is the only, or even the most significant, source for the novel, but it is certainly an important one, and as the intertextual approach demonstrates, more than simply a source. The reworking of the biblical material into *The Mayor* is fundamental to the latter's tragic vision, and the examination of this tragic vision correspondingly gives clues to a broader understanding of the tragic vision in 1 Samuel, since Hardy's poetic eye has captured the essence of the tragic in the biblical narrative. We are not dealing here merely with a conflict of generations: the implications of the intertextual study go further than that. On the basis of this examination we might go as far as to conclude that Saul without Yhwh is Henchard. Yet, if this seems to be pressing the point, at least there is clear evidence that a central feature of the tragic vision of both 1 Samuel and *The Mayor* is the ambivalence of the forces that interact with human destiny to control it.

Hardy's motivation in writing Yhwh out of the story must certainly be a consequence of his engaging of Greek tragic form. His adherence to the

---

80. *The Mayor*, p. 410.

tenets of rationalism and Darwinism is widely acknowledged, and his agnosticism, which he held in a certain tension with these other philosophical standpoints, led him to the conclusion that religious practice ought to be divested of its supernatural elements and its emphasis on the literal authority of the Bible, which he felt were obstacles to those such as himself, the 'thinking man' who wished for a return to the simplicity of Jesus' religious teaching. He was preoccupied with questions relating to the nature of God and God's conduct with respect to humanity, rather than with the question of the existence of God. Indeed, he wrote

> …the Supreme Mover or Movers, the Prime Force or Forces, must be either limited in power, unknowing, or cruel—which is obvious enough and has been for centuries.[81]

And while it was this sentiment which caused him to be labelled a pessimist (and worse!), the remark demonstrates Hardy's relentless attempts to fathom the purpose of deity who was supposed to have created a world in which, in Hardy's view, his involvement was ambivalent.

There can be little doubt that Hardy's interest in biblical narrative led him to consider using more than an occasional point of reference, and that, though the work remains the product of his own creative imagination, Hardy has conceived the biblical story in modern terms and produced a work that is, among other things, a deeply absorbing rendering of an ancient legend. Such a reading contributes much to an understanding of *The Mayor of Casterbridge*; it coexists comfortably with readings that focus on the novel as history, as psychology, and, crucially, as tragedy. Hardy drew his sources from a wide variety of texts and observations and it is essential to acknowledge his indebtedness to the Bible as a source. To do so adds a dimension to historical perspectives in providing a frame of reference for a new set of historical contexts, for example the corn trade over against the Philistine war. Such acknowledgment also informs a psychological reading by providing a background framework within which the protagonists' responses may be located. Furthermore, this idea connects with the understanding of *The Mayor* as tragedy by contributing an idea of the significance of the attitude of the deity.

This reading of *The Mayor of Casterbridge* also adds to the understanding of 1 Samuel. If *The Mayor* is an intertext (i.e. not a subtext or a supertext) in relation to 1 Samuel, a reading that stresses this relationship

---

81. Michael Millgate, *Thomas Hardy: A Biography* (Oxford: Oxford University Press) p. 302.

essentially brings fresh perspectives to an understanding of the anterior text as well. For instance, the fact that *The Mayor* is conceived as tragedy testifies to the presence of the tragic vision in 1 Samuel. The relationship between Henchard and Farfrae serves to emphasize the significance of character to the understanding of the biblical narrative. The absence of divine ordination points to an examination of the ambivalent role of Yhwh in the fate of Saul and David. Reading *The Mayor of Casterbridge* as an intertext may (and should) thus inform the reading of 1 Samuel.

Chapter 7

CONCLUSION

I have summarized my conclusions at the end of each chapter and I do not propose to repeat that task here. The intertextual relationships between Lamartine's *Saül* and 1 Samuel have been investigated, as have those between Hardy's *The Mayor of Casterbridge* and 1 Samuel. The posterior texts are related by source to the anterior text, and the enterprise of examining source relationships intertextually has been more common in biblical studies than examining other kinds of relationships, despite Culler's caveat that this is 'what the concept was designed to transcend'.[1] Before proceeding to my concluding remarks it seems fitting to explore some of the intertextual relationships between *Saül* and *The Mayor of Casterbridge*, which are not related to each other by source (except through having a common source in 1 Samuel), but which have many points of textual contact and connection. There are four categories which, on the basis of the conclusions of the foregoing chapters, suggest themselves as possible candidates for examination: plot, characterization, theme and the involvement of the deity. As this investigation is made on the basis of what has already been determined, it will not be very detailed, but will draw on and attenuate the conclusions that have already been made.

The plot of *Saül*, in which all the events occur in a matter of hours, is considerably more compact than the that of *The Mayor*, where the action spans many years, from the wife-selling incident in Henchard's youth to Elizabeth-Jane's marriage (although the years between the wife-selling and the reappearance of Susan and her daughter are not treated within the plot of the novel). There are a number of parallels: Both Henchard and Saül have known great success in their fields of endeavour. Saül has been an admirable military leader, as is shown by the scene in which Micol recites Psalms that touch on his past successes; Henchard's term of office

1. Culler, 'Presupposition', p. 1388.

as Mayor of Casterbridge has been characterized by success in his profession as corn factor. It is only at the appearance of David in *Saül* and Farfrae in *The Mayor* that events begin to overrun these heroic figures. Both are already somewhat troubled, with Saül's impending battle against the Philistines likely to end in defeat and Henchard's problem with the 'growed' wheat threatening financial loss and the whole town affected by 'unprincipled bread'.

In both cases the younger man arrives just in time to reverse a potentially damaging situation and is welcomed. Personal difficulties begin only when a threat to the older man's status is perceived. In Saül's case he is irked by David's talk of God's favour, but becomes enraged when David leads his army in battle carrying Goliath's sword. Henchard finds Farfrae's popularity threatening, but breaks off relations with him (both socially and professionally) after seeing Farfrae dance with Elizabeth-Jane. Saül attempts to influence Jonathas against David, while Henchard requests Elizabeth-Jane, in a manner she cannot refuse, to discourage Farfrae's attentions. Each man becomes father-in-law to his rival: Micol is already married to David, though by the time Elizabeth-Jane marries Farfrae Henchard knows he is not her biological father but has come to view her as a kind of surrogate daughter, and until shortly before her wedding Elizabeth-Jane believes herself to be Henchard's daughter. David takes Saül's role as leader of the army owing to Saül's mental incapacity, and Farfrae becomes mayor during a steep portion of Henchard's gradient of decline; Henchard perceives the role of greeting the Royal Personage to be rightfully his. Jonathas warns David of the risk his father poses, and Elizabeth-Jane warns Farfrae that Henchard might become dangerous. However, the perceived insubordination leads Saül to attempt to kill David after the initial battle, and leads to Henchard's attempt on Farfrae's life in the corn stores. While Farfrae is the means of saving his own life by his words to Henchard, David's life is preserved by Achimelech's intervention, which results in Saül's murder of Achimelech. However, owing to the different worlds of the two texts, Saül's relationship with David is never reversed in the manner of Henchard's with Farfrae when he enters Farfrae's employ.

Both Saül and Henchard find their paternal relationships disintegrating as they become more isolated: Saül's last dialogue with Jonathas leaves them without the possibility of reconciliation, and Jonathas dies, while Elizabeth-Jane's discovery of Henchard's lie about her true parentage causes her to reject him, and Henchard dies without reconciliation to her. In both cases this lack of reconciliation can be traced to recognition of an individual: in Saül's case Samuel, the appearance of whose ghost is the reason for Saül's struggle against the heavens, and in Henchard's case Newson, to whom he has lied about Elizabeth-Jane's death; and also Mrs Goodenough, who reveals the crime of his youth. Both *Saül* and *The Mayor* end with harmony for the wider community: Casterbridge has Farfrae as mayor and Israel has been victorious against the Philistines. However, the personal cost to the central characters has been enormous: despite Israel's victory, Saül and Jonathas are dead; Elizabeth-Jane has learned to expect hardship, Henchard and Lucetta are dead and even Farfrae has suffered some loss: his respectability has been compromised by one impure and one illegitimate wife.

The parallels of character are numerous. Henchard and Saül are two men with a similar nobility and a similar flaw. Both Henchard and Saül are heroic but gloomy characters and both are inclined to the belief that their suffering is cosmic in origin. Saül loses his reason and degenerates into raving, though Henchard's moods never descend into insanity. Both men are guilty of hubris, but whereas Saül's crime is the murder of Samuel, Henchard's is a social crime: the wife-selling, and also the lie to Newson. Neither man initially attributes the reversal of his fate to his crime. Saül simply believes that God has abandoned him and that his suffering is wholly undeserved and Henchard believes his reputation has been harmed by Elizabeth's having served in the Three Mariners. It is only with the revelation of their crimes that Saül and Henchard begin to comprehend the meaning of their suffering. Both Saül and Henchard attempt to combat the forces that cause their agony after this revelation: in Saül's case after the scene with the Pythonisse and in Henchard's case after the scene where the furmity woman appears before him in court. Like Saül, Henchard vacillates between hatred and affection towards the man he considers his enemy, but despite all efforts to control his emotions, like Saül he is eventually driven to distraction and the desire for murder. The origin, for both men, of this enmity is a fear of being usurped after learning of the popularity of the rival: Saül hears the cries of the soldiers proclaiming David 'chef et roi dans les combats,'[2] and Henchard learns from a child that the women 'wish [Farfrae] was the master instead of Henchard'.[3] Both men are self-destructive to the extent that Saül commits suicide during the battle and Henchard contemplates suicide at Ten Hatches Hole, but is prevented by the sight of the effigy of himself.

2.   *Saül*, l. 1135. Translation: leader and king in battle.
3.   *The Mayor*, p. 171.

There are also points of contact between *Saül* and *The Mayor* in the characterization of David and Farfrae. There is a father–son typology in the relationship between David and Saül, which Jonathas exploits in his hope that Saül will accept David's return, 'N'aviez-vous pas deux fils? N'avais-je pas un frère?'[4] A similar familial closeness is alluded to when Henchard remarks that Farfrae reminds him of his dead brother. Both David and Farfrae believe themselves to be beneficiaries of the goodwill of supernatural forces. David is convinced of God's help in battle, and Farfrae believes the decision of the Council that he should be mayor is a result of 'Powers above us'.[5] Both David and Farfrae are musically gifted: David's singing of Psalms is referred to by Saül, and Farfrae wins the hearts of both women and men with his singing. Neither David nor Farfrae can comprehend the emotional depths to which Saül and Henchard succumb, and both are characterized as somewhat shallow. However, Farfrae's miserly and acquisitive attitude to money is without parallel in the David of Lamartine's drama. David is the object of Micol's love just as Farfrae is the object of Elizabeth-Jane's love, and there are further relationships in the characterization of the women. Like Micol, Elizabeth-Jane is inclined to a pessimistic attitude with regard to the deity. Micol's belief that God has abandoned her is echoed by Elizabeth-Jane's fear of tempting Providence by being too cheerful or extravagant, in case Providence afflict her and her mother, 'as He used to do'.[6] This points to a corresponding similarity in perspective between Micol and Saül and between Elizabeth-Jane and Henchard.

A further parallel of character is that between Abner and Jopp. Abner considers himself to be David's enemy just as Jopp views Farfrae with resentment. Abner is Saül's general, usurped by David's military brilliance, while Jopp initially loses the opportunity of being Henchard's manager to Farfrae, and even when Henchard eventually employs him he continues to regard Farfrae as a rival. However, although Abner advises Saül to consult the Pythonisse, Henchard's decision to consult the weather prophet Fall is a decision he withholds from Jopp. Jopp contributes to Henchard's downfall by exposing his earlier dalliance with Lucetta, which results in Lucetta's death. Abner contributes to Saül's downfall by encouraging David to lead the army, which results in Achimelech's death (by Abner's hand).

4.   *Saül*, l. 302. Translation: Did you not have two sons? Did I not have a brother?
5.   *The Mayor*, p. 316.
6.   *The Mayor*, p. 158.

Thematically and stylistically there are a few similarities between *Saül* and *The Mayor*. Both Saül and Henchard perceive in nature an enemy: Saül's expression of terror at the dawn is echoed in Henchard's gloom as he regards the night after learning Elizabeth-Jane's identity. Both imagine supernatural beings haunt them: Saül speaks of 'un fantôme' (a phantom), while Henchard likens his situation to the work of 'infernal harpies'. But while Saül merely projects his state of mind onto natural phenomena, Henchard's fortunes are actually dependent on the weather, which in Chapter 26 is a significant contributory factor in his bankruptcy. Another theme that occurs in both *Saül* and *The Mayor* is that of human blindness, in a metaphorical sense. This has more to do with the fact that both texts are tragic than with a merging of textual boundaries, as the theme is recurrent in the tragic vision. For both Saül and Henchard the feeling of not knowing what fate holds prompts a consultation with an individual who claims to be able to reveal the future, but the revelation of the Pythonisse is a direct revelation of Saül's destiny, whereas Henchard's information from Fall contains no such details; it is Henchard's response to Fall's prediction which has disastrous consequences. The stylistic device of naming to emphasize a relationship is used by both Lamartine and Hardy, particularly with reference to Micol and Elizabeth-Jane, who are both characterized by this technique in relation to the tension between father and husband. Thus in Micol's opening scenes she is addressed as 'David's wife' when she is praying for her husband's safety, but later when she is concerned for Saül the technique is used to accent her filial relationship. Similarly, in Elizabeth-Jane's final scenes with Henchard she is named by the narrator in accordance with her loyalties, for example after the uncomfortable encounter with Henchard at her wedding, 'Mrs Donald Farfrae had discovered in a screened corner a new bird cage'.[7]

However, some other important themes in *Saül* have no correlatives in *The Mayor*, and vice versa. The conflict between Saül and Jonathas over what the latter considers to be blasphemy has no parallel in *The Mayor*, and the significance of social history in *The Mayor* is absent in *Saül*; even the theme of the old regime being replaced by the new order is discounted, since in *Saül* there is no background relating the election of Saül as king and no account of David's subsequent kingship. In these two matters the respective worlds of the texts are entirely different and have no contact even by virtue of their common source in 1 Samuel.

---

7.   *The Mayor*, p. 405.

Both texts handle the concept of the involvement of the divine in human affairs with tragic consequences. However, while *Saül* implies an active but invisible God, the conception of the deity in *The Mayor* is more transcendent. The chief difference is one of conviction: Saül and his companions are certain that God is active in the human sphere, and some characters in the drama, notably the Pythonisse and Achimelech, claim to speak with divine authority. Despite Henchard's 'fetichistic' nature, he never discerns meaning from sources that might be described as divine. Instead he is inclined to believe in other kinds of supernatural forces, such as the possibility that someone is 'roasting a waxen image' of him (despite his denial of such beliefs), or that he is 'subject to visitations of the devil'. Such supernatural forces are entirely absent in *Saül*; even the Pythonisse, the medium, claims to speak for God rather than performing necromancy, and there is no implication that the appearance of Samuel's ghost is the product of her work. If we infer that the appearance of Samuel is her doing, then we must be sceptical of her claim to be 'the voice of the supreme God', and such a reading would be forced. The world of *Saül* is one in which divine involvement in human affairs is taken for granted, whereas the world of *The Mayor* is a world that advocates a belief in 'Providence', a force which, whether beneficent of malevolent, is perceived by most of the characters to be justified by virtue of its omnipotence. However, the role of 'Providence' is not overt, and Henchard meets his destiny through a combination of the workings of his character and the workings of chance, coincidence and fortuity. There is no corresponding role of chance in *Saül*; each event is determined by the deity who is directing Saul's destiny. Even Saül's suicide comes at a point where he can neither continue to inveigh against the heavens nor turn back and be reconciled to God. That the battle cries he hears are those of his own soldiers is ironic, but there is no suggestion that the irony is one of accident. The characters' perceptions of divine activity in both *Saül* and *The Mayor* have strong associations with Greek tragedy, but the crucial difference between the two texts is that while Saül comes to comprehend his fate through the activity of God, Henchard can only proceed with self-questioning.

Perhaps when Tod Linafelt wrote that one might read intertextually to cite God against God there was no implication that one might read extrabiblical literature; however, having drawn a possible inference it may be concluded that reading the story of Saul in 1 Samuel and some of its intertexts may be a means of privileging Saul over against Yhwh, Samuel and the narrator of 1 Samuel, and also a means of privileging the elements that point to the tragic vision over against the arguments of scholars such as Steiner. The tragic vision of 1 Samuel is attested by these examples of interpretation and remodelling by the poetic eye of Lamartine and of Hardy, as intertextual readings demonstrate, and much of the substance of plot, character, theme and the involvement of the deity in *Saül* and in *The Mayor* points to an affinity with Greek tragedy. The matrices within which these three texts operate can never be thoroughly investigated since their components are infinite, yet an exploration even of this scale points to countless possibilities for understanding Saul and the meaning of his anguish.

Summary of Main Findings

I have found that there is a structure in 1 Samuel that lends itself to the tragic: a lengthy series of doublets and repetitions prefigures and emphasizes the weaknesses of the tragic hero and the extent of his fall. Furthermore, this series presents a hero who at every turn struggles to comprehend the consequences of his actions and the motivation of forces beyond his control. Though it has been argued that these dual accounts have their origins in a variety of sources, the editor or writer of the edition of 1 Samuel that has come down to us has juxtaposed these accounts in a structure that paints a picture of their hero in a manner so similar to ancient Greek tragedy in its world view as to warrant the label 'tragic'.

The central element of this similarity of world view between 1 Samuel and ancient Greek tragedy is the ambivalent motivation and behaviour of the deity. This ambivalence is particularly striking in view of the fact that similar themes emerge; for example when the deity visits insanity upon the hero leading to murderous behaviour towards the hero's children (cf. Heracles), or the hero's attempt to discern his fate in advance in order to cheat it and his pursuit of his fate (cf. Oedipus). Also central to this similarity of world view is the idea of the hero's attempt to thwart the deity and thereby his fate, and the idea that the hero's fate results from some error or hamartia.

While terms such as 'tragedy', 'fate' and 'hamartia' rightfully belong to the literature of ancient Greece, it must be recognized that textually these terms are part of the currency of contemporary western culture. So, to no small extent, is the literature of the Hebrew Bible. We have inherited these terms and they have become part of our literary outlook. For these ancient Greek terms to be used with reference to the Hebrew Bible, it is helpful to explore their meanings intertextually; this study has explored two texts that interface with 1 Samuel and which have made use of the tragic vision.

I have found that the concept of a tragic vision in 1 Samuel underlies both Lamartine's *Saül: Tragédie* and Hardy's *The Mayor of Casterbridge*. These texts are inextricably bound up with 1 Samuel, though their worlds are very dissimilar. What is ultimately striking is that the ambivalent deity, even *in absentia*, features strongly within the structures of plot and characterization. Although these two texts have received critical attention linking them with 1 Samuel, this attention has been very slight. Criticism on Lamartine's drama is minimal and scholarship on the relationships between *The Mayor* and 1 Samuel has been meagre and unconvincing. This study has found that there are substantial relationships between *The Mayor* and 1 Samuel, but that these relationships are best explored intertextually rather than source-critically. It has also shown that the intertextual relationships between Lamartine's *Saül* and 1 Samuel constitute the drama's significance.

Methodological Considerations

As I have stated, terms such as 'tragedy' and 'tragic' belong originally to ancient Greek literature. It has been considered problematic to use such terms with reference to the Hebrew Bible. A common approach to this problem has been to use Sewall's term 'tragic vision' to describe a tragic quality within literature that originates outside ancient Greek culture, and this appears to be a helpful solution. In this study I have implied a distinction between 'a tragedy', which requires certain formal and generic aspects, such as dramatic form and unity of time and place, and 'tragedy', used as a noun describing a tragic condition. The term 'tragic' has been used to describe that which pertains to the tragic vision. Thus *Saül* is a tragedy, but *The Mayor* is best described as a tragic novel. A categorical label for 1 Samuel in this manner is problematic because of its range; one must not forget that the text as a whole extends from 1 Samuel 1 to 2 Samuel 24 and not all of this deals with Saul. Saul's story is part of much larger composite text. For this reason I have discussed 'the tragic', or 'tragic elements' within a particular section of the narrative, viz. 1 Samuel 8 to 1 Samuel 31. It has been important not to confuse these definitions, since doing so would involve a blurring of the formal and generic distinctions between the texts.

This study has used poststructural techniques in its approach to the tragic vision in the three texts that are its objects. A literary technique, rather than for example a historical technique, was required in view of the subject matter: a non-literary approach to the tragic vision would have been somewhat anomalous. The advantage of poststructuralism is partly its philosophical focus: arguably ancient Greek literary theory has closer parallels with poststructuralism than with other theoretical approaches. In a discussion of poststructuralism, Tompkins writes,

> The insistence that language is constitutive of reality rather than merely reflective of it suggests that contemporary critical theory has come to occupy a position very similar to, if not the same as, that of the Greek rhetoricians for whom mastery of language meant mastery of the state.[8]

Furthermore, poststructuralism's political focus, as it is practised outwith the American school, has been valuable for this study. The exploration of a non-canonical text in a language other than English (*Saül*) is one feature of this outlook. A sense of political focus has also been important in view of Fiorenza's sentiments, quoted above, in which she urges biblical criticism to engage itself with the political in order to effect an ethical accountabiliy.[9] Such has been the intention of the political focus of this study. These two elements of political focus are discussed in more detail below.[10]

The choice of intertextuality as the medium for exploring textual relationships has provided the means for a fresh critical perspective on these texts. The study found that an intertextual approach was able to support a more persuasive argument in favour of the relationships between 1 Samuel and *The Mayor* and yielded more evidence than the previous source-critical approaches. Moreover, the intertextual approach to the relationship between 1 Samuel and *Saül* helps to clarify some of the material in Lamartine's drama which it would not be possible to do with a source-critical approach, particularly in respect of questions of its tragic dimension and its literary value. It must be noted that there may be some theoretical concerns surrounding my use of the concept of intertextuality, as I do not use it precisely as Kristeva constitutes it. However, following the example of Pyper, van Wolde and others, I have employed the technique in a manner common in biblical studies. In any case, the term and concept of 'intertextuality' has now been adopted by other critics and is no longer the exclusive property of Kristeva; nor should it be forced to conform to the strict definition that Kristeva or her followers might insist upon. As I have asserted in my introduction (following Clines and others), methodological discipleship can stifle insight. My usage and application of

8. In Tompkins, *Reader-Response*, p. 226.
9. See above, p. 111.
10. See below, pp. 266-70.

the term is consonant with that of other scholars who have used Kristeva's work as a springboard to uncharted territory.

Limitations of this Approach and Areas for Further Research

I argued in my introduction that the choice of Lamartine's *Saül: Tragédie* and Hardy's *The Mayor of Casterbridge* had political implications, and I would like to deal here with some of these, since they set limits on the focus of the study. Both Hardy and Lamartine wrote many works that have been given an established place in the literary canons of their respective countries of origin. Though Hardy's reworking of the Saul narrative is within the canon, Lamartine's has been overlooked to the extent that there is virtually no scholarship on it. Many of the reasons for its exclusion are associated with those I have discussed above.[11]

The concept of 'canon' is now regarded in some circles as politically problematic. In the United States in particular feminists have argued that the literary canon excludes work by female writers; similarly, objections have been voiced by those who oppose the 'white-centredness' of the canon. Themes as well as writers have acquired particular positions: the canon's relationship with social culture ensures that heterosexuality is represented as 'normal', disability as 'abnormal', childhood as a time of innocence, and old age as unfortunate. From Saskatoon to Stornoway, English-language literature drowns out non-anglophone voices. The canon is a social text and its power extends beyond educational institutions to be exerted wherever literature is made available, from bookstores to television and the tabloid press.

Harold Bloom has devoted a massive volume to the defence of the Canon.[12] In his introductory chapter, 'An Elegy for the Canon', he identifies what he terms a 'School of Resentment' (made up of feminists, Marxists and other groups of people with political agendas) whose members, he claims,

> go so far as to suggest that works join the canon because of successful advertising and propaganda campaigns. The compeers of these skeptics sometimes go farther and question even Shakespeare, whose eminence seems to them something of an imposition.[13]

11. See above, pp. 178-81.
12. See Bloom, *The Western Culture: The Books and Schools of the Ages* (London: Macmillan, 1995).
13. Bloom (1995), p. 20.

The reason for Bloom's outrage becomes clear from his first chapter, in which he argues that Shakespeare is the 'centre of the Canon'. Although he grants that there may be some truth in the argument that the nature of aesthetic value is socially constructed, he insists that political engagement with social constructs has no place in discourse surrounding the canon. In a tone redolent of mid-life crisis, Bloom begins with a metaphor of human mortality (the human lifespan is too short to allow one to read every book; the canon aids choice) and argues that the canon is constructed by authors seeking immortality. Though certain that 'Shakespeare's eminence is…the rock upon which the School of Resentment must at last founder',[14] he paints a picture of a future world in which departments of English will become departments of cultural studies, 'where *Batman* comics, Mormon theme parks, television, movies, and rock will replace Chaucer, Milton, Wordsworth, and Wallace Stevens'.[15] (It would be intriguing to discover that any western nation, apart from the United States, accords Wallace Stevens a significant place in the canon.)

A nostalgia for the past and contempt for contemporary culture permeates Bloom's argument: according to Bloom only a handful of Yale students exhibit 'an authentic passion for reading',[16] and, in similar vein, he asserts that his book is not directed towards academics because 'only a small remnant of them still read for the love of reading'.[17]

The crux of Bloom's argument is its downfall: he imagines that writers who produce works worthy of inclusion in the canon will think like him. He suggests that if Dr Johnson or George Eliot were to experience 'MTV Rap' or virtual reality they would respond with a 'strong refusal of such irrational entertainments'.[18] How can he be so sure? Though he pours scorn on the work of Maya Angelou and Alice Walker, he does not consider the possibility that young African American lesbians might experience the construction of social and textual discourse so differently from Harold Bloom that their conception of aesthetic value discourages them from reading Johnson or Eliot. Perhaps this is one of a plethora of reasons that Yale is not spilling over with African American lesbians who have an authentic passion for reading.

14. Bloom (1995), p. 25.
15. Bloom (1995), p. 519.
16. Bloom (1995), p. 519.
17. Bloom (1995), p. 518.
18. Bloom (1995), p. 517.

Interestingly, the vast majority of the authors whose place in the western canon Bloom defends are anglophone; he does not tackle the question of what may constitute the western canon in non-anglophone western countries, and some of the authors he includes (e.g. Walt Whitman) are considerably more important in the United States than elsewhere in the anglophone world.

Bloom fails to give an adequate response to the criticisms raised by the groups of activists he terms the 'School of Resentment' and the tone of his defence of the canon does little to mask the gaps in his argument. It appears that he has failed to appreciate the political implications of the existence of the canon, though he claims to recognize them in some degree, and his assertion of his views without engaging the arguments of his adversaries amounts not to scholarship but to polemic.

While Bloom argues unconvincingly in defence of the canon, Peter Widdowson is very persuasive in his critique of the canon. He, too, is preoccupied with the question of aesthetic value in the canon. Widdowson's central thesis involves the suggestion that Hardy's novel *The Hand of Ethelberta* is as significant as *Tess of the d'Urbervilles*. He argues that the process of ranking literary works according to hierarchies of value

> is neither hself-evident nor natural—although it has, crucially, been naturalized... *Tess* is not self-evidently 'better' than *Ethelberta*, except to the 'educated eye', nor does it intrinsically contain its value—any more than ivory or silver do in their ante-social, pre-utilized state.[19]

He points out that the process is one of discrimination, with all the connotations of the word, and emphasizes that the reader functions 'within a critical mindset constructed around her or him by prevailing cultural institutions and discourses, themselves already deeply naturalized'.[20] Widdowson concludes that part of the reason that *Ethelberta* is considered to be less significant than *Tess*, and to hold a lowly position in the literary hierarchy in comparison with *Tess*, is that it does not handle the themes that have become identified with Hardy's *oeuvre*. It does not fulfil the expectations of a canonical Hardy novel. Widdowson is conscious of the political function of his study in terms of its critique of the manner in which texts are 'constructed and appropriated by the dominant ideological institutions'[21] and suggests that if 'Hardy' is recognized as constructed

---

19. Widdowson (1989), p. 2.
20. Widdowson (1989), p. 2.
21. Widdowson (1989), p. 125.

within discourse, then Hardy can be reconstructed just as properly on behalf of an alternative interest. Widdowson's alternative interest is to rescue 'a radical Thomas Hardy' from his critical niche in the canon. A similar case could perhaps be argued for Lamartine.

Throughout his study Widdowson holds back from claiming outright that *Ethelberta* holds a similar literary value to *Tess*, though there are moments where one may sense a strong desire on his part to do just that. Yet his focus is on the significance of *Ethelberta*, a position which can be appropriated into this study in respect of Lamartine's *Saül*. The question of literary value has in any case been of little interest to contemporary structural theorists, and this is the literary-critical movement from which the concept of intertextuality developed. Structuralism, as a theoretical tool, may be employed in analysis of any text, from a bus ticket to the Bible. Curiously, however, structural analyses of bus tickets are startlingly rare; works by Chekhov are considerably more popular as objects of structuralists' interest. The choice of Lamartine's *Saül*, juxtaposed with Hardy's *Mayor*, is a conscious attempt to subvert canonical power and to accord equal status to both texts at the starting-point of intertextual study. While *Saül* may be considered to have little literary value in the discourse contexts that construct 'Lamartine', it is arguably of more interest than a bus ticket. Like Widdowson, I have an 'alternative interest', which is to rescue Lamartine's *Saül* from its canonical exclusion. The purpose of this rescue is not to place *Saül* within any canon but rather to call into question the political act of canon construction.

This study handles only two established texts in relation to 1 Samuel, and both of them are written texts. While they give an impression of ways in which two authors have re-conceived the tragic vision in 1 Samuel with a poetic eye, the length of the study did not permit an exploration of the manner in which the story of Saul has been understood artistically or musically. This gap could be viewed as an area for further research. Other areas for further research could include an attempt to discern a tragic structure in other parts of the Hebrew Bible, such as the book of Job, although there is a consensus to the effect that only the story of Saul realizes its tragic potential. This idea could also be explored further from a poststructural or intertextual perspective.

Summary Conclusions

In using intertextual theories I have been engaging with methodologies that are recent developments in the field of biblical studies. A poststructural approach is also something of a novelty, though it is receiving increasing support. This work is therefore applying new solution strategies to an old problem: trying to understand what happened to Saul. The use of extra-biblical literature has very little precedent in intertextual studies of the Hebrew Bible, and the fact represents a deficit in biblical scholarship. It is widely recognized that the Bible has had a more pervasive influence on western culture and society in the last few centuries than has any other single or composite text, and this influence has been examined sociologically, psychologically and source-critically. An intertextual examination provides the opportunity to explore the influence of the Bible in western culture with reference to the art a culture generates (whether it be painting, literature or music) and with reference to the structures of western societies. Such work would be beyond the scope of a single study; this thesis is a step towards the wider engagement of biblical studies with the contexts in which biblical studies occur. As such, it is determinedly conscious of concerns, such as those elucidated so cogently by Fiorenza,[22] that biblical studies operate ethical methodologies and hermeneutics.

22. See above, pp. 111-12.

BIBLIOGRAPHY

Abercrombie, Lascelles, *Thomas Hardy: A Critical Study* (London: Martin Secker, 1912).

Ackroyd, Peter R., *The First Book of Samuel* (Cambridge: Cambridge University Press, 1971).

Ahern, M.B., *The Problem of Evil* (London: Routledge & Kegan Paul, 1971).

Alfieri, Vittorio, *Saul e Filippo* (introduction and notes by Vittore Branca; Milano: Biblioteca Universale Rizzoli, 1980).

Alter, Robert, *The Art of Biblical Narrative* (London: George Allen & Unwin, 1981).

Anderson, Bernhard W., *The Living World of the Old Testament* (London: Longman, 3rd edn, 1978).

Aristotle, *Poetics and Rhetoric, also Demetrius on Style, Longinus on the Sublime: Essays in Classical Criticism* (introduction by T.A. Moxon; London: J.M. Dent & Sons; New York: E.P. Dutton & Co., 1934; reprinted 1955).

Aschkenasy, Nahama, 'Biblical Substructures in the Tragic Form: Hardy, *The Mayor of Casterbridge*. Agnon, *And the Crooked shall be Made Straight*', *Modern Language Studies* 13.1 (1983), pp. 101-110.

Bar-Efrat, Shimon, *Narrative Art in the Bible* (JSOTSup, 70; Sheffield: The Almond Press, 1989).

Bentzen, Aage, *Introduction to the Old Testament*, vols. I and II (Copenhagen: G.E.C. Gads Forlag, 1948 and 1949).

Berlin, Adele, *Poetics and Interpretation of Biblical Narrative* (Sheffield: The Almond Press, 1983).

Birkett, Mary Ellen, *Lamartine and the Poetics of Landscape* (Lexington: French Forum, 1982).

Bloom, Harold, *The Western Canon: The Books and School of the Ages* (London: Macmillan, 1995).

Bouchard, Larry D., *Tragic Method and Tragic Theology: Evil in Contemporary Drama and Religious Thought* (University Park: Pennsylvania State University Press, 1989).

Boumelha, Penny, *Thomas Hardy and Women: Sexual Ideology and Narrative Form* (Brighton: The Harvester Press, 1982).

Brown, Douglas, *Thomas Hardy* (Westport, CT: Greenwood Press, 1980 [reprint of the 1954 edn published London and New York: Longmans, Green & Co.]).

Brueggeman, Walter, 'Narrative Coherence and Theological Intentionality in 1 Samuel 18', *CBQ* 55 (1993), pp. 225-43.

Craig, Kenneth M., Jr, 'Rhetorical Aspects of Questions Answered with Silence', *CBQ* 56 (1994), pp. 221-39.

Crenshaw, James L. (ed.), *Theodicy in the Old Testament* (Philadelphia: Fortress Press; London: SPCK, 1983).

Culler, Jonathan, 'Presupposition and Intertextuality', *MLN* 91 (1976), 1380-96.

Davis, Stephen T. (ed,) *Encountering Evil: Live Options in Theodicy* (Edinburgh: T. & T. Clark, 1981).

Dike, D.A., 'A Modern Oedipus: *The Mayor of Casterbridge*', *Essays in Criticism* 2 (1952), pp. 169-79.

Draisma, Spike (ed.), *Intertextuality in Biblical Writings: Essays in honour of Bas van Iersel* (Kampen: Kok, 1989).

Draper, R.P., 'The Mayor of Casterbridge', *Critical Quarterly* 25:1 (1983), pp. 57-70.

Driver, S.R., *Notes on the Hebrew Text and the Topography of the Books of Samuel, with an Introduction on Hebrew Palaeography and the Ancient Versions, and Facsimiles of Inscriptions and Maps* (Oxford: Clarendon Press, 2nd edn, revised and enlarged, 1913).

Eagleton, Terry, *Literary Theory: An Introduction* (Oxford: Basil Blackwell, 1983).

Ebbatson, Roger, *Thomas Hardy: The Mayor of Casterbridge* (London: Penguin Books, 1994).

Eslinger, Lyle M., '"A Change of Heart!": 1 Samuel 16', in Eslinger, Lyle, and Glen Taylor (eds.), *Ascribe to the Lord: Biblical and Other Studies in Memory of Peter C. Craigie* (JSOTSup, 67; Sheffield: JSOT Press, 1988), pp. 341-61.

—*Into the Hands of the Living God* (JSOTSup, 84; Sheffield: Almond Press, 1989).

Euripides, *Medea and Other Plays* (trans. with an introduction by Philip Vellacott; London: Penguin Books, 1963).

Exum, J. Cheryl, *Tragedy and Biblical Narrative: Arrows of the Almighty* (Cambridge: Cambridge University Press, 1992).

Exum, J. Cheryl (ed.), *Tragedy and Comedy in the Bible* (Semeia, 32; Decatur, GA: Scholars Press, 1985).

Exum, J. Cheryl, and David J.A. Clines (eds.), *The New Literary Criticism and the Hebrew Bible* (JSOTSup, 143; Sheffield: JSOT Press, 1993).

Fewell, Danna N. (ed.), *Reading Between Texts: Intertextuality and the Hebrew Bible* (Literary Currents in Biblical Interpretation; Louisville, KY: Westminster/John Knox Press, 1992).

Fiorenza, Elisabeth Schüssler, 'The Ethics of Biblical Interpretation: Decentering Biblical Scholarship', *JBL* 107:1 (1988), pp. 3-17.

Fishbane, Michael, *Biblical Interpretation in Ancient Israel* (Oxford: Clarendon Press, 1985).

Fokkelman, J.P., *Narrative Art and Poetry in the Books of Samuel: A Full Interpretation Based on Stylistic and Structural Analyses*. II. *The Crossing Fates (I Sam. 13–31 & II Sam. 1)* (Assen: Van Gorcum, 1986).

Fortescue, William, *Alphonse de Lamartine: A Political Biography* (London: Croom Helm, 1983).

Frye, Northrop, *The Great Code: The Bible and Literature* (London: Routledge, 1982).

Fussell, D.H. 'The Maladroit Delay: The Changing Times in Hardy's 'The Mayor of Casterbridge'', *Critical Quarterly* 21.3 (1979), pp. 17-30.

Garsiel, Moshe, *I Samuel: A Literary Study of Comparative Structures, Analogies and Parallels* (Ramat Gan, Israel: Revivim Publishing House, 1983).

Genette, Gérard, *Narrative Discourse: An Essay in Method* (trans. Jane E. Lewin; Oxford: Basil Blackwell, 1980).

Gevirtz, Stanley, *Patterns in the Early Poetry of Israel* (Chicago: University of Chicago Press, 1963).

Gibson, John C.L., 'Biblical Tragedy', *Reformed World* 36.7 (1981), pp. 291-98.

—'On Evil in the Book of Job', in Lyle Eslinger and Glen Taylor (eds.), *Ascribe to the Lord: Biblical and Other Studies in Memory of Peter C. Craigie* (JSOTSup, 67; Sheffield: JSOT Press, 1988), pp. 399-419.

Good, Edwin M., *Irony in the Old Testament* (Sheffield: Almond Press, 2nd edn, 1981).

Gordon, R.P., 'Saul's Meningitis According to Targum 1 Samuel XIX 24', *VT* 37:1 (1987), pp. 39-49.

Gunn, David M., *The Fate of King Saul: An Interpretation of a Biblical Story* (JSOTSup, 14; Sheffield: JSOT Press, 1980).

Harari, Josué V. (ed.), *Textual Strategies: Perspectives in Post-Structuralist Criticism* (London: Methuen, 1980).

Hardy, Evelyn (ed.), *Thomas Hardy's Notebooks and some Letters from Julia Augusta Martin* (London: The Hogarth Press, 1955).

Hardy, Thomas, *The Life and Work of Thomas Hardy* (ed. Michael Millgate; London: Macmillan 1984).

—*The Mayor of Casterbridge* (Penguin Classics Edition; ed. with an introduction and notes by Martin Seymour-Smith; London: Penguin Books, 1985).

—*The Return of the Native* (New Wessex Edition with introduction by Derwent May; London: Macmillan, 1975).

—*Two on a Tower* (Penguin Classics Edition; London: Penguin Books, 1995).

—'The Withered Arm', in Peter Haining (ed.), *The Supernatural Tales of Thomas Hardy* (London: W. Foulsham & Co., 1988).

Hertzberg, Hans Wilhelm, *I & II Samuel: A Commentary* (trans. J.S. Bowden from the German 2nd revised edn; London: SCM Press, 1964).

Humphreys, W. Lee, 'The Rise and Fall of King Saul: A Study of an Ancient Narrative Stratum in 1 Samuel', *JSOT* 18 (1980), pp. 74-90.

—'The Tragedy of King Saul: A Study of the Structure of 1 Samuel 9–31', *JSOT* 6 (1978), pp. 18-27.

—'From Tragic Hero to Villain: A Study of the Figure of Saul and the Development of 1 Samuel', *JSOT* 22 (1982), pp. 95-117.

—*The Tragic Vision and the Hebrew Tradition* (Philadelphia: Fortress Press, 1985).

Ingham, Patricia, *Thomas Hardy* (London: Harvester Wheatsheaf, 1989).

Ireson, J.C. , *Lamartine: A Revaluation* (Hull: University of Hull, 1969).

Jobling, David 'Saul's Fall and Jonathan's Rise: Tradition and Redaction in 1 Sam 14.1-46', *JBL* 95 (1976), pp. 367-76.

—*The Sense of Biblical Narrative: Structural Analyses in the Hebrew Bible (1 Samuel 13–31, Numbers 11–12, 1 Kings 17–18)* (JSOTSup, 7; Sheffield: JSOT Press, 1978).

—*The Sense of Biblical Narrative*. II. *Structural Analyses in the Hebrew Bible* (JSOTSup, 39; Sheffield: JSOT Press, 1986).

—'What, if Anything, is 1 Samuel?', *SJOT* 7 (1993), pp. 17-31.

Kaufmann, Walter, *Tragedy and Philosophy* (Princeton, NJ: Princeton University Press, 1968).

King, Jeanette, ' "The Mayor of Casterbridge": Talking about Character', *The Thomas Hardy Journal* 8:3 (1992), pp. 42-46.

—*Tragedy in the Victorian Novel: Theory and Practice in the Novels of George Eliot, Thomas Hardy and Henry James* (Cambridge: Cambridge University Press, 1978).

Kort, Wesley A., *Story, Text, and Scripture: Literary Interests in Biblical Narrative* (University Park: Pennsylvania State University Press, 1988).

de Lamartine, Alphonse, *Saül: Tragédie* (critical edition with an introduction by Jean de Cognets; Paris: Librairie Hachette, 1918).

Lawton, Robert B., '1 Samuel 18: David, Merob, and Michal', *CBQ* 51 (1989), pp. 423-25.

—'Saul, Jonathan and the Son of Jesse', *JSOT* 58 (1993), pp. 35-46.

Lemche, Niels Peter, 'David's Rise', *JSOT* 10 (1978), pp. 2-25.

Lerner, Laurence, *Thomas Hardy's The Mayor of Casterbridge: Tragedy or Social History?* (London: Sussex University Press, 1975).

Levenson, John D., 'I Samuel 25 as Literature and as History', *CBQ* 40 (1978), pp. 11-28.

Lévi-Strauss, Claude, *The Raw and the Cooked: Introduction to a Science of Mythology* (trans. John and Doreen Weightman; London: Jonathan Cape, 1970).

Linafelt, Tod, 'Taking Women in Samuel: Readers/Responses/Responsibility', in Danna N. Fewell (ed.), *Reading Between Texts: Intertextuality and the Hebrew Bible* (Literary Currents in Biblical Interpretation; Louisville, KY: Westminster/John Knox Press, 1992), pp. 99-113.

Lindström, Fredrik, *God and the Origin of Evil: A Contextual Analysis of Alleged Monistic Evidence in the Old Testament* (Lund: C.W.K. Gleerup, 1983).

Long, Burke O., 'The "New" Biblical Poetics of Alter and Sternberg', *JSOT* 51 (1991), pp. 71-84.

Long, V. Philips, *The Reign and Rejection of King Saul: A Case for Literary and Theological Coherence* (SBLDS, 118, Atlanta: Scholars Press, 1989).

Maxwell, J.C., 'The "Sociological" Approach to *The Mayor of Casterbridge*', in R.P. Draper (ed.), *Hardy: The Tragic Novels* (London: Macmillan, 1975).

Mauchline, John, *1 and 2 Samuel* (London: Oliphants, 1971).

Maitland, F.W., *The Life and Letters of Leslie Stephan* (London: Duckworth and Co., 1908).

McKane, William, *I & II Samuel: Introduction and Commentary* (London: SCM Press, 1963).

Miller, J. Hillis, 'Presidential Address 1986: The Triumph of Theory, the Resistance of Reading, and the Question of the Material Base', *PMLA* 102 (1987), pp. 281-91.

Millgate, Michael, *Thomas Hardy: A Biography* (Oxford: Oxford University Press, 1982).

Miscall, Peter D., *1 Samuel: A Literary Reading* (Bloomington: Indiana University Press, 1986).

—'Isaiah: New Heavens, New Earth, New Book', in Danna N. Fewell (ed.), *Reading Between Texts: Intertextuality and the Hebrew Bible* (Literary Currents in Biblical Interpretation; Louisville, KY: Westminster/John Knox Press, 1992), pp. 41-56.

—'Moses and David: Myth and Monarchy', in J. Cheryl Exum and David J.A. Clines (eds.), *The New Literary Criticism and the Hebrew Bible* (JSOTSup, 143; Sheffield: JSOT Press, 1993), pp. 184-200.

Morgan, Rosemarie, *Women and Sexuality in the Novels of Thomas Hardy* (London: Routledge, 1988).

Moynahan, Julian, '*The Mayor of Casterbridge* and the Old Testament's First Book of Samuel: A Study of some Literary Relationships', *PMLA* 71 (1956), pp. 119-30.

Nicol, George G., 'Story-Patterning in Genesis', in Robert P. Carroll (ed.), *Text as Pretext: Essays in Honour of Robert Davidson* (JSOTSup, 138; Sheffield: Almond Press, 1992), pp. 215-33.

Nietzsche, Friedrich, *The Birth of Tragedy out of the Spirit of Music* (trans. Shaun Whiteside; ed. Michael Tanner; London: Penguin Books, 1993).

Noth, Martin, *The Old Testament World* (trans. from the 4th German edition by V.I. Gruhn; London: Adam & Charles Black, 1966).

Patrick, Dale, and Allen Scult, *Rhetoric and Biblical Interpretation* (JSOTSup, 82; Sheffield: The Almond Press, 1990).

Peterson, Michael L. (ed.), *The Problem of Evil: Selected Readings* (Notre Dame: University of Notre Dame Press, 1992).

Pleins, J. David, 'Son-Slayers and their Sons', *CBQ* 54 (1992), pp. 29-38.

Porter, Laurence M., *The Renaissance of the Lyric in French Romanticism: Elegie, 'Poëme' and Ode* (Lexington: French Forum, 1978).

Preston, Thomas R., 'The Heroism of Saul: Patterns of Meaning in the Narrative of the Early Kingship', *JSOT* 24 (1982), pp. 27-46.

Prouser, Ora Horn, 'Suited to the Throne: Symbolic Use of Clothing in the David and Saul Narratives', *JSOT* 71 (1996), pp. 27-37.

Provan, Iain W., 'Ideologies, Literary and Critical Reflections on Recent Writing on the History of Israel', *JBL* 114 (1995), pp. 585-606.

Pyper, Hugh S., *David as Reader: 2 Samuel 12.1-15 and the Poetics of Fatherhood* (Biblical Interpretation Series, Leiden: E.J. Brill, 1996).

von Rad, Gerhard, *Old Testament Theology* (trans. D. Stalker; New York: Harper & Row, 1962).

—*Wisdom in Israel* (trans. James D. Martin; London: SCM Press, 1972).

Reinhartz, Adele, 'Anonymity and Character in the Books of Samuel', *Semeia* 63 (1993), pp. 117-41.

Reis, Pamela Tamarkin, 'Collusion at Nob: A New Reading of 1 Samuel 21–22', *JSOT* 61 (1994), pp. 59-73.

Rogerson, John, 'Can a Doctrine of Providence be Based on the Old Testament?', in Lyle Eslinger and Glen Taylor (eds.), *Ascribe to the Lord: Biblical and Other Studies in Memory of Peter C. Craigie* (JSOTSup, 67; Sheffield: JSOT Press, 1988), pp. 529-43.

Ruprecht, Louis A., Jr, *Tragic Posture and Tragic Vision: Against the Modern Failure of Nerve* (New York: Continuum, 1994).

Schulz, Alfons, 'Narrative Art in the Books of Samuel', in David M. Gunn (ed.), *Narrative and Novella in Samuel: Studies by Hugo Gressman and Other Scholars 1906–1923* (trans. by David E. Orton; JSOTSup, 116; Sheffield: The Almond Press, 1991), pp. 119-70.

Schwarz, Daniel R., 'Beginnings and Endings in Hardy's Major Fiction', in D. Kramer (ed.), *Critical Approaches to the Fiction of Thomas Hardy* (London: Macmillan, 1979), pp. 17-35.

Schweik, Robert C., 'Character and Fate in *The Mayor of Casterbridge*', in R.P. Draper (ed.), *Hardy: The Tragic Novels* (London: Macmillan, 1975), pp. 133-47.

Sewall, Richard B., *The Vision of Tragedy* (new enlarged edition; New Haven: Yale University Press, 1980).

Seymour-Smith, Martin, *Hardy* (London: Bloomsbury, 1994).

Showalter, Elaine, 'The Unmanning of the Mayor of Casterbridge', in D. Kramer (ed.), *Critical Approaches to the Fiction of Thomas Hardy* (London: Macmillan, 1979), pp. 99-115.

Soggin, J. Alberto, *Introduction to the Old Testament* (trans. John Bowden 2nd revised and updated edn, London: SCM Press, 1980).

Steiner, George, *Antigones* (Oxford: Clarendon Press, 1984).

—*The Death of Tragedy* (London: Faber & Faber, 1961).

Sternberg, Meir, *The Poetics of Biblical Narrative: Ideological Literature and the Drama of Reading* (Bloomington: Indiana University Press, 1985).

Taylor, R.H. (ed.), *The Personal Note Books of Thomas Hardy: With an Appendix Including the Unpublished Passages in the Original Typescripts of 'The Life of Thomas Hardy'* (edited with introductions and notes; London: Macmillan, 1978).

Tcherikover, Viktor, *Hellenistic Civilization and the Jews* (trans. S. Applebaum; New York: Atheneum, 1976).

Tolstoy, Leo, *Anna Karenina* (trans. Joel Carmichael with an introduction by Malcolm Cowley; New York: Bantam Books, 1960).

Tompkins, Jane P. (ed.), *Reader-Response Criticism: From Formalism to Post-Structuralism* (Baltimore: The John Hopkins University Press, 1980).

Tosato, Angelo, 'La Colpa di Saul (1 Sam 15,22-23)', *Biblica* 59 (1978), pp. 251-59.

Voltaire, *Saül*, in *Oeuvres complètes de Voltaire: Tome quatrième* (Paris: Garnier Frères, 1877).

Walters, S.D., 'The Light and the Dark', in Lyle Eslinger and Glen Taylor (eds.), *Ascribe to the Lord: Biblical and Other Studies in Memory of Peter C. Craigie* (JSOTSup, 67; Sheffield: JSOT Press, 1988), pp. 567-89.

Whybray, R.N., 'The Immorality of God: Reflections on some Passages in Genesis, Job, Exodus and Numbers', *JSOT* 72 (1996), pp. 89-121.

Widdowson, Peter, *Hardy in History: A Study in Literary Sociology* (London: Routledge, 1989).

Willey, Patricia A., 'The Importunate Woman of Tekoa and How She Got her Way', in Danna Nolan Fewell (ed.), *Reading Between Texts: Intertextuality and the Hebrew Bible* (Literary Currents in Biblical Interpretation; Louisville, KY: Westminster/John Knox Press, 1992) pp. 115-32.

Wing, George Douglas, *Hardy* (Edinburgh: Oliver & Boyd, 1963).

van Wolde, Ellen, 'Trendy Intertextuality?', in S. Draisma (ed.), *Intertextuality in Biblical Writings: Essays in Honor of Bas van Israel* (Kampen: Kok, 1989), pp. 43-50.

Woolf, Virginia, 'The Novels of Thomas Hardy', in R.P. Draper (ed.), *Hardy: The Tragic Novels* (London: Macmillan, 1975), pp. 73-79.

Young, Robert (ed.), *Untying the Text: A Post-Structuralist Reader* (Boston: Routledge & Kegan Paul, 1981).

Zakovitch, Yair, '∪ and ∩ in the bible', in Exum, J. Cheryl (ed.), *Tragedy and Comedy in the Bible* (Semeia 32; Decatur, GA: Scholars Press, 1985).

Zalewski, Saul, 'The Purpose of the Story of the Death of Saul in 1 Chronicles X', *VT* 39:4 (1989), pp. 449-67.

Zvi, Ehud Ben, 'The Dialogue Between Abraham and Yhwh in Gen. 18.23-32: A Historical–Critical Analysis', *JSOT* 53 (1992), pp. 27-46.

INDEXES

INDEX OF REFERENCES

OLD TESTAMENT

CLASSICAL

INDEX OF AUTHORS

JOURNAL FOR THE STUDY OF THE OLD TESTAMENT
SUPPLEMENT SERIES